big bother

Dr Toni Johnson-Woods finished school at 14 and completed her high school education at night. She fell in love with learning and to date has three degrees, including one in Speech Pathology. Toni has taught a variety of academic and creative writing courses in Australia, the United States and the United Kingdom. She lectures in Media and Communications at the University of Queensland. She is currently writing a book on 1950s Australian pulp fiction.

why did that reality-tv show become such a phenomenon ?

big bother

Toni Johnson-Woods

University of Queensland Press

First published 2002 by University of Queensland Press
Box 6042, St Lucia, Queensland 4067 Australia

www.uqp.uq.edu.au

Typeset by University of Queensland Press
Printed in Australia by McPherson's Printing Group

Distributed in the USA and Canada by
International Specialized Book Services, Inc.,
5824 N.E. Hassalo Street, Portland, Oregon 97213–3640

Cataloguing in Publication Data
National Library of Australia

Johnson-Woods, Toni.
Big Bother : why did that TV show become such a phenomenon?

1. Big Brother (Television program : Australia). 2. Reality television programs — Australia. I. Title.

791.45612

ISBN 0 7022 3315 3

Cover photo courtesy of News Limited

Contents

Acknowledgments *vi*
Introduction *vii*

1. Home and Away: the *Big Brother* Family *1*
2. Guiding Lights: Behind the Scenes *32*
3. As the Reality World Turns: Genre *50*
4. The Box: The Show *69*
5. A Week-by-week Guide *87*
6. The Young and the Restless: The Contestants *121*
7. Daze of Our Lives: The Audience *178*
8. The Media *208*

Notes *224*

Acknowledgments

The author wishes to thank Ms Vanda Leigh, Dr Sally Stockbridge and Tim Clucas from Channel 10; Peter Abbott and James Cooper at Southern Star; Aaron Pederson and Jeremy E Cath from Southern Star Endemol Interactive; Dominique Burgess from Dreamworld; Carol Davidson, Rosie Fitzgibbon and Felicity Shea from UQP; Lurline Winfield-Woods; Dr Liz Ferrier; Julie Avery and Helen Groom from Contemporary Studies; Mark Smitheram; and my virtual friends: Anne Byrne, alsoanon, anonymous, Annabelle bbaddict, cate, dazz, helen, iamthemarquis, jeffds, judy, Karen Charlton, karren, Kaz, Lace, me_cathy, nat, nichst, russ, SS, vicki76, wattlegirl and Leo Howard Vacation School (2001 & 2002). Special thanks to Stuart Glover and to Dr William Lott.

Introduction

Cher, Tarzan, Madonna — Sara-Marie. If you live in Australia and don't recognise the last name, then you must have slept through 2001. You didn't have to watch *Big Brother* to know that the bum-dancin' blonde lost a game show but won the game.

While it might not have been a critical success, *Big Brother* put Channel 10 back on the ratings map and boosted Southern Star's finances. It made quasi-celebrities out of a dozen unknowns and proved that too much hype is never enough. A show about 'bugger all' (as Wendy Harmer put it) could hardly be classed as entertainment. But for millions of Australian viewers it was exactly that, entertaining.

Big Bother analyses the *Big Brother* world, its generic heritage, its multiple formats, the pantheon of contestants, the behind-the-scenes chaos, fandom and its discontents, and the orchestrated media madness. The book is an exemplar of how to 'read' a television show and is a companion guide for viewing *Big Brother* 2 and reality-tv programs in general.

Love it or loathe it, *Big Brother* has created television history. The first show aired in the Netherlands in 1999 and was so successful that production company Endemol was able to sell the show to more than twenty countries; two years later over 40 series have aired. At the beginning of 2002 *Big Brother* programs were showing in Sweden, Brazil and Mexico.

Who could forget the Italian housemate who was convinced he was Scottish and finished each diary session with the yell 'God

Save Scotland'? Or the Spanish contestants who, after they left the house, agreed to go to a remote part of Spain to run a hotel. While there, they witnessed a UFO landing. But it was an elaborate hidden-camera joke and their reactions were being filmed (*El Gran Marciano — The Big Martian*). Some contestants have found the confinement traumatising and have exhibited bizarre behaviours such as hoarding batteries and burying spoons in the garden.

Big Brother is one of the many 'copy-cat' television formats, like *Who Wants to be a Millionaire?*, *The Weakest Link* and *Survivor*. When a television station pays for the rights to copyrighted programs, they receive a 'bible' which contains instructions on how to run the show, a logo, backdrops, computer graphics and information about screening times and so on. Sometimes phrases ('you are the weakest link') and suggestions for prizes are included.[1] Occasionally an executive from Endemol will come out and help supervise. Despite the formulaic nature of the show, each country has slight variations: Australia ran for 85 days, the United Kingdom 64 days, Portugal 120 days; sometimes the show is aired once a night, as in Australia, and sometimes only three times a week (United States). The richest *Big Brother* is the United States' version ($1 million) and the poorest is the Russian copycat *Behind the Glass* (*Za Steklom*) at A$75,000. The houses have resembled penitentiaries (United Kingdom) and palaces (United States). There have been sexy *Big Brother*s (Switzerland) and violent ones (Portugal). Often the contestants have been odd to say the least.

In most countries the show airs nightly; so *Big Brother* requires a huge commitment, not only in terms of money but also in terms of staffing, equipment and internet technology. South Africa spent two years thinking about *Big Brother* because to stage it would involve a complete overhaul of the South African television and internet infrastructure; the television station even had to dig up their car park to build the house. The behind-the-scenes workings of *Big Brother* are unlike those of other television shows — it was a 24 hours a day, seven days a week television spectacle. Besides the usual television production team of editors, producers and camera crew, it required lawyers, psychologists and security personnel on call around the clock.

Obviously *Big Brother* was a huge gamble. It costs millions to buy (rights to *Celebrity Big Brother* and the second series are rumoured to have cost Channel 10 a further $25 million) and millions to produce. Why did television stations outlay so much money? Because television executives have seen the success of shows such as *Survivor*, which attracted 52 million viewers in 2000. And high ratings translate into advertising dollars. But ratings aren't left to chance.

Big Brother launched one of the most determined media blitzes in Australia. The words *Big Brother* were on everyone's lips, even politicians. 'This is not a government,' said Kim Beazley. 'It's an episode of *Big Brother*.' The term has come to mean something different and only time will tell if the show brings about a semantic shift in meaning.

Many critics panned the use of 'reality' in conjunction with *Big Brother*; if only they realised they were the ones who called *Big Brother* 'reality tv'. But documentaries also structure their constitutive discourses and make claims to truth. Although some claim that shows such as *Big Brother* are post-documentary, they are truly meta-documentary. *Big Brother* is a documentary about a television show and its viewers and the show is *Big Brother*.

What was all the bother about? The big attraction of *Big Brother* was the contestants. Channel 10 received around 10,000 applications for the first series. The second series attracted nearly triple the number of applications — 27,000. Why?

Most contestants are motivated by the promise of fame. Dutch contestant and serial hugger Ruud wrote a song 'Let's Hug' and went on to make a CD 'Cuddling with Ruud'. Zlatko, a 24-year-old unemployed mechanic, nicknamed The Brain (because everyone thought he was stupid) released a rap single 'I Miss You' which sold half a million copies; he now has his own television show and a beer named after him. In the United Kingdom, Nick Bateman wrote a book and hosted a game show; the winner, Craig, released a CD, as did Nichola; Darrin's care of the chickens led to an advertising gig for Chicken Tonight.

Critics feared that *Big Brother* was dehumanising, but in a way it was hyperhuman. For the first time 'ordinary people' occupied centre stage for a protracted length of time. The viewers knew it wasn't 'real life' but that didn't stop them from identifying the contestants as 'real'. As one fan said, 'I just think [Sara-Marie] is the most gorgeous little woman on this Earth. She is what I want to be because I am shy. I love watching people and thinking, "Hey they are just like me". I am normal.' The show seemed real because it contained people, images and concerns that reflect our culture.

Big Brother was rather like a game of cricket. It was not about winning; it was exciting just watching the show, even if the show was boring. Perhaps only cricket fans understand their reasoning. The show promised excitement. Of course we knew that if something did happen, we would be in the kitchen getting a cup of tea at the time, but that didn't matter. It was about being part of *Big Brother* fandom and the *Big Brother* community. Everyone — at work, at school, in pubs, at parties — talked about it. To not watch was to be, somehow, a social pariah. This balancing on the precipice of entertainment made for *frisson* television.

Many of the fans could not articulate why they watched the show. One said, 'I don't know why I liked *Big Brother*. Sometimes I would sit and watch the show thinking this is so boring what am I doing watching this — I should be doing something else. But I COULD NOT STOP WATCHING! I loved it and hated it and miss it.' Perhaps the issues are more complex than fans realise. In these days of increasing isolation, 'cocooning' as it has been called, *Big Brother* created a community. People who didn't know each other found themselves chatting about contestants they didn't know. Some viewers adopted the *Big Brother* family as their extended family — with shrinking family sizes some viewers felt they gained virtual siblings. Though it might not have been Jane Austen, it was a contemporary comedy of manners. Many viewers reported that they learned some valuable life lessons from watching *Big Brother*. The fact that their judgments were based on edited samples, quick takes and sound bites does not diminish the value of the lesson.

Generally, the show appealed to younger viewers; indeed, Triple M radio host Andrew Denton found that *Big Brother* forced him to realise he didn't 'get' young culture anymore. Older viewers have come to appreciate slick productions, tight plotting and effective acting. Younger viewers are more fluid — more accepting of new formats — for the moment anyway.

An integral part of *Big Brother* was the internet. Nearly 2 million people logged into the official website on the debut night and more than 2000 people waited to use live feeds. Overseas viewers set their computer clocks to Australian time so they knew when to log on. In the United Kingdom it was estimated that nearly £300,000 per day was lost due to people logging into the *Big Brother* website.

To the despair of many critics, *Big Brother* was an outstanding success. In Holland almost a million viewers watched Bart and Sabine satisfy their love under the doona; in the United Kingdom more people voted for contestants than voted in the general election (7.7 million voted in the final *Big Brother* eviction) and ten million people watched the final eviction (56.6% of the population). Nearly three million Australians watched the final episode and nationally the show topped the 16–39 demographic for nine weeks.

In the press, critics decried *Big Brother*'s voyeurism; but if viewers did tune in for sex, they would have been heartily disappointed (in Australia, anyway). Neither did viewers see contestants on the toilet — that was their second greatest fear. To others the show represented the thin edge of the wedge; from *Big Brother* it was a short step to televised murder. No one ever pointed out exactly how that slippery slope worked; indeed, critics' rantings were often models of illogical argument. All in all, the media panic was unfounded.

Not everyone was offended by the show. Desmond Morris found it rather fun and gossipy. One researcher claimed that watching *Big Brother* increased viewers' sex lives! But nothing about *Big Brother* was new. The desire for fame, the opportunity to win easy money, capitalising on the viewer's penchant for watching other people — it's all been done before. *Big Brother* simply reinforced what Shakespeare had already told us:

All the world's a stage,
And all the men and women merely players:
They have their exits and their entrances;
And one man in his time plays many parts.

As You Like It, Act II, Scene VII

Chapter One

Home and Away: the *Big Brother* Family

On the last night of 1999 over 50 per cent of the Dutch population weren't out ringing in the New Year. They were at home watching the final episode of a television show that had gripped the nation *Big Brother*.

News of the show's success soon spread throughout Europe. Television executives at stations who courted younger viewers were eager to try the format in their countries, and so the following year *Big Brother* aired in eight countries: Germany, Spain, United States, United Kingdom, Portugal, Switzerland, Sweden and Belgium. In Portugal, Switzerland, Sweden and Belgium the series started screening on the same day. Soon media around the world broadcast stories about the on-screen sex and nudity, critics howled, television stations clamoured and viewers watched. In 2001 several countries completed their second series and some had shown three; in October 2001 seven *Big Brother*s aired simultaneously: Argentina, Belgium, Italy, Denmark, Greece, Netherlands and South Africa. The channels that air *Big Brother* tend to be those that target younger audiences; they usually broadcast television programs such as *Who Wants to be a Millionaire?* and *Survivor*. Often the channels are fairly young channels themselves (e.g. TVN in Poland, Veronica in Holland). Most of them believe that *Big Brother* played a vital role in their gaining market share (e.g. Switzerland's Channel TV3, Poland's TVN and Australia's Channel 10).

Big Brother has been watched by over two billion people. In

Italy 69 per cent of the population claimed to have watched it, in America 52 per cent tuned in and in Germany 64 per cent watched it. But the shows have a much broader audience than television viewers; on the internet, viewers around the world can see the live feeds. You don't have to be fluent in Spanish to watch *Gran Hermano* or Polish to enjoy *Wielki Brat.* Indeed, some viewers claim that not being able to understand a word enhances the viewing pleasure. It adds *frisson* if you imagine that the madly gesticulating Henrique is discussing the size of someone's genitals and not the toothpaste tube. It reminds viewers that in some things human nature transcends geographical boundaries.

While the basic format remains the same, each country adapts the format to its own television viewers' needs (or at least their perceived needs). The Americans have a *Survivor*-type format in which the contestants vote each other off. The British producers felt that their audiences wanted a short, sharp shock — their series runs for only 64 days. The Portuguese have longer attention spans, their series is the longest at 120 days. Countries tend to have contestants who epitomise their culture: the passionate Europeans, the win-at-all cost Americans and the laid-back Australians.

The basic rules

In *Big Brother* a group of strangers agree to live in a house for a period of time. They are cut off from contact with the outside world and they are voted off until one person remains. The winner receives a significant amount of money. Only the French *Loft Story* differed significantly. Over time there have been some refinements but generally the format has changed little since 1999.

All contestants on *Big Brother* are volunteers. They can leave the house in three ways: they can be evicted; they can leave of their own free will at any time; they can be forced to leave by *Big Brother* if they break the rules or behave in an inappropriate manner (violence etc.).

Nomination processes vary: in most *Big Brother*s the contestants nominate the person they want to evict and the audience votes. In Spain, the contestants nominated each other equally so that they were all up for eviction and left it to the viewers to decide which of them was to go. France's *Loft Story* contestants were voted off gender by gender (in alternate weeks) until only two remained. The audience voted for who should stay (not leave). In the second American *Big Brother*, the contestants were voted out by each other; the final contestants faced a panel of former contestants (à la *Survivor* and *Boot Camp*) who voted for the winner. In Holland and Germany, evictions occur fortnightly rather than weekly.

Not everyone loves Big Brother; a number of contestants have left before they were evicted. One French contestant left during the first week because he felt he did not fit in. Several Danes left the house together. A Russian contestant left to patch things up with his girlfriend. Polish contestants who fell in love left when their new loves were evicted. In the South African *Big Brother*, an irate contestant demanded to be let out in ten minutes. Spanish contestants didn't leave but refused to conform to Big Brother's orders. So far, no British, Australian or American contestants have voluntarily left the house; however, the first US series was so dull that the producers offered money to any contestant who would leave; no one did. As can be imagined, Big Brother panics when a contestant threatens to leave; a lot of behind-the-scenes preparation is essential (more on this later). It seems surprising that more contestants don't leave *Big Brother*. Contestants are of course under a totalitarian regime: they must obey Big Brother at all times and 'failure to do so may result in eviction'. Obviously if Big Brother did not have such a list of 'thou shalt nots', control over the contestants would be impossible; what if they decided to sit around all day and not do the tasks or refused to recharge their batteries? Surprisingly few contestants have rejected Big Brother's exhortations. British *Celebrity Big Brother* contestant Vanessa Feltz was proud that she told Big Brother to 'fuck off' and refused to go to the Diary Room when ordered.

Big Brother can evict contestants whenever he chooses. Perhaps the most famous eviction was that of the United Kingdom's 'Nasty

Nick', who was evicted from the first British series for cheating. In the second US series, Justin was evicted because of his violent behaviour. A reduced number of contestants leaves the producers with a logistical problem: because evictions occur at regular intervals and because the series is contracted for a certain period of time, if one extra contestant leaves, the producers have to decide on certain program changes. The show can finish early, there can be fewer contestants on the eviction couch on the final night, or a contestant from the standby list can be brought in. Intruder Claire replaced Nick, but Justin was not replaced, the winner being chosen from two contestants and not three.

The 'intruder' clause allows Big Brother to bring in new (or old) contestants when he pleases. This clause states:

> At any time Big Brother may elect to send in intruders. These intruders will come as a surprise to the housemates. After 48 hrs the *Big Brother* housemates will decide which one will stay. The intruder who stays is not eligible for eviction in their first week.[1]

The intruders are introduced in a variety of ways. In Australia, contestants were told just a few hours before Rachel and Anita arrived. In the United Kingdom it was handled differently. When the contestants arrived they found a rag doll with a note on its lap that explained that after the first eviction a new contestant would arrive. Viewers were invited to vote for their preferred intruder, from three candidates. Meanwhile, the three potential intruders were sequestered in Spain so they wouldn't be able to watch the show. Thus they came to the house relatively uncontaminated, unlike the Australian intruders. So far, intruders have not lasted longer than a few weeks.

Usually there is only one winner, as the rules state: 'the contestant to survive to the end ... will walk away with the cash'. However, in France and Russia there were two winners and in the United States the runner-up won US$50,000. The Danish believe that their paltry cash prize (A$115,000) was responsible for the fact that only four applications were received for the third series.

Contestants enter the house with one suitcase of clothes and one small suitcase of personal belongings. Photographs of loved ones, limited reading material, and cosmetic items are allowed; CD players, radios, laptops, mobile phones, batteries, drugs, weapons and so on are not. Some countries allow cigarettes and alcohol, and others don't. Time-keeping seems to be an issue too; one rule states that 'one clock is allowed in the house, no other equipment is allowable, unless introduced by Big Brother for a specific purpose'. In South Africa, contestants had cards confiscated because there were calendars on them. Also forbidden are clothes displaying prominent logos, labels or well-known brand names. The contents of the suitcases are a source of interest in some countries; the UK and South African *Big Brother* websites contained photos and detailed descriptions of what each contestant brought in. Before contestants enter the house, security guards search the suitcases and confiscate prohibited items; these items are returned after eviction.

Once the contestants are inside, the house is sealed and security personnel stand guard 24 hours a day, seven days a week. Why such heavy security? First and foremost is the concern for the contestants' safety. If violence errupts (as it did in Portugal and the United States), guards can immediately remove the offender. Second, the guards can protect contestants from people who might try to get into the house and harm them. In Germany and Holland, crowd control became an issue when thousands of viewers camped outside the house. Russian viewers queued around the block for a glimpse into the Moscow apartment. Some visitors are less benign and in France protestors broke into the *Big Brother* compound to 'liberate' the contestants. Australian producers capitalised on the crowds the show attracted and put the house in a theme park where it could control (and profit from) the curious. The only people allowed into the house are the intruders and those who bring the supplies.

Big Brother provides basic provisions, vegetables and dry goods like rice, beans and flour. Other foods, cleaning products and luxury items are purchased from a weekly budget; the size of the budget depends upon the successful completion of the weekly task. The weekly allowance for each person is kept to a minimum, but the contestants won't starve. The vegetable garden and eggs from the chickens are potential other food sources. Groceries are collected from the storeroom which is opened for one hour each day.

Once a week Big Brother assigns the contestants a task. Once the task is described, contestants have 30 minutes to decide what percentage of their budget they wish to wager. Tasks are not optional and their rules are non-negotiable; tasks must be completed at a given time. In Australia, contestants were given the task on Monday and it had to be completed by Thursday. If one contestant fails, the group fails. Contestants who do not participate may be evicted. From time to time impromptu one-day tasks may be assigned. Contestants received a small reward upon successful completion of these tasks.

Everything the contestants do and say can be broadcast. There is no criminal amnesty for *Big Brother* contestants while they are in the house. Contestants are warned of this, yet they don't seem to take this to heart — or consider the consequences. In South Africa, one contestant made racist remarks which caused at least one viewer to complain to the police. Contestants are debriefed after evictions so they know what has been written about them and how they are perceived by the public. (Melanie Hill in the first UK series was shocked to find out that she had been portrayed as a flirt.)

Once a day the contestants must go (separately) to the Diary Room and record a video diary. A psychologist is available to the contestants; these session will not be filmed or overheard by the *Big Brother* production team. There is support available to contestants after they leave the house.

All contestants are given a written plan for emergencies before they enter the house. In case of medical emergencies, a health professional would treat the contestant in the Diary Room. If a hospital stay of more than one day is required, the contestant may not be allowed to re-enter the house.

Before the show starts, contestants' identities remain secret. Contestants who are seen in the press before this date are not eligible to enter the house.

Contestants receive a weekly stipend for their time in the house. This is to cover costs incurred outside the house such a rent. Rumours are that this amount can be negotiated on a individual basis. In Australia it was $500 per week.

To date, thirty-eight *Big Brother*s have aired in 20 countries. The table below charts some *Big Brother* details:

Country	**Days**	**No. of contestants**	**Winner**	**Prize**
Argentina I	112	12	Marcelo Lorazza	200,000 pesos
Argentina II	112	14	Roberto Parra	200,000 pesos
Australia	85	12/14	Ben Williams	$250,000
Belgium I	106	10/13	Steven	5 million B. francs
Belgium VIP	106	12	Sam Gooris	charity
Belgium II	106	12	Ellen	5 million B. francs
Denmark I	100	10	Jill	500,000 kroner
Denmark II	100	12	Carsten	500,000 kroner
France	70	11	Loana and Christopher	1.5 million francs each
Germany I	100	10	John	250,000 marks
Germany II	106	12	Alida	250,000 marks
Germany III	106	12	Karina	250,000 marks
Greece	112	12	George	50 million drachma
Italy I	99	10	Cristina	250 million lire
Italy II	99	14	Flavio	250 million lire
Netherlands I	100	9	Bart	250,000 guilders
Netherlands II	100	97	Bianca	250,000 guilders
Netherlands III	100	6/12	Sandy (female)	1 million guilders
Norway I	97	11	Lars Joakim	1 million kroner
Norway II	97	13	Leena	1 million kroner
Poland I	109	14	Janusz Dziêcio	500,000 zlotys
Poland II	109		Marzena	500,000 zlotys
Portugal I	120	12	Ze Maria	20 million escudos
Portugal II	120	13	Henrique	20 million escudos
Portugal III	120	13	Catarina	20 million escudos
Russia	35	6	Denis and Zhanna	flat valued at 1,200,000 roubles
South Africa	106	12	Ferdinand	1 million rand
Spain I	90	10	Ismael	20 million pestas
Spain II	90	10	Sabrina	20 million pestas

Country	Days	No. of contestants	Winner	Prize
Sweden	100	10	Angela	500,000 kroner
Switzerland I	100	10	Daniela	150,000 S. francs
Switzerland II	100	14	Christian	150,000 S. francs
Turkey	100	15	Melih	100 million lire
United Kingdom I	64	11	Craig	£70,000
UK Celebrity	7	6	Jack Dee	charity
United Kingdom II	64	11	Brian Dowling	£70,000
United States I	88	10	Eddie McGee	US$500,000
United States II	88	12	Will Kirby	US$500,000

Argentina

Two *Gran Hermanos* have aired in Argentina, one in 2000 and one in 2001. Love blossomed in the second series when two contestants became engaged on the show. The aggressive marketing has included a *Big Brother* magazine.

Both series have been phenomenally successful. Advertisers paid US$850 per second advertisement time and the slots were filled quickly. The final episode attracted a 90 per cent viewer share, and three thousand Argentines besieged the house. The second series received 120,000 applications, and 80 per cent of viewers tuned in to watch 30-year-old marketing student Robert Parra win. The two *Big Brothers* have been instrumental in making Telefé the leading television station in Argentina.

Belgium

Those sexy Belgians! In the first series, Kanaal 2, the channel that aired *Big Brother*, had to cut some of the more explicit scenes from its afternoon episodes. No wonder more than 13,000 people applied for the second series. The second series was so steamy (there were couples under the sheets in the bedrooms and frolicking in the pool) that the afternoon repeats were cancelled altogether, Flemish channel Kanaal 2 explained that 'more than half the housemates had sex with each other'.

Viewers blamed the producers for supplying the contestants with beer, wine and spirits; but a Kanaal spokesman retaliated that it was the contestants' responsibility: 'In the first *Big Brother* we had parties where people drank a lot more. The only difference is it all happened in one evening. Not we but the inhabitants are writing the story.'

A small isolation cell was built inside the house for the second series, inside which was a small bed, water and a toilet. Contestants could send anyone who was misbehaving to the cell, but Big Brother decided how long they would stay there.

Live streams were not free for the second series and people had to pay by the minute. Throughout Belgium, five *Big Brother* cafes were built, complete with large-screen television sets, so patrons could watch the daily broadcasts. Furnishings from the first house added authenticity and gave patrons a sense of being in the *Big Brother* house. Evicted contestants visited the cafes.

During the live nomination shows, the three nominees could opt for immunity by pulling a rope. If one of them did so, the house lost its weekly budget.

Denmark

Seven contestants walked out of the first *Big Brother* house in Copenhagen in April 2001. After negotiating, four of the contestants returned to the house (Jill, Naja, Nico and Suzanne). The three who did not should have read their contracts more closely, because the contracts stipulated that the contestants would be fined A$24,000 if they sold their stories to the press. And apparently that is exactly what contestants Pil, Soren and Christian had in mind. A judge ruled that TV Danmark had control over what the contestants said to the press and they were gagged. TV Danmark considered suing daily tabloid *Ekstra Bladet* which allegedly paid A$350,000 for exclusive rights to their stories.

In January 2002, it was reported in the Danish press that only four people had applied for the next series. Some believed that the prize money of 500,000 kroner, around A$40,000, did not tempt people. A year earlier, over two thousand contestants had applied for the first series.

France

From its highly stylised cartoon eye, *Loft Story* was clearly not the typical *Big Brother* format. In this slightly different format, the contestants were voted off one by one (alternating genders) until one couple remained. The focus of the show was love. The final couple then proceeded to the second hurdle. They had to live in a luxury villa in Saint-Tropez for 45 days; if they remained together, they won the money. While at the villa they were still subject to camera scrutiny but they could have guests and could leave the villa. The couple did not have to have sex to win the prize. The title change from the political *Big Brother* to the romantic *Loft Story* (echoing Eric Segal's romantic novel *Love Story*) underscores the aim of this version of *Big Brother*.

On 24 April 2001, 11 contestants (six men and five women) entered the loft in La Plaine-Saint-Denis, an industrial site north of Paris, for 70 days. Within a few days one of the contestants left, saying he didn't fit in.

Those anxious to follow the contestants' paths to love could watch in a number of ways. They could watch the free-to-air nightly episodes, and there were live feeds on a dedicated pay (satellite) channel and on the internet.

Criticism of the show came from a number of areas. The cultural elite panned the show because it was trashy. The politically inclined called it 'rampant facism'. Moralists felt there was too much alcohol and too much smoking. Some felt the contestants should be paid actors' salaries. Ethicists wondered about the contestants' rights to privacy.

Protestors defied tear gas and security guards to storm the compound where the loft was located in an attempt to liberate the contestants. As protestor Amelie Martenot said, 'When people agree to take part in such a humiliation, it's a little bit of each of us who feels humiliated'.[2] Other protestors stormed Channel M6's offices in Neuilly-sur-Seine and left literal evidence of their feelings about the show: garbage.

The Communications and Culture Minister, Catherine Tasca,

denounced the 'cynicism' of M6 for airing the show. Eventually French television regulator *Conseil Superieur de l'Audiovisuel* (French Audiovisual Council, CSA) condemned the show for failing 'to respect the dignity of the human person' and ordered that the cameras be turned off for two hours each day. Also, it ordered the producers to reverse the voting mentality; rather than vote someone out, vote for someone to stay in.

Inside the house, contestants were busy. Jean-Edouard and Loana were having sex in the swimming pool. Later the cad dropped her, but she had the last laugh. Loana became a favourite with the viewers; her 'best friend' revealed that Loana had given up a daughter for adoption and had breast implants. Young women copied her 'sluttish' look: tight clothes, skimpy tops and plunging necklines. Eventually Loana (a go-go dancer/stripper) and co-winner Christophe (a sociology student) went to Saint-Tropez. Locals complained about the traffic their sojourn has caused.

The most vitriolic criticism came from rival networks. TF1 chairman (Patrick Le Lay) pulled out all the stops when he denounced *tele poubelle* (trash tv) in *Le Monde.* He accused *Loft Story* of spawning 'pornographic sub-products'. He claimed that the show manipulated the contestants. He then signed an A$500 million first-look deal with Endemol. Conservative *Le Figaro* denounced the show's 'unequalled vulgar dialogue', branding the show 'gutter television'.

The public couldn't have agreed more: it was trash tv at its best. The publicity had heightened expectations and some viewers complained that the show didn't go far enough; it was censored as soon as things got steamy. (Only subscribers to the cable network received the uncut version.) Six million viewers tuned in for the first show (10% of the total population; 30% of the viewing population). A few days later 10 million people watched Aziz's eviction. As M6's ratings rose (from 12.6% to 16.6%), its rival's (TF1) ratings fell (8%). A second series was planned for 2002.

Germany

Germany was the second country to air *Big Brother*, but the series almost didn't air.

Politicians and public figures called for a boycott of the show. The Interior Minister Otto Schily believed that the constant confinement and public monitoring was inhumane and wondered if the conditions violated Germany's constitutional laws about human dignity. German media regulators considered closing down the show.

Despite the original outrage, the first series started in March 2000. Three series have aired and the fourth series is currently in a holding pattern.

In Germany, *Big Brother* became a spectator sport and crowds gathered outside the house, which is situated in an industrial area of Cologne. Eventually, barbed wire was erected to keep the 10,000 visitors at bay.

The first winner was John, an unemployed father from Berlin. However, viewers' favourite was Zlatko Trpovksi who was given his own television program before he even left the house. The second series winner was Alida, the 'little chicken', the youngest of the 18–30-year-old group. The contestants' faces ended up on bottles and cans of Pepsi. The third winner, Karina, the joker, is best remembered for her house-cleaning! Some of the more memorable moments included a talk-show host from a rival network parachuting into the yard and the contestants' conspicuous alcohol consumption.

The series were presented by Sophie Rosenstreter and shown daily (for 45 minutes) on RTL2. RTL2 is a youth-oriented channel with programs such as *Sexy Summer*, *Popstars* and *Boat of Love*. Although *Big Brother* debuted with high ratings and a 19 per cent market share, the ratings dropped to 11 for the second series. Even though the couples in the third series regularly had sex and changed partners as they were evicted, viewer interest was waning.

Greece

Greece was the twenty-second country to air *Big Brother* (*Megalos Adelfos*). In May 2001 a call for applications went out; the production company ENA reported that over 10,000 forms were downloaded from the official website.

Opposition from the church and protest groups tried to make it illegal for contestants to appear in the show. The same complaints resurfaced: trash tv, contestants' rights to privacy, the fear of on-screen sex. Newspaper headlines read: '*Big Brother* Divides Greece', 'War erupts over *Big Brother*' and 'Victims and Victimisers of the TV-life'. As in Germany, critics felt it breached their constitution, which states that 'respect and protection of the value of the human being constitute the primary obligations of the State'. After the show started, a couple went to court to have the show cancelled because it violated human dignity. Protestors threw eggs and dumped garbage at the Antenna station's studios.

Two unusual sources for criticism were the Athens Journalists' Union and the Greek Data Protection Authority. The Union threatened members who took part in the show's production because the program is 'aimed at the erosion of human values'. The data agency said that it was 'unconstitutional, illegal, and unethical' for producers to create a database of personal details provided by thousands of potential contestants. The application form listed 80 questions, and candidates had to give tax information and details about friends and relatives. 'For there to be a legal archive, its purpose must be legal,' the authority said. In Greek law, it is illegal to retain such data without permission from the government or the authority. The production company stopped collecting information from the applications.

Italy

The *Grande Fratello* contestants spent their days in a villa outside Rome. Two latin lovers didn't waste much time, for within four days they had had sex under a curtain behind a couch. The public didn't miss out either — the incident was aired in prime time. The first series started in September and ended in December 2000.

One of the contestants, Franceso Maria Gaiardelli, was quirky to say the least. He used to end his Diary Room visits with a shout: 'God save Scotland'. He wore a Scotland football jersey and slept with a huge saltire above his bed. When he was evicted (he made it to the final four), he marched out of the house wearing a kilt and playing the bagpipes. Apparently Francesco believes that his family is descended from a Scot who fought at the battle of Pavia in 1525. Needless to say, a Scottish tourist board heard about him and gave him a job as an ambassador.

The final show attracted more than 16 million viewers — a 60 per cent market share. One-hour highlights were screened on free-to-air Canale 5, and 24/7 coverage was available on the dedicated pay channel, TV Stream.

Television critics were outraged when *Big Brother* won a prestigious award Telegatti (Telecats) in the Customs and Culture section. After the first series, the *Big Brother* house was sold and all the contents auctioned.

The Netherlands

Holland with its preponderance of peep shows seemed to be the natural birthplace for *Big Brother*.

The first-ever *Big Brother* series started on 16 September 1999. Nine contestants competed for 100 days for the prize money. The first series produced the most famous *Big Brother* couple: Bart (23) — the eventual winner — and Sabine (25) who had sex in Bart's bed. Thousands of fans camped outside the house in Aalsmeer.

The ratings were phenomenal and broke Dutch audience records. It attracted an average 27.5 per cent audience share and four million of Holland's 15 million inhabitants watched the final episode on 30 December 1999. It was the most watched show of 1999. It was so popular that a rival network tried to get into the act and parachuted its own celebrity reporter into the compound with candy and beer for the surprised *Big Brother* inhabitants. The 100 episodes aired on the youth network Veronica.

At beginning of the summer of 2000, the first *Celebrity Big Brother* was aired, but the ratings were disappointing.

The second *Big Brother* started in September 2000 but the format was somewhat changed. There were two more contestants. Contestants paid for electricity and running water from their budget. The added workroom was stocked with tools because contestants had to carry out routine house maintenance. Security had been increased to cope with the crowds. Besides the daily 30-minute broadcast, *Big Brother* 2 had its own 24/7 dedicated pay-TV channel. It wasn't the ratings success of the first series and attracted only 1.5 million viewers.

The most radical changes were in the third series — *Big Brother: The Battle* (September 2001). As the name implies, the series was more confrontational. It began with six contestants: twelve more were hidden in a secret location, and each week two of these contestants moved into the house. The house had been redesigned and split into two: one 'basic' side and one 'upmarket' side. The upmarket side had a luxury kitchen, a jacuzzi, double beds, a garden, and endless champagne and caviar. The other side was much smaller, and had cold showers, a wooden stove in the yard and daily rations of dry bread. Contestants competed to see who got to live on which side; the producers initiated the 'battles'. The television station interrupted evening programs with news flashes from the *Big Brother* house. The prize increased from 250,000 guilders to 1 million guilders (A$800,000).

Norway

Norway's *Big Brother* might have set a viewing record (750,000 tuned in to the second episode) and given TV Norge its highest ratings ever, but some advertisers pulled out after watching the first episodes. Even so, *Big Brother* expected to earn $30 million for its production company Metrenome.

When stripper Natalie Strand was evicted from the house, she decided to setup a website, 'Big Sister'. *Big Brother* was not impressed and took legal action. Two contestants were married in the house in November 2001; naturally Big Brother broadcast the wedding live over the internet.

Poland

Of all the *Big Brother*s, the Polish one had the most militaristic underpinnings. As part of the selection process, contestants underwent lie-detector tests which monitored their responses to statements such as 'naked or dressed' and questions such as 'Have you ever stolen anything?'. One of the tasks was a 'miliary training' task with gas masks. *Big Brother* was compared to a Polish literary genre that examines life in concentration camps ; the show was concerned with 'human behavior in conditions of deprivation of the natural rights of the human being'.[3]

The first *Wielki Brat* (*Great Brother*) series started in March 2001 and was a great hit. Nearly 4 million Poles, 10 per cent of the population, regularly watched the show. Their 12 contestants were chosen from 10,000 applicants. The show was screened four times a day for 30–45 minutes and there was a later adults-only show. One of the highlights of the first series was the romance between Karolina and Grzegorz. Karolina followed him when he was voted out; Monika also quit the show when her boyfriend was evicted. The eventual winner was Janusz, a 47-year-old male.

Big Brother was shown on Poland's privately-owned network TVN. The youth-oriented station started in 1997 and has exclusive rights to all Endemol formats. According to its website, TVN reaches 60 per cent of Polish television households.

For die-hard fans, a *Big Brother* store opened in October 2001. It promised to fulfil the dreams of *Big Brother* fans; fashion and 'devices' (whatever they are) from the house were on sale.

Portugal

When Sergio and Veronica decided to have sex in the house, even the bedclothes couldn't hide what they were doing. The camerapersons should have turned away but they didn't, and Portugal's media regulator, the High Council for the Media, promptly prosecuted TVI and SIC for screening 'excessive' sex scenes without appropriate warning. A heavy fine was levied against TVI. However, the segment achieved a 60 per cent market share — 2.7 million viewers for the 9 pm timeslot.

Not only did *Big Brother* viewers witness on-screen sex, they also saw Marco (a kickboxing expert) kick Sonia in the face after she made disparaging remarks about his mother. He was removed from the house, and the public evicted Sonia soon after. Two intruders were introduced to replace the ousted Marco. His violence rekindled the domestic violence debate in the press.

Two other contestants became popular: one released a CD and another wrote a successful autobiography.

The second series (2001) was more popular than the first (2000). The second 12 contestants arrived to find only 11 beds; the producers did this to ensure an exciting start. A third series finished in 2001.

Russia

Russia's version of *Big Brother* produced the most steamy shower sequence of all when it broadcast nearly 20 minutes of Margo and Sasha washing in the shower.

Behind the Glass (*Za Steklom*) was not an Endemol production but was said to be based upon Yevgeny Zamyatin's *We* (a precursor to and inspiration for *1984*). It started in October 2001. Six contestants lived in a one-room apartment in the Rossiya Hotel (just off Red Square in Moscow) for 34 days. The viewers voted contestants off until two remained to claim the ultimate prize. They each won a Moscow flat. Anyone who left the show had to pay a fine. The program was broadcast three times a day on Russia's youth tv station and 24/7 on the internet.

The show had numerous raunchy incidents. Contestant Margo was particularly generous with her affections. First she formed an attachment with Olga a lesbian. But Olga, was voted out. Then she shared a shower with Sasha. When Sasha's his girlfriend (Macha) on the outside heard this, she flew into a rage. The producers organised an emergency meeting, which was broadcast nationally, and despite his reassurances that he didn't have an erection, Macha dumped him in front of millions of viewers. Sasha left the show to try and patch up their relationship. Margo then turned her attention to Max, and they ended up having sex on television, a 60-second encounter that made Russian television history. Margo and Max moved into an apartment together when they left the show. The viewers chose a quiet, bespectacled advertising manager (Denis) and the one woman who refused to remove her clothes or engage in any sexual activity (Zhanna, a student) as the winners.

The nudity and sexual activity outraged the Russian Orthodox Church which called the show pornographic; others were shocked by the poor grammar and consumerism of the contestants. A leading communist, Viktor Anpilov, was dismayed by the show's popularity: 'People who used to go to the museum and theatres are being corrupted by this sort of Western trash,'' he said. 'It's vulgar, sick and filthy.'[4] Hundreds of people stood in line to look through the apartment's mirrored windows.

More than 67 per cent of the population claimed to have watched the show at least once; the producers claim a 45 per cent market share. However, Endemol was not thrilled with the copycat production and planned to sue the producers.

South Africa

Of all the *Big Brother* series, South Africa was the most conscious of the racial mix of its contestants; it was touted in the media as a racial social experiment. The 12 contestants (six whites, three blacks and three people of 'mixed-race origin') entered the house in a Johannesburg suburb on 26 August 2001. Contestants were voted off fortnightly by the television audience. The contestants were aged between 21 and 31 (the average age was 26.5). Unlike other countries, South Africa has two presenters — one male and one female. After 106 days the winner, Ferdinand, claimed his 1 million rand (A$120,000) prize.

One of the contestants, primary school teacher Janine, was accused of hate crimes while on the show. Her racist comment 'The fucking whites, they want to rule the world' prompted at least one viewer to complain to the police. Hate-speak is illegal in South Africa. Janine also landed in trouble with the Board of Education when she mimicked oral sex on a cucumber. She was under investigation when she left the house and may have forfeited the right to teach in South Africa.

Another contestant, Brad, demanded to leave the house. He gave Big Brother ten minutes to let him out and he tried to unscrew the door to the outside himself. Big Brother ordered Brad back into the Diary Room and counselled him. Brad stayed.

Residents of Randburg (the suburb in which the house is located) have complained because fans drove past yelling for 'more sex', threw their garbage over their fences, set off fireworks, and generally caused traffic problems. One resident commented that if things didn't settle down residents would get angry and someone could get shot!

The criticism about *Big Brother* tended to focus on inequality; for example, one critic wrote that 'many people are more concerned with the daily struggle for existence [than with watching *Big Brother*]'[5] — this also refers to the fact that Big Brother was available on a pay television channel (M-Net) only.

South Africa had never produced a show of *Big Brother*'s magnitude. It took two years to decide if the show would be financially viable — would M-Net be able to recoup US$2.87 million paid for the format given the small size of South Africa's television audiences. Special broadcasting and recording equipment had to be imported. A portion of the M-Net parking lot had to be dug up for the *Big Brother* house. Even the official *Big Brother* website exposed the deficiencies of the South African technology. In preparation for the internet demand, M-Web connect upgraded the country's internet infrastructure. Still internet services could not cope. At one stage there were 80,000 users on the site, using up half the country's entire bandwidth, and internet services almost came to a standstill. Many internet service providers could not cope with the demand for live feeds, though they claimed they could when people signed up.

Spain

The feisty Spaniards took just three days to gang up against Big Brother. They nominated each other equally so that they were all up for eviction and left it up to the viewers to decide which of them was to go. They also seemed to be the only contestants who really cared about each other and who formed close friendships. There was a sense of solidarity and genuine commitment to each other. Love often depleted the contestant pool — two contestants took their new loves/fellow contestants with them when they were evicted.

Called *El Gran Hermano* and produced by Antenna 3-Endemol, the first series attracted 1700 applicants. It ended up with a 42.3 per cent audience share. On the final night of the first series, 2000 fans stormed the house to meet winner Ismael; he had to be airlifted from the house by helicopter.

The second series (March–June 2001) was also a smash hit. Soap operas used to be Spain's prime-time staple — *Big Brother* wiped them from the ratings map. The show even managed to rival the religiously watched soccercasts; it nabbed fourteen slots in the 50 top-rating programs for September 2000–June 2001; soccer occupied 26 slots. *Big Brother* was broadcast 24/7 on Onda Digital, and private television station Tele 5 aired daily highlights. *Big Brother* helped Tele 5 attain the best ratings in its ten years of existence (22.3%).

Sweden

Eight thousand applicants vied for the nine spots in the first *Big Brother*. The show broke previous ratings records by almost 200,000. It was aired daily on Kanal. The second series started in January 2002.

Switzerland

Despite the fact that the Swiss *Big Brother*s were rumoured to be the sexiest, there has been little written about them. The first series started in September 2000. It aired on TV3 which also shows programs such as *Who Wants to be a Millionaire?*. *Big Brother* has helped TV3 win a 10 per cent prime-time market share.

Turkey

In March 2001 the Turkish version of *Big Brother*, *Somebody Is Watching Us*, was almost banned because of its 'immorality'. The governing authority, the High Board of Radio and Television, felt that the show promoted 'perverted' family values and encouraged voyeurism. The predominantly Muslim country was particularly offended by the screening of a segment in which a 19-year-old man massaged the back of a 25-year-old mother of two.

The fifteen contestants lived in an Istanbul house. Each week viewers selected their favourite contestant, who then expelled a fellow housemate. The final prize was 100 million Turkish lira.

United Kingdom

The Brits have the shortest *Big Brother* (64 days) because they believe the format is necessary for their 'younger, sharper audience'.[6] Other than that, the rules are fairly standard: 10 contestants are evicted weekly on the audience's voting. Instead of leaving straightaway, contestants are allowed two hours to get ready before they actually leave the house.

If viewers were hoping for sex, the first *Big Brother* started promisingly when a pottery task turned into a nude wall-painting activity. But *Big Brother* 1 produced not the sexiest but the nastiest contestant of all: Nasty Nick.

Nick Bateman, a public-school-educated stockbroker, with his received pronunciation and upper-class ways, was the quintessential reality-tv villain. He lied to the other contestants. During one of the discussion topics set by Big Brother, Nick poignantly told the story of his first love — he said that his first wife had died in a car accident in Australia. But it wasn't true. It was clearly a ploy to gain sympathy. He tried to influence how the other contestants voted and broke a number of house rules. The tabloids dubbed him the 'most hated man in Britain' and tried numerous ways to let the other contestants know that he was cheating. Eventually, the contestants tumbled to him; he was confronted and evicted. His cheating made the front pages of the *Star*, the *Telegraph*, the *Mirror*, the *Express*, the *Independent* and the *Guardian*. He sold his story to the *Sun*. He went on to 'write' *How to be a Right Bastard* and to host a short-lived television show, *Trust Me*. He was replaced by Claire.

The first series ratings peaked when 56 per cent of the television viewing public tuned in. Ten million viewers watched the final show. More people voted in the final *Big Brother* eviction than voted in the European elections.

Celebrity Big Brother started in March 2001. Six British celebrities (television presenters Vanessa Feltz and Anthea Turner, comedian Jack Dee, boxer Chris Eubank, soapie star Claire Sweeney and boy-band member Keith Duffy) entered the *Big Brother* house for one week. The first instalment almost doubled Channel 4's normal share of viewers — it attracted 18.4 per cent of those watching television at the time. The 3.25 million votes cast generated £500,000 for Comic Relief and about £280,000 for BT — BT was criticised for the size of their share. The eventual winner was comedian Jack Dee who spent most of his time trying to escape in order to reconcile with his estranged wife. Vanessa Feltz emerged as the house villian and felt 'damaged' by the editing.

The second series started in July 2001 and there were a few noticeable changes. The most obvious was the improved *Big Brother* house, which had new furniture, a designer kitchen, an en-suite in one bedroom and a 'nookie hut' in the garden.

Much to the producers' dismay, the contestants did not utilise the nookie hut which was designed to give couples privacy. Indeed, generally the British contestants have been reluctant to engage in much sexual activity. For the third series, producers plan to 'redouble our efforts — to copy foreign versions of the program — one couple in every European version was filmed having sex'.[7] Apparently, they plan to do this by introducing couples into the house and then splitting them up (via public voting) and see which partners remain faithful.

The British tabloids pay a huge role in whipping the public into a *Big Brother* frenzy. Nick was the obvious target in the first series. In the second series, the *Mirror* and the *Sun* went head to head. The *Mirror* backed Brian Dowling and the *Sun* backed Helen Adams. The *Mirror* was determined to back a winner and, as the more liberal paper of the two, it was the natural place for gay Brian's exclusive story. Although Brian won the money, Helen won the viewers' hearts and the *Sun* won the circulation battle. The *Sun* secured Helen's tale and when she and contestant/boyfriend Paul Clarke were out of the house and reunited, their sex lives made front page news.

Big Brother was available on cable for up to 21 hours every day to subscribers of Sky, NTL and Ondigital. Sky Digital viewers could select from four live feeds, follow the news and information 'ticker', and even vote directly through their remote control for the contestant they wanted to leave the house. This meant that viewers could watch house 'live' (with a ten-minute editorial delay). Four and a half million viewers watched the second series.

The next *Big Brother* is supposed to be based on 'The Battle' format used in the Netherlands. The old house has been pulled down (due to zoning regulations and council laws) and so a new house will have to be built.

United States

The first *Big Brother* series was a flop. The contestants were unmemorable and the show just didn't grab the imagination of the viewing public. It sank virtually without a trace. CBS has outbid FOX and ABC and paid US$20 million for the rights. It erected a small house with a vegetable garden, a tiny wading pool and a chicken coop on one of its lots in California's San Fernando Valley. The ten contestants were chosen from 1100 audition tapes. The show was a flop largely due to the nervousness of the producers. Late-night conversations and early morning barbecues were heavily censored as the network did not want to portray the contestants as drinkers and partiers. It was so boring that even the contestants considered walking out. The producers, desperate to try and drum up controversy, offered US$50,000 to entice someone to leave the house. John deMol, *Big Brother* creator, admitted that the second series would require rethinking and revamping; he said that the 'cultural differences between American and Europeans are much, much bigger than we thought'.[8]

The most noticeable feature of the second series was the upgraded living quarters. The 1800-square-foot house, ironically not far from where *Gilligan's Island* 'seven stranded castaways' were filmed nearly forty years ago, was palatial. The new house had bedrooms divided by pexiglass wall, and a separate bedroom for the Head of the House (HOH) contained a fridge filled with luxuries denied the other contestants. Each week contestants elected an HOH — who was granted immunity from eviction.

Viewers did not vote for the winner; the evicted contestants chose a winner from the final contestants. Clearly, the producers adopted a *Survivor*-esque ideology which they hoped would increase dramatic tension. Contestants were allowed to make alliances and to discuss voting strategies. The winner, Will, was blatant in his plotting. He told the other contestants that he lied and cheated, but they still voted him the winner. The runner-up received a smaller cash prize.

The most controversial moment in the series was not sexual, but violent. Justin 'threatened' Krista with a knife. Apparently Krista was drunk and she and Justin were in the kitchen kissing when Justin held a knife to her throat and asked, 'Would you get mad if I killed you?' Viewers reported that this incident seemed to be part jokey, part sexual play. However, Big Brother was not amused and Justin was removed while the contestants were sleeping. The next morning the other contestants were told to pack up his possessions and give them to Big Brother. The full incident wasn't screened on television.

One love-in between Justin, Krista and Shannon stopped *Big Brother* cameras for ten minutes after Krista was seen feeling Shannon's breasts. The camera went to FOTH (the front of the house), a technique that irritated *Big Brother* RealPlayer viewers who had paid extra for live feeds.

There was a plethora of ways for contestants to earn/win privileges and rewards. There were food challenges (losers had to eat peanut butter and jelly sandwiches), luxury challenges, and HOH challenges. In 'America's Choice' viewers chose who received a three-minute phone call, a birthday greeting from home, a celebration dinner etc.

The host, Julie Chen, was criticised in the first series but was retained for the second. For the second series, she had her own quarters located just outside the house.

The second show was not aired nightly — there were three one-hour shows each week: on Tuesday, Thursday and Saturday at 8 pm.

General

Most of the European *Big Brother*s start in September and run until December. The two American *Big Brother*s started in mid-Summer, 5 July. Channel 10's Tim Clucas (Head of Factual Programming) believes that the timing is crucial. Australian *Big Brother* could not be shown in the summer; it couldn't compete with the weather.

Generally the contestants on *Big Brother* are young: the majority are under 35. Nearly all of the first winners have been male; only four of the 20 countries had female winners (Denmark, Italy, Sweden and Switzerland). Men are twice as likely to win as women (27 men have won and 13 women). Females are most likely to be voted out first. Quite often two or three men are the final contestants. Often the most popular contestant does not win. Sara-Marie is typical.

Central to the show are the crowds which flock to the *Big Brother* houses. Germany, Holland and Argentina have had problems with crowd control. One would have thought that by the time South Africa started filming their series they would have learned about *Big Brother* and crowds. Australia had the perfect solution: make them pay for the privilege.

The style of housing varies considerably too. From the tiny dorm-style rooms in Holland to the palatial Hollywood home, the *Big Brother* houses reflect the different cultures. Besides the two large bedrooms, the French 'loft' show had individual bedrooms for privacy. The South African house had been given an 'African feel': earthy colours, authentic ethnic art objects and even special *Big Brother* door handles. The walls were painted in colours that would enable a 'variety of skin tones' to film well. Rather than hide the cameras, the windows are framed with carved patterns. The second US house was a sumptuous mansion with double front doors and stylish furniture. One of the contestants (a realtor) claimed that some million-dollar homes didn't look as good. If the United States had the most sumptuous *Big Brother* house, the United Kingdom had the grottiest. The British *Big Brother* was set in East London on half an acre of land. Generally, the European residences look cramped and small on television. Overseas viewers have been amazed at the open design of the Australian house.

The Portuguese contestants had to fight for their beds, as did the American contestants when they entered their home, for despite the four bedrooms one person still had to sleep on the floor, in a sleeping bag.

The houses have generally undergone some refurbishment after each series. Most recently the houses have been divided into richer and poorer sections and contestants have had to earn a place in the more luxurious sides (the Netherlands, United Kingdom, United States). This, of course, increases competition. The Belgian house had a punishment cell in the living room; the Brits put a nookie hut in the garden.

Outside the houses, the yards also bear testament to the different cultures. In Australia a swimming pool replaced the sexier jacuzzi

(United Kingdom and United States); the second US house had a half-size basketball court. The gardens are supposed to provide extra vegetables and sustenance. Nearly all of the *Big Brother* houses have had resident chickens — indeed a rooster in the first UK series was almost as big a star as the housemates and soon rubber chickens were sported by the coolest fans. And generally the chickens suffer from a variety of maladies. Besides the chooks, the houses have entertained a vast array of non-human animals: dogs (Belgium, Holland, Australia and United States 1), a puppy (Portugal), a goldfish (United Kingdom), a parrot (Italy and Spain), a rabbit (Sweden), a cat (Germany) and a chinchilla 'Little Brother' (Norway). Viewers chose 'Ophelia', a Vietnamese pig, for the contestants in the United States 2 series. Some contestants don't take too kindly to the animals; Bad Brad in South Africa threatened to kick a dog if it was introduced into the house.

As is the norm, before contestants enter the house *Big Brother* staff usually have a 'dress rehearsal' in the house. The South African *Big Brother* team went wild in the house. In a moment of abandonment one of the staff stripped naked, another threw up in the bathroom and blocked the toilet with paper, and someone else decapitated a chicken! In the United Kingdom the *Big Brother* staff found that they vaguely resented the contestants entering the house; they had developed a proprietorial feeling about it. Dress rehearsals gave producers, directors and camera people a chance to preview *all* of their skills. And to check the house for dead spots (where cameras can't see or mikes can't pick up sounds).

There seems to be a general consensus that the most enjoyable task is the danceathon. Whereas some tasks develop team skills, some reveal even more. The UK pottery task hasn't been repeated, despite its sexy start to the series. Neither has the pie-eating contest. It is not surprising that Australia didn't get the bungy-jumping task; the contestants weren't allowed on the roof. Luckily, we didn't get the moon-trip task (Poland) or the inevitable Guiness Book of Records tasks (UK). However, the squeeze-food-and-people-into-a-car task sounded exciting (US), especially as the last person out of the car wins it. In South Africa the gumboot dancing task shows the cultural divide — but it sounds like fun. As does the garden-gnome sculpting — is the humble plaster statue as kitsch in South Africa as it is here? But we could forgo the Beauty Pageant.

Speaking of garden gnomes, the one in South Africa was kidnapped while the contestants, and presumably the security personnel, slept. Under the gaze of a number of cameras a couple of drunks had scaled the fence and stolen the gnome; it was taken to a local bar where the owner then auctioned the privilege to name it. A legal company dubbed the gnome 'The Lawyer' and returned it to the house. They were A$30,000 poorer but a charity was that much richer.

Love in the *Big Brother* world

The South African website stated that 'Sex is permitted, but contraception is strongly advised'. Indeed contestants having sex is the producers' wet dream. United States *Big Brother* producer Arnold Shapiro succinctly summarised his hopes for the second series 'romance — nudity — physicality'.[9] He has this in common with most *Big Brother* producers; hence the spas, pools and nookie huts which producers hope will prod contestants into minimal wear and some raunchy action.

To date, it has been the European *Big Brother*s that have had on-camera sex. Norwegian couple Rodney and Anette had sex on television; as did two Swedish women. Apparently more than half the Belgian contestants had sex with each other; one couple preferred oral sex. While the French couple had sex in the spa, sex in the loo was the go for a Swiss couple. Danish couples were considered 'boring' with their routine sex; German couples liked variety and kept swapping, depending on who was evicted. In Italy it took fewer than four days for a couple to end up under the curtains on the floor. Even in Russia one couple had sex. However, the American, Australian, South African and British versions have been much tamer. So tame, that Southern Comfort offered £50,000 to the first couple to have sex on British *Big*

Brother 1; the only trouble was that only one of the contestants knew about it, Nick's replacement Claire. For the second series, a nookie hut promised privacy, unless you count the cameras which were there to capture and broadcast every moment. A British bookmaker paid out £500 after Craig and Caroline slipped between the sheets, but there was not enough action to claim the Southern Comfort prize.

Quite often contestants strip to impress the opposite sex. Portuguese girls did and so have male contestants. Andy's shower antics were not the only ones; in Russia two naked girls slowly washed each other all over in a saucy shower scene that lasted twenty minutes.

Occasionally love blossomed in the *Big Brother* houses. German Karim and Daniela met on *Big Brother* in 2000 and married in Frankfurt a year later. Annemona and Ramsy (Norway I) married in the Big Brother house one year after they left it. In Poland, Karolina could not stand the *Big Brother* house without her fellow contestant, now boyfriend, and moved out when he was evicted. After he was evicted, Marco flew a banner over the Portuguese house which read, 'Marta I love you.' Nearly a year after their time in the house, British contestants Sada and Nichola revealed that they had fallen in love; and Tom and Claire kept their romance a secret until Claire fell pregnant. After *Big Brother* 2 finished, Paul and Helen's romance continued, even in the glaring eye of the public. The *Sun*'s headlines screamed 'Paul and Helen Bonk. She loves every position and screams Oh My God' (28 August 2001). The United States watched a blossoming love between Shannon and Will; another contestant proposed on the final night but it seems to have been a publicity stunt. Viewers in Argentina were sceptical when one couple became engaged. Sergio and Veronica (the Portuguese couple who had sex on camera) were coerced into marrying on television — complete with *Big Brother* logo in the background. So far little love has resulted from the Australian house. Although many viewers hoped that Christina and Peter's romance would survive outside the house, it didn't.

Controversy

The one constant about *Big Brother* has been the debates it has unleashed in every country that has aired the show. From the outset creator John de Mol realised that imprisoning a group of people would lead to controversy, so this was offset with careful (one might say rigorous) psychological assessment of all contestants. DeMol described his quest to counter the potential harm: 'Every psychiatrist in Holland, whether they were asked to or not, gave their opinions on how dangerous this thing could be. We had a group of psychologists advising us, telling us what to do and what not to do. They helped us oversee our casting on the Dutch version, and we have followed the same pattern each time. We take it very seriously and monitor everything as closely as possible.'

Some expressed concern on behalf of the contestants. The Netherlands Institute of Psychologists branded the show 'irresponsible and unethical'; others called it a type of mental torture. A spokesperson from the Polish Christian Psychologists Society warned of the potential harm; contestants might suffer 'a deep breakdown, neurosis or psychological disturbances'. The Polish National Radio and Television Council thought it was a 'dangerous' experiment. The president of the *Association Francaise de Psychiatrie* considered the show 'perverse exhibition', and mental health professionals warned of potential psychological harm to the cast members.

Greece was concerned not with the visual surveillance but the dataveillance of the producers of the show and their fullsome contestant records. And the journalists union threatened action agains members who took part in the show's production because it eroded 'human values'. The awarding of television honours to the Italian *Big Brother* upset television industry personnel. The screening of sex incurred heavy fines and the condemnation of MPs and the Catholic Church in Portugal.

Inhabitants of *Big Brother* houses in Belgium, Denmark and South Africa were not told of the World Trade Centre disasters.

But contestants in The Netherlands and the United States (where a contestant's cousin had been missing since the attack) were. In The Netherlands a spokeswoman said they decided that the contestants had a 'right' to know what had happened. Of course these decisions have evoked considerable debate.

The oft-expressed worry was what the show 'said' about the nature of television. The Polish National Radio and Television Council thought the show presented 'a nightmare vision of the television of the future'.[10]

Chapter Two

Guiding Lights: Behind the Scenes

'You'd be surprised how much it costs to look this cheap.'
(Dolly Parton)

Australia supports three major commercial networks: Channels 7, 9 and 10. (Their names refer to the VHF frequencies used for their main transmitters.) They are called 'commercial' channels because they are funded by advertising revenue, and although they might be 'free-to-air' this has not always been the case. Older viewers will remember the days of the television licence.

Television shows are produced in a number of ways: the television station can make their shows in-house (Channel 7 used to produce *Home and Away*, *All Saints* and *The Great Outdoors*); television programs can be bought from production companies (Channel 7 handed production of the aforementioned shows to Steve Vizzard's production company Newcom in 2000); or programs can be bought from distribution companies. Distribution companies such as Beyond International handle television programs (*Getaway*, *Our House* and *Something in the Air*). However, television programs can be handled by more than one distribution company; *Buffy the Vampire Slayer* is the property of 20th Century Fox Film Corporation, WB Television Network *and* United Paramount Network. Sometimes shows are produced, distributed and aired by the same company; 20th Century Fox Television produces *The Simpsons* and *Buffy the Vampire Slayer*, both of which aired on the Fox Network and are distributed by 20th Century Fox Film Corporation. In Australia, *Big Brother* was produced by Southern

Star Endemol in conjunction with Channel 10 (who aired the show) and Dreamworld (who provided the physical space).

Each television station has a 'personality'. If *Big Brother* had been screened on the ABC or SBS, it would have been quite a different program. These 'personalities' are fluid. Channel 10 did not always target younger audiences. In its early years it was home to programs such as *Number 96*, *MASH* and *The Mike Walsh Show*. However, by 1990 Channel 10 was in serious financial trouble and losing ratings. A new tactic was required and CEO Peter Viner decided to target younger viewers. New slogans ('Give Me Ten', 'Turn Me On' and 'Seriously Entertaining') were incorporated and program lineups changed. Gone were the endless repeats of *MASH*; instead *The Simpsons*, *The Panel* and *The X-Files* lured the 16–24 demographic. The fare is generally sit-coms and light drama rather than news and current affairs. Now it 'consistently [holds] the largest commercial share of the 16–24 year old audience'[1] In a prescient moment, it had screened a proto-*Big Brother*, *The House from Hell* (1998). Channel 10's youth focus made it the ideal channel for *Big Brother*.

The history of a television *Big Brother*

Big Brother was fathered in a think session in Holland. John de Mol described its conception:

> Three years ago [1997], we were approached by one of the public broadcasters in Holland who wanted us to create a new kind of show. So I put together a creative team, and we started brainstorming and thinking of different ideas.
>
> After many hours and one long, unfruitful evening, we finished our drinks, and suddenly one of the guys brought up an article that he had read in an American magazine about the Biosphere II. That intrigued me so much that I kept on asking about it. We had already been bouncing around an idea that would be based on a sabbatical year, if you could build a format out of that. That was still in the back of my mind, and then the guy told me about Biosphere II, and we combined that, spent a few years working on the idea, and Big

> Brother was born.
>
> First *Big Brother* was called *The Golden Cage*, and it was for one year. For all kinds of reasons, we decided to bring it back to 100 days — mainly for financial reasons. Then, the basics came about, and it took us two years to develop *Big Brother* to what it is today.[2]

The cost of producing a year-long show was prohibitive: approximately £15 million. After revising the format Endemol franchised the idea. In the mid-1990s John de Mol travelled the world pitching his shows to television executives; United States executives were unimpressed. The unexpected success of *Who Wants to be a Millionaire?* (Celador Productions 1998) had television executives reconsidering gameshow formats, and in 2000 CBS won the *Big Brother* bidding war. Similarly, in Australia Channel 7 was interested, then Channel 9 entered the fray, but the laurels went to Channel 10. According to Channel 10's Tim Clucas, part of their winning pitch was that they planned to air *Big Brother* after *Neighbours*, which is popular in Europe.

John de Mol has worked in the television industry for some time. His original company (John de Mol Productions) merged with rival Dutch company Joop van den Ende Productions to form Endemol in 1994. Since then van den Ende has left the company. Today, Endemol Entertainment is one of Europe's top television-production companies with a stable of more than 400 television formats, including *Chains of Love*, *Fear Factor* and *The Master Plan*. Endemol has affiliates in seventeen countries and is worth US$5 billion. Early in 2001, it was reported that de Mol had opened offices on Sunset Boulevard because he planned to become 'a substantial Hollywood player'.[3]

Though Endemol is the parent company, in each country different production companies are responsible for production. Sometimes the production companies are Endemol subsidiaries (as is the case in South Africa), but in the United States it was produced by CBS. In the United Kingdom, Bazal (which already had links with Endemol) was the host production company; Bazal produces other reality-tv shows such as *Changing Rooms* and *Ground*

Force. In Australia, Southern Star teamed with Endemol to produce *Big Brother*.

Not so cheap

It is generally considered a truism that 'reality' shows are cheap because there are no scriptwriters, no actors' fees, no costumes and so on. While this might be true in some cases, *Big Brother* certainly does not come cheap. It was rumoured that in Australia the show cost $20 million to produce (including $13 million for the rights).

Much of this money was spent in the host state, Queensland, and the *Courier-Mail* estimated that the show had a $19 million impact on the state economy.[4] Queensland's Pacific Film and Television Commission gave Southern Star Endemol 'access to a $2.5 million cash flow through its revolving film finance fund as well as payroll tax rebates and salary rebates … [This] assistance would have been worth about $50,000'.[5] It is anticipated that for the 2002 series a further $7 million will be spent on refurbishing the house, production facilities at Dreamworld, and promotion.

Production considerations

Filming, editing and airing a nightly show in less than 24 hours requires a dedicated team of professionals. *Big Brother* required the coordination and cooperation of people from at least four different companies: Channel 10, Southern Star Endemol, Dreamworld and Global Television.

Global Television provided the equipment and the camera crew: five of their own employees and ten specially trained university students. It was also responsible for the construction of the studio control room (seen in the opening credits to the show). The control room was 300 metres from the house and was linked by 30 kilometres of video, audio and data cable. The control room housed monitors which broadcast from the in-house equipment. There were 25 in-house cameras, 7 with remote 'hot head' control, 4 infra-red and 5 full broadcast quality on pedestals. The hot-head cameras had to be quiet so the mikes wouldn't pick up their sound movement. Audio came from 20 fixed microphones and of course the contestants' radio microphones. Blair, who was a bit of a mumbler, caused considerable difficulties: many of his conversations had to be subtitled; Sara-Marie broke several of her mikes. As can be imagined, all the equipment had to be robust. The cameras and the mikes had to cope with bad weather and contestants' antics. Microphones have ended up down toilets and in swimming pools and jacuzzis.

If *Big Brother* is remembered for nothing else, it will be remembered for providing employment and developing television skills. The South African *Big Brother* employed about 350 people: an online team consisted of six writers and two editors and 108 production crew which included camerapersons, loggers, archivists, runners, technical directors and production assistants. The United Kingdom *Big Brother* employed about 200 people including 50 camerapersons and 13 producers;[6] nearly 50 people worked on the website to cope with the 1500 daily emails.

About 220 staff from Channel 10, Southern Star Endemol and Global Television worked on *Big Brother* in Australia. The official website alone had two permanent staff at Southern Star Endemol, thirteen contractors on site at Dreamworld and volunteer moderators. Global Television was responsible for the 60-strong technical (i.e. camera and audio) crew, five permanent Global Television employees and 55 freelancers recruited in Queensland. Global also trained ten film and television students from Bond University to operate equipment as part of their course requirement (the best student won a prize from Global Television).

Because the show was filmed 24 hours a day, seven days a week, there were multiple production teams. Individual teams were relegated to either the daily shows, the 'adults-only' show, or the Saturday or Sunday shows — each timeslot required crews trained for content. Staff had to be rotated to achieve 24/7 coverage.[7]

How did a typical *Big Brother* day run? At 12 midnight the

day's footage was collated and prepared for digitisation. The material had already received one edit (by camera operators and control room editors). The footage was re-viewed by a smaller group under the guidance of *Big Brother* Executive Producer Peter Abbott (of Southern Star Endemol). He and a supervising producer, an editor, the Classification Officer and Tim Clucas viewed the collated material between 9 and 11 am. During these two hours, many issues had to be resolved. One of the most important considerations was that the material was kept in strict context; that is, there was no unfair representation of the contestants. The Classification Officer (Ms Vanda Leigh) remembered that Peter Abbot was most emphatic about assumptions: 'You don't know what "x" thinks', was a common refrain.[8] Similarly, Tim Clucas believed that it was imperative that the material be as 'factual' as possible. The final edition had to be sent by satellite to Sydney before 4.30 pm or it would interrupt the news which also had to be sent down. Missing the 4.30 pm deadline would incur enormous costs — as would later amendments to the show.

Sometimes, despite several viewings, a swear word passed undetected; this had to be culled and then the re-edited section patched down to Sydney via satellite. A 30-second broadcast delay for live shows gave the Classification Officer time to delete inappropriate content. Sara-Marie's fear that her visit to the toilet during a Sunday eviction had been broadcast live was unnecessary, but Big Brother couldn't tell her that such material would be inappropriate for television.

Twenty-fours hours a day the control room was busy. The producers watched the many monitors, always looking to see what events were transpiring and indicated to the directors the appropriate actions when necessary (e.g. 'x and y are talking in the yard'). In turn, the directors gave instructions to the camera crew (e.g. 'close up on x and y's conversation'). The camera crew were first-line editors; they had to be aware of the potential of sending out pictures (the Internet coverage was live) which could be inappropriate, especially regarding the viewing time.

Assisting the producers and directors in the control room were the 'logging staff' who would record information for the archives. The 'logging system' labelled nearly every scene with information such as names and topics (e.g. 'gossip', 'Peter', 'bitching') so that the relevant material could be retrieved and collated to create a narrative should the need arise. The logging system proved invaluable for the compilation clips shown during the various weekly shows (Saturday nights, eviction nights and Thursday night adults-only show.)

'Expect the unexpected' had to be the catchcry for *Big Brother* production staff. On screen events unfolded with seeming ease, but behind the scenes it was a different story. People sat with fingers poised over bleep buttons because, despite their best-laid plans, anything could happen. Big Brother warned contestants not to drink or swear during live broadcasts and beer bottles were placed out of view. The contestants had been given written instructions for emergencies, but when a parachutist tried to get into the compound, Big Brother ordered the contestants inside the house. During the first eviction show, Gretel tripped and sliced off the top of her finger; she carried on hosting and staff rushed around looking for bandages and patched it up during a break.

But what happens if one of the contestants leaves before an eviction?

Nasty Nick's exit from *Big Brother* 1 in the United Kingdom is a case in point. For a week before Big Brother evicted Nick, producers had been preparing for his departure. Because of the massive coverage in the tabloid press, they knew his departure would be a media circus. Diversionary plans were necessary. On the day of Nick's confrontation, the *Big Brother* team moved into high gear. Several cars arrived at the house. While a dummy car lured reporters in one direction, Nick was taken to a secret location. Waiting for him at the hotel were a psychologist and a press agent; the psychologist counselled Nick and the agent fielded the avalanche of offers Nick received. Back in the house, they were now one contestant short, but standby contestant Clare soon arrived.

Legal issues and *Big Brother*

Viewers might have thought that the most that Channel 10 had to worry about was letting the odd swear word or inappropriate shot go to air. But there were more worrying issues than expletives or cleavage. Each show's content had to be appropriate for its timeslot. So that everyone understood the regulations, Sydney's Channel 10 Classification Officer, Dr Sally Stockbridge, trained all production, camera and internet staff. She also trained an on-site assistant, Ms Vanda Leigh, who was onsite at Dreamworld. The two women were in constant touch. Sally tells of one instance when Vanda rang her while she was shopping. She was in the vegetable aisle looking at the carrots when Vanda asked about the appropriateness of a shot. Sally's question 'Can you see pubic hair?' attracted some startled looks from nearby shoppers.[9]

Throughout the world the television industry is governed by a set of protocols. In Australia, the Australian Broadcasting Authority (ABA) is the government body (federal) which regulates the broadcasting industry (radio, television and internet). The *Broadcasting Services Act 1992* sets out what is and what is not acceptable. Among other things, the Act prohibits tobacco advertising, 'R' rated material (e.g. sustained violence, depiction of sexual acts, detailed genital nudity, very coarse language, encouragement of illegal drug use and promotion of suicide), programs that 'simulate news or events in a way that misleads or alarms the audience' and shows that 'depict the actual process of putting a person into a hypnotic state'. Breaches of the Act incur heavy fines (currently A$2.2 million) and may result in the revocation of a broadcasting licence. Despite the hue and cry about sexual content on the internet, R-rated material is available only to registered users (those over 18 years of age).

Australia's commercial television stations are governed by the ABA's Commercial Television Industry Code of Practice. The Code regulates the content of commercial television so that it reflects community attitudes, especially in relation to program classification, and covers issues such as:

- the portrayal of physical and psychological violence
- the portrayal of sexual conduct and nudity
- the use of offensive language
- the portrayal of the use of drugs, including alcohol and tobacco
- the portrayal of matter that is likely to incite or perpetuate hatred against, or vilifies, any person or group on the basis of ethnicity, nationality, race, gender, sexual preference, age, religion or physical or mental disability.

There are six classifications for television shows, and each classification outlines the times a show can be aired. Roughly, they are as follows:

- Children/Preschool (C/P): can be shown at any time
- General (G): can be shown at any time
- Parental Guidance (Parental Guidance Recommended): 5 am – 6 am, 8.30 am – 4 pm, 7.30 pm – 5 am
- Mature (M): 8:30 pm – 12 midnight, 12 midnight – 5 am, 12 noon – 3 am
- Mature Audience (MA) for viewers 15 years and over: 9 pm – 5 am
- Adult Violent Content (AV) 15 years and over: 9:30 pm – 5 am.

Viewing times vary slightly for weekends and during school holidays.

For many people the constant surveillance of the *Big Brother* contestants roused fears of inappropriate material being broadcast (sex acts cannot be shown either on television or on the internet) — fears that were largely circumvented by the training given by Dr Stockbridge and the dilligence of Ms Leigh. In Portugal, the television channel that broadcast sex scenes was fined. In the United States, *Big Brother* internet cameras cut to the front of the house whenever it appeared that sexual activity might occur; cynical net-viewers speculated that it was really to save the more interesting events for night-time viewing. French pay-per viewers were similarly disappointed: the cameras turned away when things were too sexy. *Le Parisien* dubbed it the 'no-sex scandal'.

But there were other things to worry about besides sex on telly. What if a contestant should defame someone (legally labelled 'slander' if the defamatory statement is oral only) — even simple statements such as 'Oh "x", he's a big poof' could be contentious. What if one of them confesses to a crime? What are the copyright laws about singing a song? For these and many other reasons, a duty lawyer had to be available at all times.

The Internet and *Big Brother*

After entertainment came infotainment, *Big Brother* married two mediums — television and internet — for 'intertainment'.

Around the world the official websites have been inundated with viewers. France had nearly one million page views per day; Germany had 4–5 million page views and Holland had 52 million page views throughout the series. Between 8 am and 9 am on the first morning of Italian *Big Brother* 200,000 registered visitors viewed over 1.3 million pages at the official website. Thirty-two million page views were registered during South Africa's first week, equal to a new user every three seconds. The Norwegian website attracted 9.7 million hits on the first weekend. The Australian website was the single most visited website in Australian history.

The popularity of the Australian *Big Brother* website was almost its undoing. On the first day over a million visitors crashed the site; in the first four days the website had over 48 million page views. One hundred thousand people registered in its first two weeks of operation; in total 964,067 users registered. During the show's run, the website scored over 83 million page impressions and averaged 70,000 visitors each day; it recorded nearly seven million visitors. Over thirteen million streams were delivered.[10] While this was good news for *Big Brother*, others in the community haven't been so thrilled. In the United Kingdom it was estimated that £300,000 was lost in productivity every day because people logged on to the *Big Brother* website. Many companies have blocked *Big Brother* so staff can't watch it.

Each *Big Brother* website adopts the same format and look (except for *Loft Story*): the mid-blue background, the logo, and small pictures of the contestants. All of the websites are multimedia and contain graphics, audios and even videos. The UK website offered two additional viewing options: pancam and fancam. The pancam was a centrally located panoramic camera (one in the lounge room and one in the kitchen) which allowed viewers to choose their viewing angle. Fancam was an additional camera dedicated to following one particular contestant for 24 hours. Every day, viewers voted for their favourite contestant; the contestant with the most votes was then tracked for 24 hours.

Generally, the websites have their own domain name (Australia www.bigbrother.com.au; Portugal www.bigbrother.pt; South Africa www.bigbrothersa.com) and are housed at independent sites; however, some television stations hang the *Big Brother* website at their own (United States, Belgium, Spain). Though websites used to close down after the show ended, more recently they have remained opened and are regularly updated with the latest *Big Brother* news (Belgium, Norway and Australia). In order to view the live feeds, viewers had to have the right software. Generally, *Big Brother* uses RealPlayer. Although the basic software is free, some countries charged for access to *Big Brother* feeds. In the United States *Big Brother* 2 viewers were charged up to US$20. Despite the added cost, 56,026 new viewers signed up and 41,814 existing RealPlayer consumers accessed the feeds on a regular basis. CBS executive David Katz reported that the 'numbers far exceeded our expectations ... This thing was highly profitable'; the total revenue from the webcasts was around US$1 million.[11] Belgian viewers also had to pay for live feeds for their second series. Australian internet service providers (ISPs) responded quickly to the *Big Brother* phenomenon; many of them rescinded their unlimited downloads when the show started. Primus made the most of the opportunity to sign up new customers — they advertised unlimited free downloads for a set monthly rate.

Many critics objected to 24/7 surveillance, but it is not a new concept. For nearly six years people have voluntarily subjected themselves to 24-hour surveillance via the internet. In 1996 Jennifer Wringley became famous when she installed web cameras and started broadcasting her life at her internet site, www.jennicam.org. Others soon found the idea of being watched 24/7 appealing and webcam sites mushroomed. One website (www.webcamsearch.com) lists over 25,000 webcam addresses. Webcams are not only in people's bedrooms; they are in offices, on street corners, even on pets. There is little nudity or sex on many of the webcams — one particularly popular one is trained on a coffee urn. Webcams instil the web with a reality which defies its 'virtuality'.

Live feeds were not the most popular way to watch *Big Brother*. The shots were too small and lacked the smooth streaming and clarity of the television episodes. Often the video and audio were out of sync too. Live feeds may have promised the potential for sex, but more astute viewers would have realised that ABA restrictions also apply to the internet. The Southern Star Endemol Interactive team were trained by the Classification Officer and took advice from in-house lawyers about defamation and contempt issues. The live feeds did not have a time delay and thus directors had to have their fingers poised on the switch button. In the United States, *Big Brother* 2 frustrated viewers with its FOTH shots; like the French, viewers felt that they had paid to watch *everything*. Other *Big Brothers* (France, Germany, Greece, the United Kingdom) have resorted to pay television channels in order to circumvent censorship issues. Not all webviewers panted for sex; many of the fans preferred the live feeds because they were unedited and thus they learned more about the contestants and could witness the gradual unfolding of the events.

The website was perhaps the single most important marketing tool for *Big Brother* because it kept viewers interested between shows.

Marketing

Australia was the first country to capitalise on the crowds drawn to the *Big Brother* houses, and Queensland theme park Dreamworld turned *Big Brother* into one of their main attractions. After the show started, people could walk around the auditorium, watch the live feeds on large screens, wander around the stage, peek into the *Uncut* room and look over the shoulders of staff in the editing suites. They could even snoop through the house — between the first and second series the house was opened to the public. Sunday visitors to Dreamworld could pay an additional charge and be part of the audience for the live evictions.

And, of course, fans could visit the onsite shop and have their photo taken in a replica diary room chair or purchase *Big Brother* paraphernalia such as bunny ears, signed contestant photos, hats, videos, CDs and coffee mugs. Not everything in the shop was a marketing success; during the first days whips were put into the shop, until Dreamworld staff realised that they were hardly appropriate for a family park and were removed.

Dreamworld might have the only *Big Brother* attraction, but it doesn't have the only *Big Brother* shop. *Big Brother* stores have opened in Poland and Denmark. Merchandise can be purchased online at the official South African website, but most official websites don't sell directly to the public. There are virtual shops such as www.buybigbrother.com and www.amazon.com where *Big Brother* merchandise is available. Several countries have different versions of the board game (United States, United Kingdom and South Africa); Australia had an 'uncut' version which was originally available online but was later available in stores. Similarly, each series usually had its own music and video. So far, only three official *Big Brother* books have been written: two in the United Kingdom and one in South Africa.

Big Brother madness has generated a diverse range of merchandise aside from the prosaic tee-shirts and coffee mugs. In Australia it was bunny ears and Pooh-Bear pyjamas; in the United Kingdom rubber chooks were popular during the first series. Other less predictable *Big Brother* items included condoms, chewing gum and beer. A few *Big Brother* video games have been released, for example 'The Revenge of Marjorie the Chicken' from the United Kingdom *Big Brother* 1.

Advertisements and the television industry

Television is like an apple; the programs are the core and the advertisements are the flesh. Commercial television stations exist *only* because advertisers buy advertising time. Advertisements also reflect how viewing audiences are perceived by advertisers.

Typically viewers were exposed to about eight minutes of commercials during a half-hour episode of *Big Brother*. On 24 May, the following advertisements were aired during *Big Brother*:

X-Files (Channel 10)
Joe Dirt movie promo
TD Waterhouse (humour: woman and would-be mugger)
Overflow
MacDonalds
Pizza Hut
Small Soldiers movie promo (Channel 10)
Pizza Hut
ING (humorous Billy Connolly advertisement)
Eclipse chewing gum (humour: old guy and young nurse)
Dreamworld *Big Brother* attraction
Courier-Mail
Lynx, Baileys and Mitsubishi — combined ad
Dawson's Creek (Channel 10)
Pepsi
Primus
McDonald's
Dreamworld *Big Brother* attraction again
As Good As It Gets (Channel 10) movie.

Overall the ads were for products generally associated with youth (i.e. Pepsi, McDonald's, rap music and teen flicks) and they tended to have young people in them. The movies advertised included *Joe Dirt*, *Evolution*, *Tomb Raider* and *Tomcats*. *Tomcats*, with its male-mediated gaze of sexualised female bodies and riotous partying, mirrored the house antics in a glamorous and idealised way. Most of the ads were humorous — even the 'serious' ones such as ING and TD Waterhouse. Naturally Channel 10 filled the most important spots (i.e. those at the end of the ad break before returning to *Big Brother*) with promos for their own programs. After Channel 10, sponsors grabbed the lion's share.

Sponsors' ads often reflected some aspect of the show. Freedom Furniture's exhortation to 'think outside the box in which you live' subtly reflected the *Big Brother* house as prison. The Primus adverts reflected the surveillance aspect of the show: a man stands in a shower and addresses a soapbar with a camera inside. Pizza Hut had a series of *Big Brother* advertisements which were only aired during the show. These followed a delivery boy's attempts to break into the *Big Brother* house; the last advertisement in the series (aired during the final show) was particularly clever: the delivery boy breaks into the house only to find that everyone has left. Subtextually, the ad refers to the desire to get into the house — by fair means (via the television or as a contestant) or foul — even if it means undermining Big Brother, who is represented as the security guards. A Dreamworld ad has two men running around the *Big Brother* auditorium. They ask an off-camera 'mum' if they can go in, as 'it looks really good'; a camera zooms in on a sign and particularly the words 'live, adult themes, nudity' while the voiceover says '*Big Brother* exposed, live uncut at Dreamworld'. The two young actors re-define viewer as contestant as visitor: they look like the contestants and they 'look' like viewers/visitors. They ask permission from their mother as a visitor would; yet they run around the stage as if they belong there. The focus on the words 'adult themes' and 'nudity' gestures to teen male desires and underscored the voyeuristic aspect of *Big Brother*.

Other ads mimicked viewers watching tv programs: Pepsi has Kylie Minogue step out of the television and onto a male's lap; in McCain's Lasagne an Italian-esque grandmother breaks into the kitchen while the family watches television; a group of twenty-somethings sit around watching television and eating biscuits in the Tim-Tam ad. Product placement further layered the ads. The contestants were using the products in naturalistic ways as the viewer might: contestants sat on Freedom Furniture, Pizza Hut pizzas were brought in on special occasions, and Heineken beers were consumed.

Different ads were shown during the hour-long shows. The Saturday and Sunday shows featured ads aimed at the family, with their amalgamation of furniture, car, frozen food, furnishings, home improvement, appliances and department store sales. Adult products such as alcohol could only be shown on later shows. The Baileys ads had twenty-somethings in bar situations; they combined alcohol and sex in relatively humorous and traditional ways. On the other hand, the Heineken beer ads were curious indeed. The two main adverts were male-only affairs. In one advertisement, a solitary man pours the last drop of beer into a glass, while behind him people are partying. The other focuses on three males at a sporting event; two jump and high-five each other, inadvertently spilling the third man's beer. In both ads the men are not alone but are positioned as loners; in the second ad the man whose beer is spilled looks ready to start a fight.

The advertisements also influenced how viewers 'read' the show; the humorous advertisements cheered the viewers and made them more inclined to be amused by the show in much the same way as a warm-up person works. They also 'framed' the show in such a way that often the two seemed melded; the contestants ate Pizza Hut pizzas which the delivery boy was trying to deliver and which the viewer could have delivered.

Big Brother knock-offs

Big Brother's success spawned a host of imitation shows. From parent company Endemol came *Big Diet*. Ten overweight candidates (five women and five men) move into the *Big Diet* house, where they are filmed struggling with exercise regimes, diet issues and temptation for 91 days. Those who lost the least weight were expelled and viewers chose the winner — who was rewarded with their entire weight loss in gold. Endemol also developed *The Flat*: five busy women select a male 'housekeeper' from online applicants; he has to do everything — washing, ironing, cooking etc. — for two weeks. One of their most popular formats was *The Bus* which is essentially *Big Brother* on wheels; contestants are confined to a specially equipped bus for 100 days. The 'passengers' are filmed 24/7 as the bus toured throughout the countryside. Once a week the group voted to kick out a contestant, who got off at the next 'stop'. The show was popular in a number of European countries.

Business is the focus of three quasi-*Big Brother* shows. In *The Bar* two teams run two competing bars. Teams are given start-up cash and basic equipment. Viewers could drink at the bars or follow events live on the internet. The series was popular in Portugal, Norway, Spain and Sweden; the English version was called *Bar Wars*. Early in 2002 the Russian *Behind the Glass 2: The Last Beefsteak* had twelve contestants together for six weeks while starting up two new cafes. They were filmed 24/7 — the only trouble was that the television station was shut down only days after the show started (due to 'bankruptcy').

At the action end of the *Big Brother* genre is *Jailbreak*. Ten contestants were incarcerated in a 'prison'; they were monitored 24/7 by 36 cameras and real ex-prison guards. From the £250,000 prize pool, the first person or group of people to escape wins £100,000. The audience participated by sending hints in Jailmails, and the producers selected five which the prisoners read. Like *Big Brother*, the interactive website was central to the success of the show; it didn't have live feeds but it did have daily edited videos, updates and live chat forums. Australia had a radio version of *Jailbreak*, 'Escape to Pentridge'. Eight contestants spent three weeks inside Pentridge; they were subjected to 24-hour surveillance (broadcast over the internet), and they could be woken up at any time. They were awarded points for completing various tasks; the person with the most points won $20,000 and a trip to Switzerland. 'Escape to Pentridge' was the most *Big Brother*-ish of a number of reality radio stunts that coincided with the rise in reality-tv shows.

No one was surprised when the porn industry tried to cash in on the penchant for voyeurism so decried by *Big Brother* critics. *Sex Survivor 2000* promised hard-core material for online viewers willing to pay US$70 to watch 28 porn 'actors' compete for US$1million. Locked in a Los Angeles 'pleasure palace' the contestants tried to outperform each other in various parlour games — 'Musical Blowjobs', 'Blindman's Muff', and the 'Great Dildo Scavenger Hunt'. Within days the troubles began: several stars didn't turn up (no up-front money); hours later most of the 44 cameras weren't working; and the online viewers didn't vote (only seven people voted in two and a half hours), so producers decided that contestants had to vote each other out. Then the fights started. To cap it off, the ISP hosting the website closed it down when a cheque bounced. Finally, the producers declared the two 'winners' and the show finished. Despite *Sex Survivor*'s failure, a few months later *Pornstar Survivor* starred. Billed as the 'ultimate reality game show', it fared no better. This time eight contestants (four amateur males and four female porn stars) went to live in a Malibu house; the eventual winners were to share US$100,000. Viewers paid US$30 per month for access to the daily 30-minute highlights on the website. Each week four male contestants were chosen on the basis of 100-word essays submitted to the website; the men tried to 'survive' games such as 'topless football' and 'lapdance torture'. The porn stars voted out a guy each day, and on the fifth day the winner spent the day frolicking with the four women. At the end of six months, the weekly winners were to return to battle it out. The show didn't last that long. Despite the critics' prognostications, few people supported porno *Big Brother*.

Big Brother is generally regarded as one of the first reality-television shows which combines a number of disparate television genres. Still critics struggle for an adequate description — is it a gameshow? or a documentary? or a soap opera?

Chapter Three

As the Reality World Turns: Genre

Imitation is the sincerest form of television (Fred Allen)

If you think there's nothing new on the tube, you're right. From *Outer Limits* to *X-Files*, *The Flintstones* to *The Simpsons*, Coles' *£6,000 Question* to *Sale of the Century*, 'new' television shows are rarely that. Exploring *Big Brother*'s television heritage reminds us of the imitative nature of television. Today's programs are the mongrel children of fifty years of television production.

Since 1961 television fare has remained the usual mixture of police drama,[1] family sitcoms (or dramas),[2] quiz shows,[3] and 'reality' television programs[4] for night-time viewing. Soap operas,[5] cooking shows, quiz shows[6] and children's programs fill the daylight hours. The only things that seem to change are the clothes and hairstyles.

Each decade has a slight bias towards one type of program: in 1961 westerns were popular,[7] 1971 favoured family sitcoms,[8] in 1981 police dramas occupied the most air time,[9] Australian soaps continued to be night time viewing in 1991.[10] In 2001 reality-tv programs dominated the viewing line-up.

Genres in general

The word 'genre' comes from the Middle French word for 'kind' or 'class'; it describes types of films and books: western, romance, science fiction etc. Television has its own set of genres, some of which are unique to the medium: sitcoms, quiz shows, talk shows, soap operas and so on.

Genres are generally defined by a set of central characteristics or generic markers. A police drama has a crime, criminals, law enforcers and generally a resolution at the end of the show; it is presented in a realistic dramatic mode. A quiz show has a host, contestants, possibly a barrel girl and generally involves contestants answering a number of questions; it is presented in a realistic factual mode. Television viewers might agree that *Sale of the Century* is a quiz show and that *Blue Heelers* is a police drama, but not every show is so readily defined. Is *ER* a hospital drama or a soap opera? Is *MASH* a hospital drama or a sitcom? Some shows do not belong to one generic classification; for example, *Buffy the Vampire Slayer* has horror underpinnings, teen drama, and comedy elements. Of course new genres are developing all the time and recently a number of *Buffy*-like shows such as *Charmed* and *Dark Angel* have evolved. In a few years there may be a generic term for horror/teen/comedy television programs like *Buffy*. So genres are not objective classifications nor are they static; they can change over time and across cultures.[11] Producers/script writers might deliberately manipulate generic boundaries and viewers might prefer one reading over another.[12]

Take *The Bill* as an example. In its earliest form *The Bill* was a 'realistic' police drama: the half-hour episodes concentrated on crime and its resolution. More often than not the ending was ambiguous, reflecting the open-ended nature of 'real' life. However, in the past few years *The Bill* has developed more soap conventions: some episodes are 'to be continued', and often the stories concentrate on characters' relationships rather than crime resolution. Some viewers might consider *The Bill* a police drama, others a soap opera.

Although defining what *Big Brother* is might seem to be a pointless exercise, there are pragmatic considerations. If it is a 'reality' show then does it come under the heading 'factual programming'? *Big Brother* has won awards in categories as diffuse as 'Best Game Show' (*Loft Story*), 'Best Light Entertainment'

(UK *Big Brother* 1), 'Most Popular Factual Programme' (UK *Big Brother* 2); 'Entertainment and Non Drama Production' (UK *Big Brother* 2) and 'Customs and Culture' (Italian *Big Brother*). In 1999 the Emmys had 'Outstanding Non-Fiction Program (Reality)' for shows such as Mike Moore's *The Awful Truth*; but this was insufficient for the new breed of shows and so 'Outstanding Non-Fiction Program (Special Class)' was added in 2000 for *Big Brother* and *Survivor*. Australia has responded by adding a 'Most Popular Reality Program' to the Logie lineup.

Reality TV

'Reality tv' is an umbrella term encompassing a host of television programs: from the news to talk shows. News and current affairs shows are perceived as unmediated by direction and scripting in the way other 'reality' shows are — and are generally bracketed out of 'reality tv'. In the broadest definition, reality-tv shows are unscripted and their participants are non-professional actors. But other than such general guidelines, the term 'reality' can describe a wide range of television programs, from *Popstars* to *Who Wants to be a Millionaire?* Because it is such a broad (and misleading) term, it is easier to subdivide reality-tv programs into genres such as lifestyle shows, talent shows, documentaries, talk shows and quiz/game shows.

'Infotainment' describes those shows that educate viewers in an entertaining way. Once upon a time this term might have meant cooking and gardening shows, but nowadays 'lifestyle' shows are as plentiful as they are popular. Years ago, shows such as *Your Home*, *Living Graciously* and *At Home with Rosemary* were relegated to daytime television, however, since 1997 lifesetyle shows have become prime-time fare. Nearly 15 television hours of the week are devoted to 'lifestyle' shows. There are shows with the house as project (*Burke's Backyard*, *Changing Rooms* and *Better Homes and Gardens*) and ones with the house as commodity (*Hot Property*, *Location, Location*, and *Hot Auctions*). Chefs rarely cook in studio kitchens any more; they now travel the world or at least to viewers' homes (*Surprise Chef* and *Guess Who's Coming to Dinner*). Viewers are advised where to go for holidays (*Getaway*), what to do in their local city (*Click on Ten*), and how to manage money and health (*Money* and *Good Medicine*). Lifestyle shows have created their own-brand celebrities (or reintroduced 'old' celebrities such as rock stars and actors). And they rate well. In November 2001, ten of the twenty most popular television programs came under the 'reality' rubric.[13]

Television and radio have always provided a space for 'ordinary' folk to showcase their talents. *Popstars* (a New Zealand concept) and *Search for a Supermodel* have evolved from talent shows such as *New Faces*. Newcomers to the field include *Pop Idol*, in which the public votes off their least favourite star. In *Bands on the Run* cameras record four bands 24/7 as they tour. In *Soapstars* hopefuls lived together in a house and the camera followed their attempts to get soap parts.

Big Brother creators were careful to avoid the term 'reality' and with good reason. Their preferred term, 'docusoap', melds two such disparate genres as to be almost an oxymoron, like 'reality tv'.

Documentaries

> It is difficult to produce a television documentary that is both incisive and probing when every twelve minutes one is interrupted by twelve dancing rabbits singing about toilet paper. (Rod Serling)

Some people boast that they read only biographies or non-fiction; some claim to watch only the Discovery Channel or nature shows. Why? Because, since the nineteenth century, realism has been the preferred mode of textual production whether it be a book, a film, a painting or a television program.[14] Of course, 'realism' is simply another mode of representation and documentaries hide their own constitutive discourses better than others. Nevertheless, it remains that in a television program pecking order, documentaries rank more highly than sitcoms or quiz shows.

All television shows tell stories. Although documentary narrative processes are more subtle, they are as contrived as those for other film productions — a fact that John Greirson allowed for in his 1926 essay which coined the term 'documentary' and elaborated it as a 'creative treatment of reality'.[15] Consider the nature documentary. The viewers are guided through the animal narrative by several means. The most obvious one is the authoritative narrator who introduces the show and (usually) provides the voice-over for the duration of the show.[16] The choice of host sets the 'tone' for the show (John Cleese for humour, David Attenborough for authority).[17] The film is edited into a chronological order (usually), for instance Ken Burns' *Civil War*. Photographs, historical documents and newspaper articles add 'authenticity'. Cinematography plays a particularly important role: time-lapse photography reduces a nine-month pregnancy to a number of seconds (*The Human Body*), juxtaposition of shots gives the impression of the capture of an event,[18] and computer manipulation/graphics illustrate seemingly 'real' events.[19] And one must consider the production values — consider the sophisticated and glamorous *Blue Planet* as opposed to the amateurish fly-on-the-wall *Cops*.

In 1989 *Cops* ushered in a new type of reality television program — *video-vérité*. The half-hour show appeared to present viewers with an unmediated version of crime law enforcement. But the condemnatory authorial voice and racial bias of the show made critics uncomfortable. It was the dawning of savage *schadenfreude* and critics still haven't forgiven or forgotten these murky reality beginnings. *Cops* looked cheap, was cheap to produce and rated well. Naturally it spawned a number of caught-on-camera shows which used police footage of car chases and the like.

Prompted by thrills of police life, producers took their cameras to other exciting work-places: airports, hospitals and the armed forces. Camera crews followed all types of people, from strippers to vets. One website lists over one hundred such programs under the generic label 'docusoaps'.[20]

Docusoaps

Docusoaps have been around for years, but only recently has the term been adopted. First, as the name suggests, there is a 'fictional' element in the docusoap. This doesn't necessarily come from the material (which is generally the documentary part, in that it is non-scripted footage of non-professionals) but rather from the editing process; hundreds of hours of footage are reduced to one-hour programs. Those hours spliced together create a handful of cohesive storylines. Generally, the most controversial narratives are chosen. The shots might be 'real' but they might not be related. For example, a shot of someone at the hairdresser followed by a shot of someone in hospital suggests that the person at the hairdresser doesn't care (this was done in *Sylvania Waters*). Sometimes scenes are provoked by the camera crew, who may ingratiate themselves with their subjects and prompt certain discussions or confessions.[21] Not surprisingly, participants in docusoaps have complained about their inaccurate portrayal on television.

In 1973 Craig Gilbert filmed *An American Family* for American PBS. Gilbert's fly-on-the-wall series documented the Loud family breakdown and was watched by 10 million viewers. The show has been criticised for its sensational portrayal of the Loud family,[22] as was Australia's *Sylvania Waters* (1992), an ABC/BBC documentary about the Baker–Donaher family. *Sylvania Waters* followed the life of the blended family living in its eponymous Sydney suburb. Like *An American Family*, the series provoked considerable debate about the nature of documentary making, mainly because of the editing.[23] Critics agreed that *Sylvania Waters* was less a documentary than a soap opera constructed for a British audience.[24]

While *Sylvania Waters* and *An American Family* focused on family life, MTV's *Real World* and Andrew Denton's *House from Hell* documented the twenty-something house-sharing experience. In 1982 MTV screened the first *Real World*. In return for free accommodation (and presumably the promise of fame), seven twenty-somethings agreed to be filmed. The show has been enormously popular and its tenth season aired in 2001. The show aimed at fuelling viewers' share-accommodation fantasies rather than recording the realities of house-sharing; the digs were too perfect, the jobs too pert, and the contestants too perky. The slick production reinforced American middle-class lifestyle and values.

Closer still to *Big Brother* was *House from Hell.* In 1998 radio co-hosts Andrew Denton and Amanda Keller carefully selected six of the most incompatible people they could find and put them in a house in Sydney. Triple M paid the rent, bills and living expenses and installed four internet cameras. For the first two weeks, the contestants had to remain in the house, then they could resume fairly normal lives. Denton devised some cruel stunts to get the contestants to leave — the power was turned off, sometimes they only had Spam to eat — before the end of twelve weeks. Anyone who stayed three months received $5,000 from a mortgage company. It was a huge success on the radio and seven one-hour episodes were aired on Channel 10. It is the introduction of tasks and the lure of money that establishes *House from Hell* as a precursor to *Big Brother*.

Soap Operas

The name soap opera comes from the soap-powder sponsorship of early shows. Despite the genre's longevity and intense fandom,[25] soaps are little respected. Their over-the-top style and unrealistic storylines have made them a natural target for parody (*Soap*, *Soap Dish*, *Tootsie*); yet millions watch them.[26] Because of their high dramatic moments, their female gaze and their concentration on 'domestic' themes, soaps have generally been relegated to the lowest end of the television pecking order.[27]

Most people typically associate soaps with daytime shows such as the perennial *Days of Our Lives*; yet over the years there have been horror soaps (*Dark Shadows*), small-town soaps (*Peyton Place*), hospital soaps (*General Hospital*) and glam night-time soaps (*Dallas*). Prime-time soaps such as *Melrose Place* and *Bev-*

erley Hills 90210 have been superseded by dramas with soap elements: *ER* and *West Wing*.

Across cultures there are different approaches to soaps. Hyper-hysterical *telenovelas* examine the lives of the rich and famous;[28] American soaps tend to concentrate on powerful dynastic families (conspicuously wealthy families); Australian and British soaps prefer a more domestic and suburban sensibility (*Neighbours*, *Home and Away*, *Coronation Street*). Australian and British soaps tend to have mortgage rather than merger issues. Despite the cultural differences, soaps travel well: *Neighbours* in Europe, *Rosalinda* in America and *The Bold and the Beautiful* in Australia.

Australia has a rich soap history: the multicultural urban *Number 96* (1972), to the rural *Country Practice* (1981), the corporate *The Box* (1974), the bleak *Prisoner* (1979) and the perky *Young Doctors* (1976). We have had a historical soap, *The Sullivans* (1976), a contemporary soap, *Sons and Daughters* (1982), and a glam soap, *Return to Eden* (1985). In 2002 not only are there websites that celebrate these cult shows that started over 20 years ago, but some soaps are being repeated on television (e.g. *Sons and Daughters*, with a very young Guy Pearce).[29]

What are soaps' generic markers? As Sue Turnbull noted, the wide variety of soaps means that a soap definition is relatively difficult.[30] The most obvious marker is the cliff-hanging ending, the teaser which tempts viewers to return for more. From here, it all gets a bit tricky, as many of the generalisations don't hold true for all soaps. Overall, the performative mode is melodramatic. This is reinforced for American soaps and telenovelas by romantic filmic techniques such as an overabundance of close-ups, softly lit rooms filled with flowers and glittering surfaces, and glamorous costuming and make-up. The characters tend to be stereotypical (the bitchy female executive, the ruthless businessman, the person with a mysterious past) and lurch from crisis to crisis. The most outrageous storylines can be found in the American daytime soaps, while prime-time ones such as *ER* and *West Wing* are predicated on their 'reality'.

Nearly all soaps position the wedding at their narrative centre.

Narrative techniques such as spoken inner thoughts and the recapitulation narrative keep casual viewers up to date. Soap opera time moves either excruciatingly slowly or at breakneck speed, though Australian and British soaps have a more 'realistic' temporality.

Big Brother appeared to have the format of a soap opera: a continuing story (or to paraphrase Sara-Marie 'and then …'). It shared soap's concern with relationships, especially romance. Unfortunately, the romance between Christina and Peter was too sudden to reach soap-epic proportions. Still, as Gordon told Christina and Peter, 'You're tv's new favourite couple. You're more popular than *Neighbours*' couples. Cos it's real, you're not acting like you're a couple. You guys may or may not have something on and we don't know, no one knows. That's the tension and we can market it for at least six weeks'. While melodrama may have been in short supply in the Australian *Big Brother*, it was a central element in its popularity overseas (specifically Nasty Nick in the United Kingdom and Sabine and Bart's romance in Holland). So while *Big Brother* had soap *potential*, it failed to fulfil that potential. It did, however, generate a soap-like fan community (this is discussed in Chapter 7).

Big Brother is more than a documentary with soap tendencies; closer examination reveals the influence of talk shows, game shows and even sitcoms.

Talk shows[31]

Television talk shows developed from shows such as *Meet the Press*. Nowadays the shift has been from educating the public (except in the case of *Oprah*) to entertaining; shows such as the *Jerry Springer Show* are so over-the-top as to be a parody of a talk show.[32]

Phil Donahue pioneered the format in the 1970s; by the mid-1980s he was joined by Oprah, and Geraldo. Shows competed to present the most controversial topics, and some shows became violent. In the 1990s talk shows became more and more outrageous and sensational until two murders put talk shows on trial.

In 1995 Jonathan Schmitz shot Scott Amedure after they had appeared on a *Jenny Jones Show*. Amedure had revealed that he had a crush on Schmitz during a 'Secret Admirers' episode (the episode was never aired). Schmitz felt so humiliated by the whole experience that he shot Amedure three days later. During the trial, his defence attorney claimed that Schmitz was the victim because he had been pushed to the limits by the *Show*; Schmitz had been 'ambushed'. Apparently he had repeatedly asked producers if his admirer was a female and had been led to believe it was. After the murder trial Schmitz's parents brought a civil suit against the *Jenny Jones Show* for negligence; the *Show* was found negligent and ordered to pay US$25 million in damages, plus burial costs. The trial exposed the machinations of talk-show producers and, for many, confirmed their fears that producers manipulated guests in order to get good television.

After the *Jenny Jones* murder, many talk shows cleaned up their act and quite a few were cancelled.

A few years later, Jerry Springer had to respond to similar criticism after one of his guests was murdered. Nancy Panitz was beaten to death only hours after her appearance on the *Jerry Spring Show* was aired (on 24 July 2000). She and her ex-husband, Ralf, had appeared on 'Secret Mistresses Confronted'. Supposedly Ralf brought Nancy on the show to tell her about his recent marriage to Eleanor (who was also on the show). Apparently the three of them were living in the same house, and so after the show Nancy got restraining orders to force Ralf and Eleanor out of the house. She was killed a few hours later. Ralf was arrested but has not gone to trial.

Most typically each talk-show episode centres on one 'issue', and a number of guests who typify that issue sit on a stage and explain their 'problem'. The host stands with the audience and acts as a conduit for guest, audience, expert and viewer. Sometimes the host will invite members of the audience to comment.

The show usually ends after an expert has delivered his or her opinion.

As can be seen from their titles, the host is central to the talk show; he or she sets the tone and the agenda. Oprah's show has transmogrified from trash talk to middle-class new-age positivism. Ricki Lake caters to younger viewers; her guests and audiences tend to be black and vocal and the language is largely vernacular and idiomatic. Sally Jessy Raphael and Jenny Jones select issues that appeal to older viewers.[33] But of course the *Jerry Springer Show* is the epitome of 'trash' tv. His outrageous topics[34] and unpredictable guests[35] have earned him a reputation as the king of sleaze. His studio is a circus (he calls himself the ringmaster) filled with riotous guests and a vociferous audience. When critics complain about trash talk shows, Jerry Springer's is the one they have in mind.

The talk-show host is the audience's guide; the host is positioned (often literally) between the guests/expert and the audience/viewer. They direct the action, introduce the issues and keep the show moving. They ask questions that the audience can't and often gloss the responses. Because the host's scripts are naturalistic, audiences forget that they are scripted/rehearsed and that the host receives prompts from producers throughout the show. Like the documentary host, the talk-show host sets the tone: some are personal and intimate (Oprah and Ricki), others are distanced and judgmental (Sally Jesse and Jerry). Often they themselves develop a following ('Go Ricki', 'Jerry! Jerry!').

Experts have become major players in the talk-show world. The role of the expert is not merely to discuss the issues but to educate the viewers/audiences. Sometimes their exact 'expertise' is not clear; they may be vaguely labelled 'relationship expert' or 'counsellor'; for example, a disc jockey on the *Ricki Lake Show* offers relationship advice. After a few minutes the expert understands the problem and dispenses advice; their therapeutic talk gives the audience a sense of closure. The philosophy is 'common sense' which seems obvious to everyone except the people involved. In some cases, it seems that the host, expert and audience are complicit in their summation of the guest's situation.

Props of importance to talk shows are the mike and the couch. Both metaphorically represent power and help. The mike is the host's sceptre and is bestowed on others only fleetingly. The host has the primary power position because he or she explains the issue and directs the questions etc. The couch is a comfort zone, and suggests the analyst's couch. Springer has chairs that can be tossed and that can fall over for dramatic effect.

Audiences read talk shows as 'real'; they believe the people and the issues or topics to be true largely due to the ungrammatical, rambling and repetitive language. The guests on talk shows, like the contestants on *Big Brother*, are obviously non-professionals.[36]

The game show

One of the oldest forms of reality tv is a show in which people compete for prizes: the game/quiz show.[37]

The game show is a contest and its variations are seemingly endless:[38] quiz shows,[39] action/adventure contests and dating 'games'. Sometimes knowledge is rewarded (the esoteric *Mastermind*, *Sale of the Century*, *University Challenge*); at other times, chance is a key ingredient (*Wheel of Fortune*). Sometimes individuals compete (*Sale of the Century*), sometimes teams compete (*Family Feud*) and most recently individuals as teams compete (*The Weakest Link*). *The Price Is Right* introduced the audience as potential contestants, and *Who Wants to be a Millionaire?* incorporates the audience and the viewer as actual participants. Different skills are involved; sometimes dexterity is as important as knowledge (i.e. pressing the buzzer); in other shows physical skills help (*Survivor*); analytical ability might be essential (*The Mole*); or you might need to be able to cook (the British shows *Anything You Can Cook*, *Masterchef*).

Each show has its own method of creating suspense. In some of the early quiz shows contestants were locked in soundproof booths. Clocks ticked the seconds away. Rapid questioning adds dramatic tension in *Sale of the Century*. *Who Wants to be a Millionaire?* creates a different kind of tension; the clock does not tick but the lasers flash and the host doggedly paces the timing of the show. In *Survivor*, tension mounts as the elimination votes are tallied.

Studio game shows reflect a tawdry fascination with bright lights, loud sounds (buzzers) and glittery props. Afternoon game shows (*Catch Phrase*, *Wheel of Fortune*, *The Price Is Right*) tend to have lower budgets, which is reflected in their home-spun glamour. Evening shows have more bells and whistles, more glitz. Occasionally one prop is the central feature — the wheel, the squares (*Hollywood Squares*), a robot (Dexter in *Perfect Match*), the soundproof booth. Technology is presented as progress. In the original *$64,000 Question* (CBS 1956) the first four questions were provided by an IBM sorter — cutting-edge technology. The machine created the impression that questions were picked randomly, when in fact all questions were pre-selected. Today computers have replaced the hosts' cards. Lasers punctuate the show. Cameras swing giddyingly around.

Game-show performances have changed. In the early days, the audience looked on or listened in. It was formal and polite. Dignified even. Then there was the controlled mayhem of *The Price Is Right*, the embarrassing revelations of *Perfect Match*. Today game-show hosts are informal, chatty.

As in documentaries, the host plays an important role, a role which has evolved over the decades. It used to be that the host was a middle-aged avuncular male (Bob Dyer in *Pick a Box*, Terry Deare in *Concentration*). Today they are younger and there's a wider choice: mumbling Glen Ridge, the schoolmarmish Cornelia Frances[40] and the smug Eddy McGuire. They might have little or no impact on the show (Ridge) or they might control the show (Frances). Sometimes they upstage the contestants (*The Weakest Link*). They can stand with the contestants (*Wheel of Fortune*), across the studio floor (*Sale of the Century*, *The Weakest Link*) and even 'off-screen' (*Survivor*, *The Amazing Race*). They dress in a style in keeping with the image the show wants to project: *The Weakest Link*'s black, *Survivor*'s casual outfits.

The ultimate goal in the game show is to win. Generally, the prizes are displayed for both the viewer and the contestant. (Of course, some game shows offer 'joke' prizes, when the contestant has to choose either a door or a box, turning the contestant's success into a cruel joke.) The showcase is the ultimate consumeristic arena.[41] In some instances, the showcase is a central fixture in the studio (*Let's Make a Deal*, *Sale of the Century*, *The Price is Right*). Goods are positioned as items of desire rather than items of use or need: the luxury car, the $30,000 wristwatch. *The Price Is Right* capitalised on the consumeristic gaze as products were not only rewards but were sites of knowledge: knowing the correct price won the contestant the prize/s. When money is offered as a reward, it is fetishised and abstract; the numbers are illuminated with garish lights and muzak abounds.

The game-show philosophy is quite subversive. The promise of easy rewards undermines the Protestant work ethic and feeds viewers' fantasies that life is about luck. Expensive items are no longer the privilege of the wealthy. Quiz shows often deliberately undermine the authority of institutionalised learning. The academic or teacher is no longer the storehouse of information. The quiz show celebrates the knowledge of the non-expert.

The metanarrative of game shows is that anyone can win. Part of the appeal is that the contestants are not 'professionals' but ordinary people. Ratings winners are those contestants who capture the public's imagination — the taxi driver with an encyclopaedic knowledge of opera. Overnight, especially in the 1950s, contestants became stars. Perhaps the best known is Dr Joyce Brothers. Dr Brothers was originally rejected as a potential candidate for *$64,000 Question* despite her intellectual abilities. Once she understood the appeal of the contestant as freak, Dr Brothers reinvented herself as a boxing expert and went on to win.[42] Soon producers exploited the audience's identification with certain kinds of contestants and this caused a scandal in the 1950s.[43]

Though game shows are closed texts — either contestants are

eliminated or they go on to win everything and retire — producers can capitalise on contestants' fame. Winners return to compete in championship challenges or 'celebrity' challenges.

Some felt that *Big Brother* demeaned the contestants. In the 1960s contestants donned turnip costumes to be on *Let's Make a Deal* — contestant dignity was a thing of the past. For years whacky game-show clips, usually from Japan, have amused viewers. Most recently, in 'Sweepstakes Boy' an actor agreed to be locked naked in an empty apartment until he could win US$10,000 in prizes from magazine contests. He had to survive on the prizes he won. His reward, he was told, would be fame. After 18 months of being confined to an apartment, eating a large shipment of free dog food, Nasubi, his hair and beard grown out into a scraggly mess, was escorted from his apartment to a bare anteroom. The walls collapsed around him, leaving him naked and blinking in the middle of a roaring studio audience. Until then he did not know he'd been on television the whole time. Spain has *El Gran Juego de la Oca* complete with nudity and horrifying endurance contests; players have escaped from flaming coffins and bomb-rigged cages. Even the British aren't adverse to mayhem on telly. In one episode of *Endurance UK*, contestants ate maggot quiches while wearing eye-masks filled with maggots and having their feet tickled. Certainly no *Big Brother* contestant was asked to do anything as remotely disgusting.

Almost single-handedly *Who Wants to be a Millionaire?* snatched viewers from cable channels and returned them to network television. The show's overwhelming success has seen a resurgence of interest in the game show. For that reason, television executives started hunting around in wastepaper baskets for formats they had previously rejected (such as *Big Brother*).

Reality-tv game shows

One of the shows that executives had passed over was the precursor to *Survivor.* In the early 1990s British television producer Charlie Parsons approached a number of television executives with an idea for a show he called *Survive!*. They rejected it, but a few years later 52 million viewers tuned in to *Survivor*'s first finale. Since then, the *Survivor* formula has been adopted in other countries.[44] *Survivor* and its ilk are the new generation in game shows. The format is simple: contestants are subjected to physical or mental challenges; contestants and/or viewers vote each other off, and the last contestant left wins the prize. There are several versions of the format, such as the adventure/action *The Amazing Race*, *The Mole* and *Boot Camp*, and the psychologically testing *Fear Factor*, *Scream Test* and *Boy Meets Girl*.[45] The rewards of the 'dating' game school of survival, *Temptation Island*, *Chains of Love* and *Love Cruise*, are the possibility of solving a relationship issue. Generally, entrants in *Popstars*, *Soapstars* and *Search for a Supermodel* aim at fame.

Survivor, with the magic 'one million dollar' prize, is the yardstick by which most reality game shows are measured. Why was it so popular? Visually, *Survivor* comes from the spectacular school of television-making. From its opening sweeping shots with the stirring tribal music, everything in the show is carefully constructed for maximum visual and emotional effect. The tribal theme, Australian, African or Polynesian, is exotic and enticing. Throughout the show, rituals add to the primitif aesthetic: from the night setting of the tribal council with its flattering lighting and careful choreography to its symbolic props. The dousing of the contestant's flame literally and figuratively gestures to extinction.

Each show follows the same format: highlights of the previous episode, interviews with contestants, two challenges, tribal council, highlights of the next episode. And other reality game shows such as *Boot Camp*,[46] *The Mole* and *The Amazing Race* follow roughly the same formula.

Most of these game shows do not come cheaply. *The Mole* relies on state-of-the-art technology; *The Amazing Race*'s preproduction must have cost hundreds of thousands of dollars; *Survivor* and *Boot Camp* require large numbers of onsite production staff. The high post-production values gesture to big budget productions. Old claims that reality-tv shows are cheap productions just don't hold true for reality-game shows.

Reality-game-shows have combined soap, documentary and game-show elements: the cliff-hanging ending, the 'realistic' locations and the temptation of money. Ultimately, though, success hinges on the right casting. In order to attract an audience, it is necessary, because of the soap opera elements, for the producers to have the casting gene. As most of the footage consists of contestants, it is important that they appeal to viewers. Two filming techniques help to increase empathy: the video diaries in which contestants reveal their thoughts to the viewer/camera and selective editing of the material. It helps if contestants can be moulded into stereotypes: the hard-working mother, the sassy young female, the plotting villain. And if contestants can be roughly divided into 'goodies' and 'baddies', then the show is sure to attract a following. This heightened attachment to the contestants has earned these shows the title 'emotainment'.

Big Brother — the hybrid

The trouble is that *Big Brother* is not one show but several: there are the nightly episodes and the weekly shows and each resembles a different genre. The nightly episodes are docusoaps; the Thursday night shows are most like talk shows; the Saturday and Sunday shows are a cross between talk shows and variety shows.

The nightly episodes had the format of a soap opera, a continuing story, but the difference was that there was an end. In this way the show resembles the *telenovelas* which run for short periods of time. The nightly shows were documentary in nature; the voice-of-god narrator guided viewers, the setting was 'naturalistic' and the conversations and actions unscripted (generally). It captured people, à la *Candid Camera*, in the act of being themselves, but the cameras weren't hidden.

Sometimes the shows included other 'reality' program elements. Lo and behold when *Big Brother* contestants were given virtual babes — they were also assigned home improvement chores. It wasn't as if the rooms needed a coat of paint, nor did the yard need returfing. The show was mimicking lifestyle programs. The painting and returfing increased the perception of the house as a 'real' house. It closed the gap between the house as a studio set and the house as home. When Johnnie smacked into the side of the pool it was an ouch moment straight from *Funniest Home Videos*.

Many of the fans identified humorous elements of the show. But in reality there were very few funny moments, so it appears that viewers were 'reading' the show as a sitcom. Which is not surprising. Since *I Love Lucy*, sitcoms have become more and more 'realistic': *Friends*, *Seinfeld* and *The Royle Family*.

Like talk-show guests, the contestants often revealed painful and personal secrets. Many of the critics felt that the contestants, like guests on talk shows, were being exploited. However, *Big Brother* took its responsibilities more seriously than most talk shows and contestants were carefully screened and evaluated before, during, and after the show. During filming, contestants had 24-hour-a-day access to a psychologist and up to five years access after the show.

The weekly shows were a combination of daytime talk shows and night-time chat shows. Thursday night's AO shows had a host (Gretel) and a number of experts in cosy intimacy decoding and examining the contestants' behaviours. Much of the focus was on their sex talk. The contestants' conversations would not have been out of place on a Jerry Springer 'Real Life Sex Confessions' episode. The sets with their chairs and couches maintained a talk-show look; Gretel controlled the mike and the show in true talk-show-host style. The Saturday and Sunday shows resembled *David Letterman*, *The Panel* and *Rove Live*. Gretel opened the show with typical hosts' patter. She interviewed several guests. There were mock game shows, musical interludes and some audience interaction.

At the end of the day *Big Brother* was a game show. Contestants were not rewarded for talent (as in *Popstars*), an achivement (as in *Big Diet*), or their physical prowess (as in *Survivor*); they were rewarded for simply being liked. It was a popularity game show. Appropriately we had a female host (the show was set in a house) who was 'hip'. Throughout the series, the contestants competed in various mental and physical challenges.

As one of the reality game shows, *Big Brother* was not like *Survivor.* The premise was roughly the same: remove a bunch of strangers from their normal habitat, give them a number of tasks and have them vote each other off. But *Big Brother* didn't have the high post-production values or cohesive symbolism. It didn't utilise large sets for challenges; nor did it have much in the way of technology. It failed to build drama into each show's episode: discussing strategies were forbidden. The bigger-budget shows are shown weekly; *Big Brother* remained true to its soap roots and aired nightly. The exotic environment was replaced with a familiar one, the home. It rejected the masculinity of the adventure shows and concentrated on the female domestic environment. Other shows required endurance and strategising; *Big Brother* required compatibility and patience. The winner would win by, well, to paraphrase Seinfeld, competing in a show about nothing.

Chapter Four

The Box: The Show

For a show about nothing there was a lot happening in *Big Brother*. It was a soap-umentary-game show and therein was the main problem. It was a game show without a contest; it was a soap opera without a villain; it was a reality show predicated upon careful editing. The contestants were real but the situation was not.

Filmmakers can craft their material into a unified product; lighting, music, actors, script, costuming, props should all work together to give the film a certain 'feel' and reinforce its subtext. Television producers don't always have that luxury, though shows do have a certain cohesion (e.g. the urbane lifestyle of *Frasier*). But these shows are costumed and have scripts and sets which conform to their generic requirements; the shabby chair in *Frasier* comes to represent the anti-thesis of the show and is accordingly an object of ridicule. *Big Brother* did not have the same cohesion. Not only was the show a grabbag of genres across the week but the nightly shows had no unifying theme or genre.

Big Brother ran for twelve weeks. Typically, the *Big Brother* week consisted of eight shows: five half-hour episodes and three hour-long episodes, an average of five and a half hours of programming per week.[1]

The art of programming

Scheduling a television program is an art. In the earliest days, television shows started and finished at roughly any time; thus a show could start at 2:05 pm and run until 2:45 pm. Today most programs start and end on the half-hour or hour. And shows are now made to fit this time-frame. While this made viewers' lives easier, it made programmers' lives even easier. Nowadays programmers run shows overtime so that viewers who stay until the end find it's too late to change to another channel, so they stay tuned. For example, on Channel 7 *Temptation Island* tended to run late and after a very short break the not-so-popular *The Amazing Race* started. Ask any VCR programmer about the frustration of the 'pull-through.'[2] Another less obvious, but more ubiquitous, practice is that of 'strip programming'. Strip programming means that a programmer blocks a period of time for the same show each week (e.g. *The Simpsons* at 6 pm every weeknight). The practice wasn't evident in the 1960s, but by the 1970s it had crept into television schedules and by the 1980s it was quite common. In fact, viewers have come to rely on strip programming and when a show is moved it is quite frustrating (e.g. Channel 9's changes to *Boot Camp* and Channel 7's changes to *The Amazing Race*).

Effective programming requires some finesse. The program must be aired in a timeslot that will attract the desired demographic; the program must be able to compete with, but not be swamped by, the competition. *Big Brother* programmers responded to Channel 7's screening of the movie *Titanic* by putting on a special show; and they wisely delayed broadcasting the first show because they felt they couldn't beat the Logies on Channel 9.

Big Brother followed the popular soap *Neighbours*; by placing the two shows together, the programmers hoped that the show would grab *Neighbours* fans. If viewers didn't watch *Neighbours* but did watch *Seinfeld*, which *Big Brother* was replacing, there was always the chance that regular *Seinfeld* fans would tune in.[3] And it worked. One fan remembered that 'it took over *Seinfeld* and I had nothing else to watch so I got hooked!'.[4] Another viewer watched *Uncut* 'because it was after *X-Files*'. The comment 'nothing else to watch' reflects that the *Seinfeld* viewer felt that the other free-to-air-stations didn't offer programming that suited them. At 7 pm the choices were between a game show (*Sale of the Century*), a soap opera (*Home and Away*), news (Channel 2) and sports (SBS).

The framing of *Big Brother* impacted upon its reception: how viewers 'read' the show. *Neighbours*' watchers were attracted to its soap elements, but it had the added advantage of being 'real'; as one fan said, 'It's not fake like *Neighbours* or *Home and Away*'.[5] *Seinfeld* viewers perceived the show as humorous. Television shows are shaped by the material that surrounds them: the competing shows, the preceding shows, even the advertisements. Thus programming is a delicate and potent brew which needs the right ingredients.

Saturation programming has benefits. By insinuating *Big Brother* into everyday viewing, à la soap operas, viewers become more enmeshed in the goings-on in the house. On the downside, if there is no tension, the show can become repetitious and boring. So how did the programmers, directors and editors craft a show which was interesting enough to keep viewers tuning in?

Action

Producers had a bag of tricks to circumvent viewer boredom; they spiced up the show with intruders (Week 6), Christmas Day (Week 10), and a money challenge (Week 11). They also changed the programming when necessary. The first round of nominations was brought forward. It was thought that Australian audiences would not be patient enough to wait the usual two weeks and so the first nominations occurred on the Friday night at the end of the first week. An adults-only show was planned from the beginning (no doubt influenced by the r-rated antics in overseas *Big Brother*s) and started in the second week. This was think-on-your-feet television. But how did producers circumvent every-night-viewing boredom?

The domestic confines of *Big Brother* limited its potential for 'action'. Many of the days the contestants slept in late, sat around the pool, read books and performed the many mundane activities that constitute normal life. However, *Big Brother* had other ideas and, like a child observing an insect in a glass, prodded them with a metaphorical stick. Challenges are part of the reality game-show format: *Survivor* has food and immunity challenges, *Amazing Race* has its detours.

Ideally, the challenges should follow a pattern: the first tasks should create bonds; second-level tasks should challenge these social groups or challenge the contestants' abilities/ethics/morals; the final tasks should demonstrate the individuals' abilities. By ordering the challenges in this way, a key requirement for a game show is fulfilled — which is ultimately (in this instance) for the viewers to identify a winner. The challenges should provide viewers with enough information for them to decide who should win. To paraphrase Hamlet: the game's the thing in which to trap the personality of a player.

More pragmatically, the challenges should provide television moments. They should be visually exciting (think of the larger-than-life 'primitive' equipment used in *Survivor* or the scenic backdrops of *The Amazing Race*). They should be dramatic (the exciting dash to arrive at the markers in *The Amazing Race*, the race against time in *Survivor* challenges). The best ones test the contestants in some way and give them a sense of accomplishment (physical, such as completing a task, or personal, such as overcoming a fear of heights). In other words, they should be entertaining. Unfortunately, this was the weakest part of the *Big Brother* programming. Of the eleven challenges, the most memorable one was the dancethon. The music was pleasing, and there were a number of amusing moments: Gordon and Jemma, Johnnie's interrupted meditation and the boys' enthusiastic dances. The first tasks (memory task, fire-sitting) provided contestants with opportunities to learn about each other and create bonds, but they did not make for compelling viewing. The body sculpting, the treasure hunt, the synchronised swimming and the physical endurance tasks were simply boring and this is reflected in the limited amount of air-time they received. Strangely enough, one of the most engaging tasks was the virtual babies — it made for hilarious viewing on the internet but didn't capture much screen time.

The producers also had developed in-program strategies to retain viewers. After the opening sequence each night, the narrator announced the highlights of the show. 'Tonight on *Big Brother*: the housemates awake to a big surprise (clip of Blair, Chrissie and Sara-Marie looking into the yard) … rare contact from the outside world (clip of Ben and his teddy bear) … but what's it done to Christina?' (Chrissie on the bed crying). These teasers tempted viewers to stay tuned. The remote control (and channel surfing) has changed television shows considerably. Until recently the forecasting of dramatic moments was generally the provenance of soap operas and was considerably more subtle — there was no voice-over. However, it has become standard fare for some television programs, especially talk shows. At the end of the show viewers were titillated with 'Tomorrow on *Big Brother*: can Johnnie stop the wedding? Or will Peter and Christina tie the knot?' (Week 4); 'Will lagging Lisa and sleeping Sara Marie lose the task for the other housemates?' (Week 5); and 'What's troubling Christina? And will she confide in Sara-Marie' (Week 10). Gretel also directed viewers when to tune in again. On Thursdays, she invited viewers to come back and watch her on the Saturday and Sunday shows; at the end of Saturday's show she reminded viewers that Sunday's show was 'live on stage'; on Sundays she dared viewers to miss the exciting week and warned 'Big Brother is watching you'.

The nightly show format

The nightly shows were, like soaps, divided into discreet narratives. Each segment contained one storyline: a narrative about one contestant or incident. In all there were four segments; for example, Day 31's were fitness in the house, dreams, the body doubles task and the *Big Brother* song. The segments ended with voting information and teasing previews of the highlights to come. The episodes, in true soapie style, ended with cliff-hanging questions. (See complete episodes at the end of Chapter 5.)

The Saturday and Sunday night formats

The pre-recorded Saturday night 'evaluation' show examined Australia's reaction to *Big Brother*. Gretel sat on the couch and interviewed various people, evictees, relatives, celebrities and interested others about the show. The evictees told her what they had been up to that week. Reporter Sami Lukis roved the country talking to people in the streets and celebrities; she visited contestants' hangouts and chatted with their friends, co-workers and families. The 'highlights of the week' clip gave viewers who had missed episodes the opportunity to catch up. The show ended with a media round-up segment in which Gretel examined the press's reaction to *Big Brother*. It was a thinly disguised marketing exercise. The show was chatty and comfortable, Gretel provided the voice-over and Sami bounced around providing a little light comedy.

The Sunday shows were divided into two parts: pre-eviction and post-eviction. The first part might have included the audience but Gretel was firmly in charge. She had the clipboard and microphone to prove it. The camera included many audience shots but often they were merely a backdrop for Gretel, literally and figuratively. Just as the show crossed live to the house, the audience were told to be as quiet as mice — like one would tell children. The show included a clip of the past 24 hours and Gretel chatting with the nominees' relatives and friends who were sidelined for the main event. The dramatic point of the show and the highlight of the week was the announcement of the evictee. The camera then followed the evictee's journey from the house — the 'buggy ride of shame', an intertextual game-show reference. Gretel escorted the evictee (giving them advice about 'going with the flow') through the symbolic mirror hall and onto the stage. The camera followed the pair and viewers could see the contestant's view of the crowd. On stage Gretel quizzed the evictee and then reunited them with their significant others. The Sunday show was considerably faster paced than the others; but this could have been the artifice of the fast-moving laser lights and swinging camera angles.

Gretel perched on a lounge chair on Saturday and Sunday, but for *Uncut* she sat in an intimate red room, complete with flowers and candles.

The 'Uncut' format

Big Brother Uncut was the most cohesive show because it was constructed around one topic: sex. For the *Uncut* show Gretel wore 'sexier' clothes: more plunging necklines and fishnet stockings. She sat in a softly lit red room and chatted with her guests — sexperts and evictees. Their conversations were hushed and intimate. To reinforce the sexy theme, the opening sequence was altered. Red replaced the blue opening credits. Shots of slightly blurred naked bodies and body parts dominated: a scantily clad female climbing over beds, naked bodies in the shower, breasts, females and males dressing. Although *Uncut* promised a lot, it gave little; for example, one introduction stated: 'Tonight … every switch way. Peter's same-sex shenanigans; lip-gloss Jemma's perfect pash; and Sara-Marie can't get the wood from the tree'; but the show consisted of little more than Peter and Johnnie showering and some pseudo-sexual rough-housing, a couch conversation about kissing and Sara-Marie talking about penises — 'there's doodle everywhere in my life at the moment' (Week 5). The first weeks were filled with Andy's antics (clips which resurfaced in later shows) and full-frontal male nudity. But later, because there was little sexual activity, *Uncut* relied on sex talk. In Week 10 it re-aired the tried and true sex clips: Andy and her whips, various kissing encounters, Sara-Marie bum dancing and masturbation talk. By Week 11 (the final *Uncut*) the producers resorted to sexy outtakes from various overseas *Big Brother*s. Overall, *Uncut* preferred medium-range shots of Gretel and her guests; the pace was slower and romantic — as if to counteract the raw sexuality of the material being screened.

Staging the show

In *Big Brother* the house was writ large. Since the earliest days of television, producers have utilised the family home as a stage (*The Honeymooners*, *The Brady Bunch*, *Neighbours*), and with the advent of lifestyle shows such as *Surprise Chef*, *Our House* and *Changing Rooms* real homes have taken the place of studio homes. The ordinariness of the *Big Brother* house increased viewers' perceptions of the 'reality' of the show. Basically, the house looked like a typical, albeit a middle-class, suburban home. But of course it was the antithesis of the suburban home: it was a public performance space.

Each *Big Brother* designer has tried to create a unique look. Mike Bridges, the Australian designer, rejected the institutional look of the British house and the palatial design of the American one. He opted for an eclectic Australian design. He used corrugated iron for a 'shearing shed' look which was offset by the tiled floors and blonde woodwork. On television the house appeared to be much larger than it was in real life.

Aside from having to accommodate twelve contestants, the house also had to accommodate the necessities of filming. The rooms had to be fully illuminated at all times, except for the bedrooms where the lights were turned off at night. The 90 panel mirrors dominated the house-scape and provided the camera crew with clear access to the contestants' actions. They also reminded contestants of the mirroring of their lives. Cameras and microphones were designed to be as unobtrusive as possible but were strategically placed in order to catch everything.

The bedrooms were spartan. There were six beds in each room, and rooms were differentiated by doona covers (plain orange for one room; blueish-grey for the other). Privacy was severely limited — mirrors dominated the rooms, the cameras behind them whirred and the beds were within an arm's reach. Some contestants tried to create their own personal space (Johnnie and his meditation). There were no places to make a physical private space either — no drawers, no wardrobes — so contestants left their clothes in their suitcases or hung them on clothes racks.

Ultimately Big Brother controlled the room; 'he' turned on the lights in the morning and would not allow contestants to drag mattresses onto the floor (and out of the camera's range). Occasionally the bedrooms were sites of mayhem. On the night the contestants finished their record they yelled and screamed and jumped up and down on the beds — Big Brother orchestrated that. Beds were often shared (Andy and Johnnie, Peter and Christina, Sara-Marie and Blair) but not usually for sexual activity. Which is hardly surprising; the bedrooms were functional and not romantic.

The open-plan living area (combined kitchen, dining and living room) made for easier filming. Generally, the kitchen is the heart of the house, and a place for more relaxed conversations, as it was on the first night when the contestants gravitated to the fridge. However, the contestants were drawn to the couches to talk. While couches are functional, they also signify the analyst's couch and mirror the talk-show couch. The dining room, midway between kitchen and lounge room, tended to be used on more formal occasions such as celebratory nights (e.g. the first night, the cocktail party).

One of the most important rooms was the Diary Room. Under the rules, the contestants had to visit the Diary Room once a day. With its distinctive chair, it was the institutionalised space for confession. (The lounge room provided the public space and the bedrooms were used for more intimate conversations between contestants.) The Diary Room's filmic value was largely due to the nomination process and the contestants' reasons for nominations were repeatedly aired. Otherwise, little footage made it from the Diary Room to the television screens, though what went on there was often referred to in the internet updates on the official website.

Outside were the gazebo, the pool, the chicken coop, the herb garden and the barbecue. The gazebo was the outside stage, complete with disco ball, for the danceathon. The contestants ate, danced and sunbaked in the gazebo. Under the pool was a small room where the cameramen could film the contestants underwater. The chickens provided some televisual excitement — Peter 'kicked' one of them and Sara-Marie chatted to them. Sara-Marie colonised the herb garden. When she lay on her back she looked at the sky, the world beyond the house and Big Brother. Viewers could almost smell the soothing fragrance of the herbs. While a garden traditionally is a place of pleasure, leisure and creativity, the *Big Brother* herb garden was a curative place. It was the outdoor confessional for Christina when she revealed her secret desires.

Basically the yard was a supervised playground for the contestants, and Big Brother kept an eye on the contestants while they played, exercised and sunbaked. It provided the contestants with their most bewildering morning — when they woke up and found the yard transformed for Christmas in almost-July. The only thing missing from the backyard was the iconic Hills Hoist. Sometimes the laundry area was a body-washing area — the contestants rigged a hot-water shower and later Blair bathed in the laundry tubs.

By Week 7 the contestants had come to think of the *Big Brother* house as 'home'. Johnnie told Blair, '*This* has become my home'; Blair agreed and reiterated that he too thought of the house as his home, 'and my garden, and I'm very protective of what goes on here ... it's a beautiful thing'. Johnnie felt that he had bonded with the house and 'that's why I like to clean it'; he didn't care about how that looked on television. He added:

> This is my house and I live here ... I want to forget them [pointing to mirrors]. It's not about them, it's about me and how I feel ... I have NO control over them and how they feel and how they portray me — I can't worry about that at the end of the day.

One of the *Big Brother* rules states that the contestants 'may occasionally be required to clean the one-way mirrors through which camera operators film'. Keeping the mirrors and windows clean was essential for filming. But other than this chore the contestants certainly didn't fill their days cleaning. One of the most repeated observations on various websites and discussion groups was the messy state of the house; as one internet viewer noted: 'it looks like a hurricane hit the house'. Viewers are used to television houses where everything is usually neat and tidy. Watching someone doing housework is hardly exciting television viewing — *Big Brother* didn't need that much reality. However, every evicted contestant was asked who was the cleanest contestant.

Generally, a home is a private not a public space. Homes are not located within theme parks. The theme park location for *Big Brother* reflects a number of subtler issues. First, the theme park with its carnival atmosphere reflected the prevailing mood in the house. The fact that it was a Dreamworld attraction underscored the irony of the *Big Brother* house: it was always accessible (on the large video screens) yet not available (until the show ended). It collapsed private and public space and conversely projected a private space into a public arena. The house was flanked by a fantasy park on one side and the bush on the other side. Behind the security fences, locked gates and heavy doors lurked the house. The house had seven rooms: two bedrooms, one bathroom, one kitchen, one living/dining room, one storeroom, one pantry, and a diary room. But no laundry. The *Big Brother* house was an 'attraction' in the same way that freakshows or sideshows of a carnival or fair are; it was a funhouse.

The carnival is over

If one word could be used to describe *Big Brother*, it's carnivalesque.[6] During a carnival, the 'normal' world is turned upside down; the ordered world is gone, replaced by a riotous one in which sexuality and bodily functions are celebrated, language is coarse, sexual identity is challenged and games of chance rule. This time of mayhem and confusion allows the underprivileged (not purely a class distinction) to explore and even redress some of the inequalities and frustrations of their everyday life. It gives a voice to the disenfranchised. Of course, society doesn't sanction the carnival — it's too undisciplined and too childlike; basically it's too much fun. The carnivalesque is apparent in celebrations such as Saturnalia, pantomimes, Mardi Gras and 'professional' wrestling. The *Jerry Springer Show* is a carnivalesque *Oprah*; *The Price Is Right* is a carnivalesque *Mastermind*.

Certainly the contestants' world was turned upside down. They were treated like celebrities on the first night — limousines, crowds and cameras. There was Christmas in July. They had no outside contact yet the whole world could watch them. They rebelled by inverting normal household routines. They slept on floors and outdoors. They washed their clothes in the shower and their bodies in the garden. They stayed up late and slept in until midday. They acted like kids away from their parents for the first time.

From the outset, the atmosphere was one of exuberance. On the first night, contestants kissed and hugged and chatted excitedly. Their cacophony of voices rose until it was almost impossible to understand what they were saying, but understanding was of minimal importance. *Big Brother* was not a sociological experiment. It was a party. The contestants lacked the seriousness of contestants on shows such as *Survivor* or *Weakest Link*. Their 'non-professional' behaviour reminded viewers that this was not a 'real' house; it was merely a performance space.

The contestants were perfect for the carnival atmosphere. Todd threw things and pounded on his djembe. Sara-Marie screamed and talked childlike gibberish. Peter farted and sniffed his armpits. Blair picked his nose. Contestants jumped up and down. They cross-dressed and parodied each other. The boys performed an appalling ballet sequence. And there were plenty of costume changes. Lisa wore a wig, Andy donned Jane gear and Sharna dressed as a French maid; they wore 1940s formal wear, Halloween skeleton costumes and circus outfits. Despite a few tears, they genuinely seemed to enjoy their time in the house.

Parody is central to the carnival. The contestants parodied television, *Big Brother*, and even themselves. When Todd played his djembe, another contestant said, 'Welcome to Tribal Council', and they all laughed (Week 1). Sara Marie's 'bread aerobics' mimicked exercise shows — and was especially ironic as she was known for disliking exercise. Johnnie used a sock puppet to parody *Big Brother* eviction nights: 'Hi, I'm Gretel, what's going on this week — we have the highs and the lows — so who's sitting on the nomination couch this week — ' (Week 9). Peter admonished Roger the Rooster: 'This is Big Brother, would Roger please put on his microphone' (Week 6). There were the amusing self-parodic elements. Sara-Marie censored her own coarse language. Christina felt that she was 'one of those dumb girls on reality-tv shows who cries ... I hate those girls!' (Week 6). Sara-Marie showed her ability to use talk-show speak and 'broke-up' with Johnnie because he had 'issues to sort out in [his] life' (Week 9).

Public displays of the body are part of the carnivalesque. There was nude volleyball and showering in the garden, and face masks on the wall. The boys raced 'greyhound style' with champagne *muselet*s on their penises! Sara-Marie made a plaster cast of her breasts and bum-danced; she placed a bottle under her breast and poured from the bottle into a glass. Andy adorned her body with a number of geegaws and adopted a sexual fantasy-dress.

Sexual jokes and coarse language are also typical carnivale. And as many noted, there was plenty of coarse language and sexual joking in *Big Brother*. Swearing was commonplace — not just in Australia either. In the Danish and Norwegian shows 'swearing was more a rule than an exception' and even the US winner 'loved to swear'. As the wine flowed and tongues loosened, the contestants' sexual linguistic talents became more apparent. Although they might have been linguistically challenged in day-to-day conversation, most had a broad repertoire of sexual terms (except for Gordon who was not quite able to define group sex). When they swung into confessional mode, they gave graphic verbal and non-verbal descriptions of sexual activities.

The eviction nights were particularly riotous. Fans dressed in outrageous costumes parodying their favourite (or least favourite) contestants. They booed and hissed the villains and cheered and hooted for their favourites. They jumped up and down in front of the cameras waving placards — they too had caught the carnival spirit.

Soundtrack

The show's techno-tune reinforced the high-tech nature of the show. Music often replaced the voice-over narration: the Eurythmics' 'Would I Lie to You?' provided the background for one nomination and the words 'would I say something that wasn't true' underscored the duplicity of the nomination process.

Big Brother's authoritative voice commanded the contestants and contrasted with the contestants' naturalistic talk. Television viewers are used to listening to scripted material, but reality-tv programs, especially talk shows, are characterised by the naturalistic and vernacular language of the participants. Language reveals more than it conceals (as any forensic linguist knows) and everyone has their idiosyncratic speech and language patterns. In *Big Brother* there was Sara-Marie's loud, ungrammatical stream-of-conscious chat, Peter's linguistic competence, Sharna's vituperative response to nomination, and Christina's hesitant apologetic style.

Over the course of the show the language changed too. At the outset the talk was fast and furious. On the first night the raised voices demonstrated, more than anything else, the competitive nature of the contestants as they battled to be heard. In the first weeks there was a lot of swearing, and the late-night conversations tended to concentrate on sex. As the numbers dwindled, the swearing declined and the sexual flirtation stopped too.

What didn't make it into the program was revealing: Ben's sense of humour was lost due to television's sound-bite nature; Lisa's extensive vocabulary and thoughtful conversations didn't survive the editing either; and some of the more sentimental conversations were too saccharine for the producers to keep in. Andy postulated that using long sentences and taking forever to make a point would be difficult to edit and so a contestant who spoke like that wouldn't make the sound-bite cut (Week 1). One particularly telling linguistic relationship was that between Peter and Sara-Marie. Peter tended to correct her grammar ('youse'). Unbeknown to him, the effect was not flattering. It may have established his linguistic superiority, but it highlighted his patronising attitude towards her.

Generally, most conversations were 'cocktail party talk'. Though loud, the talk was rarely confrontational. Rather, it was the excited babble of a group of friends with stories to tell. In linguistic terms, these 'phatic communications' signal friendship or at least lack of enmity. In the house swearing was naturalised and contagious, but occasionally contestants realised that it was not appropriate for television: Sara Marie's comments that 'There's no need for language like that on morning television' reflected her awareness of appropriate television language.

Because Big Brother realised the importance of the contestants' conversation to the show, 'he' set a number of discussion topics. The topics had the potential to give insight into the personalities, backgrounds and morals of the contestants. But most of them were pretty mundane ('What were you at school?' and 'How do you think you are perceived and how should you be perceived?'). In the United Kingdom, the 'true/false' topic provoked Nick to confess that his first love had died in a car accident — a classic *Big Brother* moment. Unfortunately, none of the discussions in Australia made such good television.

The housemates' sayings became their trademarks. During a Saturday night show, Gretel staged a mock quiz. Each participant had a 'buzzer' with a typical contestant saying. Sara-Marie's was 'and then', Johnnie's was 'I know' and Ben's was 'Jota'. Sara-Marie's 'Hercules' was commodified by a group of the same name who then wrote a song about her. 'Man down' was a house saying whenever anyone fell over or slipped, which explains the title of their movie.

Some of the conversations were quite bizarre. One night Johnnie, Blair and Ben were bonding and talking about how much they loved each other. It would have been quite touching but it seemed so corny. At one stage Blair remarked, 'The only thing is we all love each other … I can't get over how much we love … each other. Maybe that makes for good viewing, or maybe not, but at the same time'. This was followed by a couple of minutes of dead silence. On another occasion, Jemma told Blair she'd almost feel guilty winning because then it would seem like a competition (Week 7)! One day they were talking about what it would be like to be 'on one of those reality shows' (Week 10).

Voice-overs

The contestants weren't the only ones talking on *Big Brother*. Mike Goldman guided the viewer through the nightly episodes; for example: 'Day 31. The housemates have been living together for more than a month and they're starting to feel the side effects of a long confinement … The morning exercise routine does not only promote physical fitness it also helps with morale. Fitness fanatic Gordon is carrying an injury.' His well-modulated voice was authoritative and aesthetically pleasing. As Ben Elton observed in *Dead Famous*, the narrator's role was to imbue 'the most wrenchingly boring observations with an air of significance normally reserved for matters of life and death'. His fictional narrator has a Scottish accent which 'sounds more sincere'.[7] One male Big Brother had a rather high-pitched voice which caused much amused speculation among the contestants and viewers.

Inside the house, the Big Brothers[8] were the voice-of-god. 'He' controlled the contestants and judged them. The producers were trained to keep their voices neutral and they were not to engage in personal banter, though they have admitted that it was difficult not to laugh at the contestants' antics. Particularly Orwellian was the relationship that formed between Big Brother and the contestants. In the final week, Sara-Marie hoped that her 'boyfriend' Big Brother was under 30. On her last day, she ruminated that she was nearing the end of 'three months of being told what to do'. One female Big Brother was 'hot' according to Ben, who guessed her age to be about 24. When considering his last hours in the house, the person Ben most wanted to meet in the outside world was? Big Brother. The contestants had come to love Big Brother.

Characters

Gretel Killeen played house mother and mine host. All of the *Big Brother* shows have had female hosts — and they have all been clever, articulate women in their 30s. Generally, they have a reputation for quick wit — often they have been comedians. Why? The show is young and hip.

Each host treats the contestants differently: Davina McCall (United Kingdom) treated the contestants like siblings, Julie Chen (United States) treated them like news items, and Gretel treated them like wayward children.

The host's role is pivotal to the success of the show. The fact that on *Big Brother* they are women underscores the woman's role as homemaker and expert on all things domestic. If the show were about surviving in the desert or racing around the world, the host would be male. Male hosts are for blokey shows like *Survivor* and *Boot Camp*. The contestants came to think of Gretel as their den mother and when she came into the house for the $100,000 Challenge, Sara-Marie kept saying, 'I can't believe you're here'.

Gretel also acted as a conduit for the audience. She asked questions that viewers couldn't. She glossed what the experts said and she explained things for us. She welcomed the contestants on the first night and guided them through their final nights.

Hers was a scripted role generally. On Thursdays and Sundays her patter relied heavily on metaphors: bed linen (*Uncut*), gardens and sports (eviction shows). A theme park metaphor was particularly apt: ride of our lives, tunnel of love, emotional rollercoaster, eviction tower of terror (Week 11).

The contestants straddled the reality fence; they were both real and not real at the same time. Some of them were ciphers for the editors/directors; some seemed to be stereotypes moulded by *Big*

Brother. Yet overwhelmingly, despite the editing process, many viewers felt that we did come to know the contestants. Well, in a way we should have, because they were under the microscope for twelve weeks.

Symbolism

The opening collage of images, cameras, the *Big Brother* eyes, the microphones and the television screens gestured to the voyeuristic nature of the show — something producers clearly wanted to exploit. Not only were the images shown at the beginning, but they were repeated several times throughout each show. They were compiled into a variety of 2- or 3-second clips ('interruptors') which separated each narrative. These interruptors were accompanied by the show's theme music. Eyes and cameras were signifiers for the show.

The Diary Room chair was another important signifier; a replica was used by visitors to Dreamworld who had their photos taken in it; sometimes they were filmed 'nominating' in it too. In the United Kingdom, the chair 'toured' the country. Of course the bunny ears were mostly associated with Sara-Marie, but the ears came to represent the playful nature of *Big Brother*.

Chapter Five

A Week-by-week Guide

Weekly challenges

Week 1	Memorising facts
Week 2	Fire-minding
Week 3	Circus
Week 4	Danceathon
Week 5	Body sculpture
Week 6	Assault course
Week 7	Treasure hunt
Week 8	Making a film
Week 9	Virtual babies
Week 10	Synchronised swimming
Week 11	Physical endurance

(The information for these summaries comes from a variety of sources: the television show, webcams, internet discussion groups, the *Big Brother* website, personal discussions. Much of the dialogue is not verbatim.)

Week 1 (Tuesday 24 April–Sunday 29 April)

The first (hour-and-a-half-long) episode introduced the housemates.

When the housemates were sealed in the house, spirits were high. Todd jumped around like a maniac and seemed to have planned to eliminate his competition by killing them off. One of his projectiles landed under Andy's eye. Andy showed herself to be a bit of a wuss, but Blair earned brownie points by being sympathetic.

Sex was on the menu straightaway. Sex talk included anal sex and virginity. Andy nabbed the double bed and spent much of the week trying to get someone into bed with her. Johnnie was the first to oblige. Though the television promos made much of this offer, viewers were left scratching their heads: didn't she (of ALL people) realise he was gay? Andy's spectacular showering left live viewers (and cameramen) gasping. Andy buddied up with the other most outrageous housemates, Sara-Marie and Gordon.

It seemed that Todd was going to be the practical joker; he planted a hair-conditioner-filled condom in the kitchen.

In the first week there was a lot of exercising going on. The kitchen sink was used as a makeshift place to wash hair (Todd's). Most of the girls wore Andy's bunny ears at some stage. Jemma injured her wrist during volleyball and was taken to a doctor.

By Friday Christina and Peter were sharing a bed. This put a stop to the contest between Peter and Blair for Christina's affections/attention.

The Friday night nominations (Sara-Marie, Andy and Gordon) were broadcast on Sunday night and Gretel crossed live to the house for their reactions.

Clearly, the rules hadn't been properly explained to the housemates, as Sara-Marie naively asked Big Brother (in the Diary Room) if the nominations were going to be filmed. When Big Brother responded that they were, she hesitated as if reformulating her reasons for her nominations.

For some reason many viewers expected each night's episode to be of that day's activities, but clearly that was not possible. Each night's show was a recap of the previous day's events. This sometimes was confusing; viewers who wanted to keep up-to-the-minute checked the official website.

Week 2 (Monday 30 April–Sunday 6 May)

The highlight of the week was the combined birthday party for

Blair (the youngest contestant) and Sharna (the oldest). A plasma screen was rolled in and messages from the families were shown. (Weren't they supposed to be cut off from the real world?) Blair gained more fans when he cried over his brother's message. Sharna just screamed through her message. Big Brother supplied alcohol, body paint, streamers, cake and presents. The girls dressed up: Andy in a Jane-esque bikini, Sharna in a French maid outfit, Lisa donned a red wig. The contestants got very drunk while babysitting the fire (this week's challenge). Big Brother set 'first love' as a topic for discussion, but the revelations were pedestrian (though Johnnie confessed that his first love was a female). Andy proved to be a party lightweight and fell asleep on a bedroom floor. The promos made much of this shot.

Sara-Marie almost blew the first task when she left her fireside vigil. She and Peter went head-to-head over her failure to stay by the fire. Despite her bravado, Sara-Marie was worried and went to the Diary Room and asked Big Brother for a ruling. Big Brother wouldn't give her a ruling.

During the week grooming seemed to be the major pastime. Todd got the first of what was to be a series of haircuts. This was all so Desmond Morris, that it could have been scripted: squeezing, combing and plucking.

Unsurprisingly, Andy dominated the first *Big Brother Uncut* show. She whipped Todd after dinner one night and demonstrated her toys. Her aim was to 'shag' five people before she left the house. The most awkward moment of the week was Gordon's conversation with Andy about group sex. Clearly, he was out of his depth and he was undecided about whether he preferred threesomes or foursomes. Andy was polite in listening to his stumbling explanation of what constitutes group sex. The audience tittered. The scenes of Andy and Sara-Marie and Gordon reeked of theatricality and lacked any sexual tension. Sharna and Johnnie shared a bed, and her cryptic comment 'You are so not gay' caused much speculation when she left the house. (Although she said she couldn't remember what prompted the comment, the audience jumped to its own conclusions.) It had only been a couple of weeks and already the boys were in drag for Christina's ballet lesson. Jemma, Lisa, Christina and Sharna discussed surprise orgasms. Sara-Marie warned Andy about the dangers of sex with the other housemates; this was the viewers' first glimpse of Sara-Marie as Agony Aunt. Christina and Peter starred in the famed 'dancing doona'. There was something for every viewer in the shower scenes: Johnnie's penis, Gordon's bum, Christina's and Andy's breasts.

The website provided additional information such as the entire shopping list and prices. Heineken was only $30. Clearly the website and television producers had decided to conquer and divide. The most obvious way they did this was in the different versions of the conversations on first love; according to the website, Johnnie's first love was a guy.

The quote of the week was Johnnie's comment 'Australian tv has hit an all-time low' as he watched Andy and Sara-Marie attempt to sexually tease Gordon. Johnnie hadn't forgotten that this was a television show.

The intriguing event of the week was Andy's voodoo spell. Did she cast it hoping to win Gordon?

The joke of the week was Blair's quip after Johnnie's claim that 'I was a police recruit': 'And then I was a construction worker, and then I was an Indian.'

One of the mini-tasks was to create and decorate face masks for the *Big Brother* wall of fame. Andy's was the most theatrical and effective (televisually at least). It was surprising that none of the psychologists did an in-depth analysis of the masks.

Though the 'Save Andy' campaign dominated the media, she was the first evictee. She and her husband were comfortable in front of the camera — and, despite constant probing from Gretel, they seemed well-adjusted. (The rumour of the week was that they weren't 'really' married.) Andy's was one of the most dignified exits of the series.

Week 3 (Monday 7 May – Sunday 13 May)

This was the famed 'dummy spit' week which added 'doing a Sharna' to the Australian vernacular. After Tuesday's nominations (Christina, Peter and Sharna), Sharna slammed the door and refused to talk to the other housemates, thus ensuring that she would be evicted.

The circus task was pretty boring. The make-up and outfits subtly implied that this was not a human zoo but a human circus. The make-up also made it difficult to differentiate among the housemates. Ben asked Big Brother to excuse Jemma from the challenge because of her arm injury. Last week he thanked Big Brother for the party. Although cynics construed his thanks as vote-winning tactics, he seemed sincere.

Big Brother encouraged the housemates to write and perform a *Big Brother* song. Overseas songs have been chart toppers. Clearly, the housemates weren't singers or songwriters. But viewers who'd heard the German version agreed that the Aussie version was much better. When performed and mixed by professionals it didn't sound bad.

It was no surprise that Andy co-hosted *Big Brother Uncut*. The episode was most notable for its full-frontal of Gordon, a shot which earned him a mention on the BBC news website. Despite her interest Andy hadn't seen Gordon naked; nor did she know about Christina and Peter's doona dancing. A cuddle between Blair and Johnnie showed that Blair, the confessed 'raging heterosexual', was coming to grips with having a gay housemate. The sex talk included 'walk job' and first masturbation experiences. Blair, Sara-Marie, Johnnie, Christina and Peter went to the Diary Room to remind Big Brother that there were no condoms after Andy left — they were added to the first aid kit. Blair dropped his trousers; Christina looked into the camera and said, 'My god it's huge'. Exactly what she was referring to was uncertain. Andy talked about being a dominatrix and demonstrated some of her bondage booty. During the making of the face casts, Sara-Marie made a breast cast and the footage was shown. The most humorous segment was (drunken) Blair's exploration of Sara-Marie's breasts: 'They're like fucking melons, man . . . it's like giving birth to a new nation.' Whatever that means. The best use of music was 'Just Be Real to Me' which punctuated the collage of Andy and Gordon.

The Truman Show was the Sunday movie — a nice piece of companion programming.

The misrepresentation of the week was the heavy editing of Sharna's apologies to the housemates. In reality, she apologised to each one and was quite sincere. Big Brother's edit proved that omission can be as damaging as fabrication in the editing world.

In the Saturday show *Big Brother* reporter Sami Lukis visited Johnnie's gym. Apparently Christina and Peter had been doing more than doona dancing — one producer confessed that they had been warned about whispering. (This was another piece of creative editing; their whispering wasn't shown at all on television.) A group 'bum dance' was filmed. The Dreamworld attraction was plugged — there were clips of visitors in the nomination chair giving their nominations for the week. Gretel reported that 1.2 million Australians watched *Big Brother* last week and *Big Brother Uncut* was one of the top five shows of the week.

With a whopping 76 per cent of the votes, Sharna was voted off.

Week 4 (Monday 14 May – Sunday 20 May)

The housemates showed their community spirit by volunteering to undergo the World Vision 40-Hour Famine.

Three-quarters of the budget was bet on this week's task — the danceathon. This was one of the most enjoyable challenges. Each housemate was given a signature tune:

Peter: 'Where Do You Go?' (No Mercy)

Gordon: 'Sweet Dreams' (Eurythmics)

Blair: 'Ballroom Blitz' (Sweet)

Jemma: 'I Want to Kiss You All Over' (No Mercy)

Sara-Marie: 'Sing Hallelujah' (Dr Alban)
Lisa: the *Big Brother* theme (Unknown)
Ben: 'Slam Dunk the Funk' (5ive)
Johnnie: 'Lucky Star' (Custard)
Todd: 'Broken Bones' (Love Incorporated).
Christina: 'Real to Me' (DJ Honda)

The housemates had to be on the dance floor (the converted gazebo) within 45 seconds of hearing their song, with a partner, and they had to maintain body contact. When the house songs (Boney M's 'Daddy Cool' and Strauss's 'Blue Danube Waltz') were played, they all had to be on the dance floor. Big Brother showed 'his' devilish side when 'he' selected Johnnie's song three times in a row, while Johnnie was trying to meditate in the bedroom. The housemates were allowed to sleep between 2 am and 9 am during the challenge, but just in case, Jemma and Sara-Marie slept on the gazebo floor one night. The highlights included Ben's morning glory, Sara-Marie's early-morning dash and Jemma trying to dress and dance. They threw themselves into this task and were quite energetic. Ben's song was the housemate's favourite.

One of the mini-tasks this week (and part-reward for participation in the 40-Hour Famine) was a cocktail-creation contest. The housemates dressed up in 1940s' formal wear for the event. They chose fake names (Blair was Sir Roger-a-lot) and paired up. Sara-Marie looked great in her blue dress — it was a pity she had to do the bum dance in it. Chrissie and Peter were the most regal couple. Blair and Johnnie were pretty fetching too.

Edited out were Sara-Marie's screeching and late-night noises. She was very annoying to watch on the live-feeds but entertaining on the television show.

The surprise of the week was Christina's intuitive revelation in the Diary Rooms. 'Tell me he [Johnnie] didn't vote for me', she dared Big Brother and looked the camera, or the audience, right in the eye.

The housemates weren't the best housekeepers and Big Brother supplied paint for Todd's chess pieces (named Stonehenge) only after they had cleaned up. Speaking of Todd, he continued to be the joker and tried to tempt everyone to hold a surprise mock wedding for Christina and Peter. Johnnie stepped in and suggested that the couple should be told of the plan. The matter was laid to rest; it was a weird idea.

Big Brother Uncut had the usual conglomeration of sex-related dialogue. A sexpert joined Gretel in the Red Room. Sara-Marie demonstrated to Lisa and Christina how to give a lap dance, and her ability to clasp a bottle under her breast and pour its contents into a cup proved to be almost as popular as her bum dance. She was starting to act like a performing seal. A conversation about penis size was a particular highlight. Jemma's 'chunka hoochie mama' was linguistically rich. The website added an 'Uncut' section.

Libby Gorr joined Sharna and Gretel for a girly session on Saturday's show. Triple M's *Big Brother Parody Song* was played during outtakes. An astrologist predicted that certain relationships would develop (Sara-Marie and Gordon; Peter and Johnnie) and that the winner could be Ben, Blair or Lisa! Already there were lookalike contests (Blair).

On the Sunday show an older man got a 'Gordon' haircut, proving not everyone who watched *Big Brother* was fifteen and female. Todd's eviction was the first really emotional one. And for the first time the housemates seemed to realise that they would be losing a pal each week. Two people rushed the stage to hug Todd. More of the audience members were in costume. Todd's charity, male teenage suicide, showed that he was a socially aware person.

Week 5 (Monday 21 May – Sunday 27 May)

The weekly task was to make papier-mâché body doubles of each other. Only two of the nine sculptures passed. There seemed to be an editing conspiracy against Sara-Marie, as episodes suggested that she and Lisa were lagging behind the others and thus might be jeopardising the task. Still Sara-Marie found time to photocopy her breasts! Did Jemma's remark 'If Johnnie doesn't quit farting

I'll nominate him' qualify as collusion? Jemma provided the show's most controversial moment so far by practically telling Lisa and Johnnie that she was going to nominate Gordon.

A humorous note was struck when Peter farted while Chrissie was trying to fit chicken wire around him for the body sculpture.

Ebony, the kelpie, was a surprise addition. The housemates were given strict instructions about dealing with the dog. Sara-Marie slept on the couch with Ebony. (Why did the website have Kelly, the red kelpie? Was there a last-minute switcheroo?)

The 'Best Song Ever' (what an awkward title) won't go away. One television episode showed the housemates jumping up and down, playing air guitars and screeching (well, Sara-Marie was screeching). This 'spontaneous outburst' was really a directed sequence. Big Brother told them what to do and the housemates were rewarded with movies.

The dumb quote of the week came from Gordon, who told Jemma about his girlfriend, whom he described as attractive but 'not model good-looking'. Jemma suggested that he tell her that, but to leave out the 'not model good-looking' part. His response was, 'Well, I'd never tell her that', unaware that he had just told thousands of viewers who hoped she was not watching. Or that she at least had a sense of humour.

Lisa seemed to have decided that now was the time to fall off the fence and she ripped into Gordon.

The plasma screen was wheeled in to show Peter his chook abuse. Of course the housemates were shocked at how they looked on television. A few grumbled about Big Brother showing the scene on television. Didn't they realise that *Big Brother* could show whatever 'he' liked? The incident occurred several days earlier. Why hadn't it been shown until then? The RSPCA had complained to Channel 10 — it seems like everyone wanted to get in on the act. As punishment, Peter had to be responsible for the chickens for a fortnight or the housemates would lose 50 per cent of their food budget. The incident appeared to amuse the housemates — so much so that Big Brother stepped in and warned them about the seriousness of the matter. Among the later fallout was Sara-Marie's nomination of Peter because of this.

The weirdest nomination excuse came this week; Jemma nominated Peter because he used to go through her clothes and wear them!

Dr Cindy Pan joined Gretel for Thursday's *Big Brother Uncut*. The material had started to wear a bit thin. Sara-Marie had replaced 'cock' and 'dick' with 'doodle'. It was evident that the amount of swearing had dropped considerably since the show started.

On Saturday's show Todd was a great interviewer. He was at ease in front of the camera, and the public responded well to him as he vox-popped his way around Dreamworld.

No one seemed particularly surprised that Gordon attracted the most votes, and his eviction from the house elicited little emotional response. Controversy ensued about his mention of Stella Artois beer. The show ended on a mysterious note when Gretel announced that everything was going to change during the next week.

Week 6 (Monday 28 May Sunday 3 June)

The week focused on the two intruders. In the lead-up to their arrival, the press was filled with various rumours: some speculated that an ousted housemate (most thought Andy) was going to return; other reports claimed that Jemma was for the chop after her careless talk.

After nominations (Lisa, Sara-Marie, Christina and Blair), Big Brother gathered the housemates into the Diary Room and announced the surprise: intruders. Blair took the news the hardest and asked Big Brother to apologise. No one else seemed very worried. Later he and Ben realised, 'Johnny's gay, Pete's taken … there's one girl each then'. Anita and Rachel arrived and everyone welcomed them. Jemma was particularly gracious; she certainly knew how to be the nice-girl.

Rachel seemed the funnier of the intruders. She matched the boys Simpson joke for Simpson joke. But Anita had prepared well and had brought playthings and had memorised parlour games. The housemates played a number of her games — 'psychologist' was hysterical on the internet but didn't get any air time. One wonders why the other housemates hadn't thought to prepare similar games.

The first evictee of the week was Ebony. Again Ben came up trumps in the Ebony episode: his concern for the dog's well-being was touching. Apparently, Ebony had just whelped and was fretting for her pups. The producers drew some flack on the website for this ill-considered move.

The most intriguing moment was the boys squirting water in an effort to attract the newbies' attention. It was puerile and obvious. In hindsight, Blair's attempts to impress Anita are a hoot.

Another I-know-I-am-on-telly moment occurred when Christina howled, 'I'm one of those dumb girls on reality-tv shows who cries … I hate those girls!' Her romance with Peter looked a bit rocky this week. Christina confided to Sara-Marie that she wanted more bed space. Sara-Marie showed her best side when she was consoling someone. Peter showed his unsympathetic side when he spent more time cleaning mascara from his shirt than comforting Christina. His vow of silence didn't help matters much either. Ben's summation? 'What a knob.'

The backyard assault course, the week's task, took a back seat to the new arrivals. Little of it was aired. Was that some bonding going on when Blair's team spent four hours in the water? The pool was jinxed for Johnnie who scraped his nose on the side of it after an over-enthusiastic dive. He wore a beanie and dark glasses for a few days.

Big Brother Uncut concentrated on masturbation. Gordon assisted Gretel on this week's show. Sara-Marie provided the most insightful quote of the week: 'I understand when I'm a root and when I'm a girlfriend and that's okay.' Blair didn't win any friends when he and Peter confronted Jemma about her modest showering/dressing techniques. It was obvious to viewers that the boys were primed on alcohol but Jemma won the day. Blair regained lost ground when he apologised to Jemma.

During the week there were a few tense moments. Big Brother had to reprimand Anita for revealing information about the show to Lisa. A one-hour special on Friday night crossed live to the house for an intruder eviction night. Judge Johnnie presided over the eviction court; some viewers seemed to find this another instance of his arrogance, but in reality the other housemates had appointed Johnnie. (Johnnie also had the deciding vote if the jury was deadlocked.) He did an admirable job and the audio feeds did not interfere with his performance. The jury decided that Anita would stay. The housemates looked taken aback when their votes were read aloud.

Lisa couldn't recover from her fence-sitting label and ended up on the couch with Gretel. Which is a pity for she was one of the few who had listed a decent book in her biography. The audience booed Johnnie.

The most bathetic moment of the show was Johnnie's 'Goodnight, Lisa' as he gazed into the distance the night after Lisa's eviction; though he seemed sincere, it looked awkward on television.

Week 7 (Monday 4 June–Sunday 10 June)

Anita spent the majority of her time crying (when she wasn't complaining about the other housemates, that is). An ouch-that-hurt-award goes to Anita for her conversation with Johnnie about his being perceived as a gay icon. The wheels turning in Johnnie's head were almost audible. Anita had immunity this week and couldn't be voted off. It was merely a matter of time though.

Viewers learned more about Peter's Crohn's Disease. This helped him to regain some lost ground, but it was unlikely that he would recover from his 'never say that to a boy' comment to Christina. It seems as if he didn't take Sara-Marie's warning too seriously ('If you break her heart, I'll break your balls'). His washing routine (wearing his clothes while he showered) was novel.

One of the most boring and senseless tasks was this week's

treasure hunt. It was never going to make good viewing and revealed little about the housemates.

Roger the Rooster took a vacation from the house. It is difficult to understand the need for the chickens (in both UK *Big Brother*s the chooks have become ill and some have died). Though they provided eggs, their main role seemed to be to make work for the housemates.

For some reason, the task in which the housemates swapped roles grabbed only a few seconds on television. This was a pity, because if the Ben/Christina and Johnnie/Peter swap was any indication it would have been amusing.

Jemma continued to dig her own grave: comments about which lip gloss looked good on television cast doubt on her intelligence. She admitted to watching *Big Brother* overseas (rumour has it that she studied the tapes prior to the Australian show). Of all the housemates, she might have been the most 'prepared' — her boyfriend Grant commented that she wasn't paid to wear the clothes, though she was 'given' some to wear on the show.

Big Brother Uncut added another term to the vernacular: 'greyhound racing'. The build-up to the race was far too long in the *Uncut*, although it made interesting (if a bit cringe-making) television. But who made Ben and Blair think of putting a champagne *muselet* on their penises anyway? Peter. *Why* they did it is less easily answered.

On Saturday's show the wryest observation came from Tim Ferguson, who noted that Sara-Marie had gone from 'She's too much, arrggh!' to 'She's too much, yah!'. Sami Lukis asked celebrities at *Cirque du Soleil* about *Big Brother*. Celebrities? Brooke Satchwell, Leah McLeod, Carlotta, Chloe Maxwell, Scott Cam & Jamie Durie, Deni Hines, Stan Zemanek, Annalise Braakensiek, and one of the Wiggles!

The Sunday crowd had become more inventive in their costuming. The girl in the shower was visually exciting (and eventually won the prize for the best costume overall). The Sara-Marie fanclub had grown.

Peter's recent behaviour earned him the buggy ride of shame. Viewers learned later that he was hospitalised after being evicted.

Week 8 (Monday 11 June – Sunday 17 June)

This week's task was to make a movie. *Man Down* was a melodrama/murder mystery. Jemma wrote the plot, Johnnie directed and Anita supplied the histrionics. The *Charlie's Angels* influence was obvious: Ben as Eduardo, Blair as 'The Chad'. As was to be expected, the acting was heavy-handed. Ben was better as the interviewer of the 'stars' as they arrived at the 'premiere'. But the highlight was Anita's outburst about her contribution. She was reading a well-thumbed copy of *Wild Swans*; other books spotted around the house included *Lord of the Flies* and *Of Mice and Men.*) Poor Anita will go down in *Big Brother* history for her remark to Blair about his 'smirking'. The shot of the week was the bemused look on Ben's face as Anita gave vent to her frustrations.

After Jemma's accidental breast flash was not shown on *Big Brother Uncut*, there were howls on the official website from emailers who sniffed a conspiracy. This in turn led to more speculation about Jemma's contract with *Big Brother*. Discussions extended to include the contracts each housemate had negotiated. Eventually Big Brother came online and explained that to show the flash would have 'exploited' Jemma who clearly had intended to keep covered up while in the house.

Big Brother Uncut contained a discussion about 'innies' and 'outies' in the vaginal sense. Another 'sexual' moment was the Sara-Marie/Johnnie tongue kiss.

On Saturday, Gretel aired a tape of Christina doing her comedy act. She was surprisingly good — which further demonstrated to viewers that perhaps the editing didn't do justice to some of the contestants.

After her outburst, Anita attracted 79 per cent of the vote and broke Sharna's record. She seemed relieved to leave the house, but not as relieved as the other housemates.

Week 9 (Monday 18 June–Sunday 24 June)

Anita got the ouch-that-hurts award again, this time for her farewell video. Her broadside to Blair really knocked him for a six.

The mechanical babies disrupted the house. Now the family image was complete — the housemates had moved in, 'fallen in love', had children and renovated the house. They have been completely domesticated — even Sara-Marie, who Ben and Blair seem to tolerate much better these days. Ben and Sara-Marie bonded during this task. Ben's comment about Sara-Marie's mothering, that 'the baby will grow up deaf', caused much viewer amusement. Sara-Marie looked good throughout this task. The editing did not favour Jemma, who managed to look as if she couldn't care less. They all thought that this was good 'training'. Apparently the babies can be set to various levels and each couple was given a 'different' baby: an easy, a medium or a difficult one. Watching the housemates get up and down all night was hilarious.

The renovating tasks were odd. They seemed to be merely busy work designed to stretch the housemates to their limits.

Jemma-gate provided the other dramatic highlight of the week. She and Johnnie were in the bathroom placing bets of chocolate on who would be nominated this week (particularly Sara-Marie and Chrissie). Chrissie walked in and realised what was going on. She walked around looking thoughtful for a while before she approached Jemma and Johnnie and very reasonably explained how hurtful such conversations were to her. The next day Big Brother called Christina to the Diary Room. She had to tell the group what had happened the previous night. Jemma went to the Diary Room and came out with her version of what Big Brother had said to her — she was clearly upset. The rest of the group supported her protest about being disqualified from the nomination process. Sara-Marie didn't look impressed.

Big Brother explained to Jemma and Johnnie that, even before Chrissie had told them, Channel 10 had been receiving phone calls about their conversation. The internet population were quick with their dial fingers. It was interesting that Jemma didn't apologise to Sara-Marie and Christina but Johnnie did.

When Blair lost a game of chess to Ben (whom he had taught the game), he wasn't pleased. It looked like the pressure was getting to him.

The cross-promotional highlight of the week was *Rove*'s remark that the show wasn't having a *Big Brother* guest because 'it's Anita'.

During the *Uncut* show viewers learned what 'freeballing' means (what happens when you wear boxer shorts rather than Y-fronts). Doona dancing was replaced with doona kissing, and the kissing experimenting between Sara-Marie and Ben/Blair reminded viewers of how young the housemates were.

Johnnie's eviction was the most emotional to date. It marked a turning point in house dynamics — the housemates realised that Sara-Marie might be unbeatable.

Week 10 (Monday 25 June–Sunday 1 July)

After Johnnie's eviction the house mood was glum. Three of the six remaining housemates were up for eviction.

The highlight of the week was Wednesday's Christmas-almost-in-July. While the contestants were asleep, the crew had set up a Christmas tree and covered the backyard with bubbles and ice. Everyone received presents and Blair played Santa Claus; Big Brother gave the housemates a mechanical dog. Christina was upset because her father did not sign her card. She started pondering her family life and this set her on a thinking path which led her to the herb garden. With Sara-Marie as a confidant, Christina revealed that she was adopted and had not met her biological mother and brother. Sara-Marie's sympathetic nature was foregrounded.

The week's task was synchronised swimming. They had to perform as a group and as individuals. Clearly, Boney M was a favourite of one of the production staff; 'Daddy Cool', 'Mary's Boy Child' and 'By the Rivers of Babylon' have all figured in the challenges. (Which prompted viewers to ask — what's wrong with a little Abba?) The challenge mimicked the popular danceathon, but it didn't have the same entertainment value. Surprisingly, Sara-Marie's dummy spit over her costume was not broadcast on television. Internet viewers debated whether this was a conspiracy by the producers to keep the public's favourite looking good. The amount of time the housemates needed to spend practising had some unfortunate side effects including conjunctivitis and rashes.

One of the most humorous moments was Sara-Marie's self-censoring beeping when she dropped a piece of wood on her finger in the chook pen. In the same vein, her swearing while doing bread aerobics prompted her to tell herself, 'There's no need for language like that on morning television'. This demonstrated how domesticated she had become.

The *Uncut* show was a compilation of all the best of the *Uncut*s to date. More interesting was Saturday's show which aired a reunion of seven of the evicted housemates; they got together for lunch with Gretel and discussed their particular experiences. Also on the Saturday show was Johnnie and ex-Rugby League star Ian Roberts. Roberts expressed his annoyance at reality tv and at Johnnie's portrayal as a bad guy. Again the talk centred on Johnnie's sexuality. 'Gay' must have been the most used word in this episode. Gretel ended speculation that Jemma was *paid* to wear certain clothes; but Gretel did reveal that someone had *given* Jemma clothes to wear while in the house.

The unawareness quote of the week was, 'I love doing my makeup. I obviously don't do it much in here, but it makes me feel like I'm going out.' Guess who said it? Jemma.

Big Brother gave the housemates a chance to put *Big Brother* staff faces to voices, using an identikit.

Jemma was evicted. It was a fairly dry-eyed event, until Sara-Marie went to her bed and found a flower that Jemma had left for her. It was a touching gesture.

Week 11 (Monday 2 July–Sunday 8 July)

And then there were four: two boys and two girls. Jemma's eviction tape was such a sweet one that it seemed almost too saccharine. It lacked the emotional impetus of Johnnie's. Most obvious to viewers was how empty the house had become. Although not reaching previous highs, 41 per cent of the budget was spent on alcohol.

There were lots of shots of Sara-Marie and Blair declaring their 'love'. Surely this was not an attempt to develop a narrative about a romance between them? Some viewers seemed to buy it, but it was so obviously another performance. Overall, the endless declarations of love palled. One wonders which housemates will really bother to keep in touch outside the house.

The week's challenge was a physical endurance challenge, 'The Australian Big Brother Games'. The housemates wagered 90 per cent of their budget. The group had to climb the equivalent of the ten highest mountains in Australia, using gym equipment. Then they had to cycle the equivalent of the Great Ocean Road, row the length of the Murray River and walk around the base of Uluru. It prompted an amusing argument between Ben and Blair about distances. The best part of the challenge was the 'and then …' exchange between Sara-Marie and Ben. Ben didn't seem at all perturbed by her loudness now.

Wednesday night was a special one-and-a-half-hour show, slotted to compete with Channel 7's showing of the movie *Titanic*. (Ratings revealed later that the majority of viewers turned to *Big Brother* for the first part of the show but then switched channels.) The celebrity 'intruder' was Gretel who came in for the $100,000 Challenge. Rumours leading up to the show were rife, the most popular being that the money would go to one housemate only. In fact, the housemates got to share the money equally, each receiving nearly $20,000. The Challenge was boring and some of the tasks were poorly planned. The tasks were the Haunted Room (complete with authentic Sara-Marie screeching), Charades (again kudos to Sara-Marie for her Peter kicking impersonation), Leaky

Buckets, Scavenger Hunt, Pictionary and Bridge over Troubled Waters. Pictionary does not make for good television viewing. One of the funnier moments was when the housemates threw the robotic dog into the box of alphabetical items — items which were to be removed from the house — and Gretel took the dog out. The dog had come from one of the sponsors of the show, Sony.

The housemates seemed to get more and more pampering from Big Brother. As well as the $100,000 Challenge and a visit from Gretel, they had an outdoor barbecue (complete with Aussie delicacies) and sushi (for doing the *Big Brother* News show). Sara-Marie showed that she was no contender for *Sale of the Century* (she sensibly declined to appear on such shows later). Her lack of general knowledge meant that she came last in the quiz and spent the night outside in a tent.

The promos promised a sensational revelation from Christina. It was a cheap beat-up. She'd posed for the men's magazine *Ralph*. Viewers might have been disappointed, but Ben was impressed.

Uncut was a compilation of overseas video clips.

The promised Sara-Marie/Christina pash didn't occur, thanks to a cold sore.

Blair was the only one not nominated this week. So he made it to the final three. Chrissie reached Sara-Marie's nomination record.

Christina was evicted.

Week 12 (Monday 9 July–Sunday 15 July)

With only three housemates remaining, Sara Marie grabbed most of the viewing time.

Viewers were finally told how the final evictions were to be done; there had been speculation about this for some time.

The funniest moment of the week was Ben's sleep-talking about chickens.

The three housemates were given a seafood banquet; the chairs had cut-outs of the faces of ex-housemates on them. It was quite spooky. Naturally Sara-Marie sat beside 'Anita'.

One of the mini-tasks was to paint a mural, but not much of that was televised. They also had to prepare a time capsule and complete a job application.

Sara-Marie promised (rashly) to plunge nude into the pool if she made it to the final three. Why was she so modest now? She didn't cover up when Andy was around. She and Blair were almost parodying Peter and Christina with their lurve talk; although some speculated that they were forming an attachment, it was clearly not a love one.

In another weird viewers-watching-housemates-and-videos moment, the chore for the week was to create video diaries. Viewers watched the housemates being filmed filming each other. The boys also spent considerable time playing with the cameras. And then viewers got to watch the housemates watching a preview of *The Secret Life of Us*. Sara-Marie's flattering comments about it being the 'best movie' she'd ever watched made some viewers wonder if this had been scripted.

Blair bathed in the laundry tubs — with his underwear on. He had been filmed showering nude for a number of weeks, so why the sudden modesty? And after mouthing off at Jemma.

Gretel interviewed a UK *Big Brother* producer. Viewers learned, among other things, that Australia was the only country in the world that had live audience evictions each week.

On Sunday night Sara-Marie was evicted. It was a close thing as to who was the more overcome, Sara-Marie or the crowd. She was positively quiet. The inevitable bum dance happened, though it looked like the audience might see more of Sara-Marie than was necessary when her skirt slipped. Her lack of focus was at times annoying but she did show her usual spark. At the end it really had looked as if she was going to win.

Finale (Monday 16 July)

After Sara-Marie's surprise eviction there were complaints about vote-rigging but nearly every *Big Brother* has faced similar complaints.

All the housemates gathered and outtakes dominated the final episode. There were some live feeds which showed Ben and Blair dancing around obviously unaware that the cameras were on them.

'And the winner of *Big Brother* is ... Ben', with 62 per cent of the votes. Blair left the house and had his moment on the couch with Gretel, while the camera returned to a pacing Ben. Although it was Ben's night, he got little air time. His jump into the audience surprised Gretel and security; what kind of audience were they expecting?

One viewer thought that it would have been effective to have all the housemates walk onto the stage in the order of their eviction, then Ben! That would have been a real telly moment.

A sample of some complete episodes

A nightly episode (aired 24 May, Week 5)

'Day 31. The housemates have been living together for more than a month and they're starting to feel the side effects of a long confinement ... The morning exercise routine does not only promote physical fitness it also helps with morale. Fitness fanatic Gordon is carrying an injury.' Cut to Johnnie asking about Gordon's elbow.

'With no gym equipment in the house, lots of wood might make good weights.' Cut to Lisa and Jemma looking for gym equipment. 'When your lifestyle is back to basics you learn to improvise.'

'Gordon's finding it difficult to contain his feelings about Lisa.' Cut to Gordon gossiping about Lisa to Sara-Marie as they laze by the pool.

Cut back to Lisa and Jemma searching for stuff to put in milk cartons. They raid the herb garden for rocks.

Interruptor: music, blue and green fuzzy pictures — this signals a change in time.

Back to the house. Inside Jemma and Lisa are exercising. The time is shown as 11:07 am. Chrissie walks past them and is invited to pass judgment on the improvised equipment. 'The back yard has become the exercise yard.' Cut to a camera following Peter jogging around while Johnnie, Lisa and Gordon watch from the verandah steps. We hear their conversation. Johnnie and Lisa talk about exercising; Johnnie gives advice. Cut to the kitchen and Gordon admits to feeling unhealthy. Johnnie gives some advice: 'Johnnie's not the only one feeling unhealthy.' Gordon comes out and gets ready for a run. Cut back into the house and to everyone in the kitchen making breakfast. Sara-Marie joins Johnnie and Lisa and they kiss. 'In his other life Johnnie is a gym instructor; now it's his own fitness he is worried about.' Johnnie feels he is 'like I am 18 again' and yet 'falling apart' .

A graph of the voting appears on the screen. 'Who will be evicted from the house this week? Once again the voting is neck and neck. Your phone call will make all the difference.' Instructions on how to vote are given and the costs of the phone call. 'Next on *Big Brother*, Sara-Marie under fire for being lazy.' Cut to a confrontation between Sara-Marie and Ben.

Ad break

The *Big Brother* eye appears. 'Yesterday Ben asked Big Brother to excuse Sara-Marie from the task. She's just found out.' Cut to Sara-Marie talking in Diary Room. She talks to Ben about her back. Group talks about backs. 'It's four weeks since the housemates left their other lives. Now they can only dream of home. Christina dreams about her pet dog.' Chrissie tells Peter a dream about her dream. Back to group talking on the couches — about dogs.

Interruptor

Shot of everyone working on the body doubles. 'The house has bet 60 per cent of its shopping money on completing the body replica task. Most of the housemates have nearly finished. Sara-Marie is just starting on her model of Lisa.' Cut to Lisa and Sara-Marie in a bedroom where Sara-Marie works on Lisa's body double. Cut to others working on the sculptures. Back to Sara-Marie and Lisa in a bedroom.

Interruptor

'If you want Peter to be evicted from the house vote … if you want him to stay …'

'Next, *Big Brother* the single.'

Ad break

'One of the first things the housemates did when they arrived is set about writing the lyrics to a house song. Once they finished them Big Brother let them chose a tune and had it recorded professionally. Tonight they hear the guide track for the first time. All they have to do is to perfect their performance.' Cue song and they sing along.

Interruptor

'Big Brother wants them dressed up to make a music video.' Housemates in bedrooms; Jemma talks about her outfit, while Gordon and Jemma offer Lisa clothes.

Interruptor

Collage of clips of the housemates singing and dancing, inside and outside. 'And now Big Brother has a task — to make the performance sound in tune.'

Interruptor

'If you think Gordon should be evicted from the house call … if you want him to stay vote for either Lisa or Peter.'

'Coming up on *Big Brother*, Scary-Marie.'

Ad break

'The rare chance to hear music has sent the house into a dance frenzy and has lifted the spirits of the house since this morning's low point.' Everyone is in one of the bedrooms, jumping on beds, screaming.

'Here's a special reward for all of their musical efforts.' Johnnie reads a letter from Big Brother.

'Tonight someone else has done the cooking.'

Blair says, 'Just because I worked in a pizza shop you make me carry these bloody things.'

They prepare to watch a movie and comment about the quality of DVD.

'After a month locked up in Australia's most unusual household a night in front of the tv is refreshingly normal.' Watching them watching *Charlie's Angels* on DVD.

Interruptor

'On *Big Brother* tomorrow will lagging Lisa and sleeping Sara-Marie lose the task for the other housemates?'

Credits roll

'Hi, it's Dean here, catch up on all the overnight action in the *Big Brother* house each weekday morning on Triple M's Sammy and Dean Morning Show. Or read about it in the *Courier-Mail*.

Big Brother Uncut (aired 24 May, Week 5)

'Good evening, this is *Big Brother Uncut*. I'm Gretel Killeen. Well, life is not clean and simple. It is not a crisp white freshly laundered bedsheet. Life has creases. It gets grimy. It has yucky stains. People swear, they kiss each other, their underpants fall off, and they sometimes have very unclean thoughts. *Big Brother Uncut* is the adults-only laundry where we drag in the grubby sheets from the *Big Brother* house and give them a good going over and a nice public airing. What comes out in the wash? Well dirt, the dirt you can't get when the kids are still awake at 7 pm, the dirt that can change the way you look at life in the house.'

'So there are nine left in the house. Nine lives or nine live ones?' This week they have been cavorting through the *Big Brother* abode in very curious ways, so we called in an expert to navigate us through one very stormy sea of sexuality. Welcome Dr Cindy Pan. Now, you are our sex and relationship expert this evening.'

Gretel asks: 'What five words would you use to describe what's going on in the *Big Brother* House?' Cindy gives four words which leads to a discussion of Gordon and Jemma.

Gretel: 'Ah yes, every time I watch Gordon with Jemma I hear the theme song from *Jaws*. While we've been watching Gordon try to check Jemma's tan lines, another sexual pursuit is starting to race all over the house. Running: Johnnie, Capricorn, 30 years old, attractive, fashionable, inner-city boy. Chasing: Pete, Gemini, 28 years old, attractive, fashionable, inner-city boy. Does it add up? You do the maths.'

Clips of Peter and Johnnie in the house, sharing a shower (nude shots) and on beds together. Peter corrects Sara-Marie's use of 'beated up'; beaten up' says Peter. Peter and Johnnie are chatting and Johnnie calls Peter a 'latent homosexual'.

Gretel and Cindy discuss Peter's motivation. Cindy thinks that Peter is using Johnnie and Christina — by 'exerting power' over both of them, by being 'sexually ambiguous', Peter gets it both ways. Outtake of Johnnie calling out 'Pete' in his sleep. Gretel and Cindy discuss sleep-talking.

Ad break

Gretel talks of Ben's erection at the danceathon. Outtakes of this and other occasions when various housemates discuss erections and penises. Gretel asks Cindy about Peter's penis.

Ad break

This segment concentrates on Sara-Marie and penises. It is comprised mostly of Sara-Marie, Christina and Peter in the gazebo. Sara-Marie says that she is 'drowning in doodle'.

Ad break

Outtakes from bedroom where Johnnie and housemates discuss his sexual experiences; cut to Johnnie fondling Sara-Marie's breasts; back to bedroom and talk of boys' wake-up erections.

Lisa tells of her 'sexy' half-dreams. Gretel and Cindy discuss Lisa and sex.

Ad break

Gretel introduces the segment — housemates are on the couch discussing kissing techniques.

Gretel and Cindy consider the kissing talk. Gretel suggests that Peter and Christina's relationship has taken a weird turn.

Clip of Peter and Chrissie's pillow talk; cut to them on the couch during the day looking like a loving couple; back to pillow talk, sometimes subtitles.

Cindy and Gretel discuss Peter and Christina's relationship.

Ad break

Gretel introduces the *Big Brother* cocktail party. Outtakes of the cocktail party give Gretel and Cindy a chance to talk about alcohol and sex. Bedroom shots show Chrissie massaging Sara-Marie by walking on her; there is laughing talk of golden showers.

Gretel and Cindy talk of the use/abuse of alcohol.

Ad break

Gretel introduces a segment on sexual-technique conversations; Jemma is coy about using certain terms, Peter by comparison uses all words. Jemma asks what the boys don't like. Gretel wonders why Jemma is asking this question. Cindy hypothesises that Jemma has a 'queen bee' complex.

Gretel promises viewers that Big Brother will be keeping an eye on the increasingly 'bizarre' behaviour of the housemates. Gretel signs off reminding viewers she will be back for the Saturday and Sunday shows.

Saturday show (aired 9 June, Week 7)

Same opening credits as nightly show.

Gretel introduces the show and gives an outline of the show while clips play: Lisa, Tim Ferguson, Johnnie's friend, celebrity news, who watches, highlights of the week and the last 24 hours. Sami Lukis walking along Bondi Beach. These clips are interspersed with clips of Anita and the background music is 'Best Song Ever'. Sami goes to Anita's favourite coffee shop; she interviews the hostel manager where Anita works; Anita's mother tells us that Anita wants to be an actress; Sami interviews her father, nephew, sister, grandparents and boyfriends (past and present); it is revealed that Anita is part-Israeli and part-Hungarian.

Ad break

Lisa talks about being out of the house. Clips of men-in-the-street comments about women who say 'We must have a talk'. Back on the couch with Tim Ferguson and Lisa. Lisa is surprised at the camera angles and close-ups. They talk about Anita. Tim suggests that Ben is under everyone's radar and talks about the audience turnaround on Sara-Marie. Another song from Triple M is aired: Sara-Marie's 'and then' refrain.

Ad break

Security guard Dan talks of being afraid of being pulled into the house; clips of guards at doors.

Clips of the past 24 hours: Chrissie shows Peter how to use eyelash curlers; Sara-Marie cleans toilet; boys in the yard work out how to use the pool blanket; Chrissie washing clothes. On the couch Jemma talks about the monotony and says 'We're like dole bludgers'; Anita doesn't appreciate the analogy; she thought she would enjoy lazing around but she doesn't. Sara-Marie is in the vegetable patch singing; she claims she had the bum dance before *Charlie's Angels.*

Ad break

Gretel chats to Johnnie's female friend; she's wearing a tee-shirt with the words 'Johnnie Rocks' in a star. The expert guest is psychologist Dr Bob Montgomery who talks about *Big Brother* as a competition; he says that we all lie to each other several times a day; we don't plot that 'I want you to like me', or form fan clubs etc.; mentions that in brainwashing you deprive people of information and then feed them only certain types of information, and little hints have a thousand times more clout.

Ad break

People in the Diary Room at Dreamworld giving their nominations. The week's highlights, with Gretel's voice-over. Sami Lukis interviews people in front of *Cirque du Soleil* about their reaction to *Big Brother.*

Ad break

Media news: Johnnie was the poster boy for *DNA* magazine; Andy is on the A list; she was at the premiere for *Pearl Harbour*; Andy and Damon's unconventional marriage causes comment in the press; Lisa's bungy jump on *Rove*; *NW* article 'Hot Toddy'; someone copies Peter's high kick and ends up tearing ligaments!

Gretel reminds viewers to tune in for the eviction tomorrow night.

Sunday eviction show (aired 3 June, Week 6)

The show opens with sweeping shots of the audience, who are jumping up and shrieking. The camera pans in on fans:

Sara-Marie's are in pyjamas and bunny ears; some have fake breasts.

Christina's are in tutus.

Lisa's are in dark wigs.

Blair's are in footy jerseys.

Gretel introduces the show, using sporting metaphors such as 'It's half-time' and 'We've had injuries'. Cross to house — the nominees are seated on the couch; the others stand behind them. She asks:

'Anita, how are you settling in?'

'Johnnie, are you so lacking affection in the house you had to kiss the pool?'

'Pete, what's this with your vow of silence … are you planning on becoming a monk when you leave the house?'

Back to the stage/ studio, where Gretel introduces the potential evictees' supporters: Sara-Marie's father; Lisa's friends Sue and Zoe; Chrissie's mother, Gwen, and an attractive blonde girl who is not introduced; Blair's mother and his brother Gavin, and a girl who is not introduced.

Clips of the past 24 hours in the house: Chrissie and Pete; Chrissie retiring to bed with a migraine; Johnnie's pool accident; Blair's apology to Jemma in the bathroom; Lisa admits she'd rather leave halfway than before halfway.

Ad break

Gretel interviews Sara-Marie's father. Clips of nominees: Sara-Marie playing volleyball by herself; Lisa arguing with Gordon; Chrissie and Peter hugging; Peter rubbing mascara off his shirt (boos from the crowd); Jemma comforting Lisa after a fight with Sara-Marie; Peter's 'never say that to a boy' incident; Blair giving Lisa a hug; Lisa crying in the Diary Room. Quick images of all nominees: Chrissie laughing, Sara-Marie leaping around in her bra, Lisa looking happy, Blair laughing and with a tennis ball in his mouth.

Ad break

Blair talking to the camera in the garden: 'Hi Dad. Do the windscreen wiper thing.' He is interrupted by the helicopter. Gretel talks with Blair's mate and mother. Blair collage: thoughtful after nomination, reading a letter, being very happy about the new housemates, some of the argument with Jemma.

Ad break

Gretel: 'The lines are closed.' Back to the house live. Gretel reads the verdict: 'Lisa, it's time to go.' In the house there are hugs and kisses from all; Jemma dissolves into tears. Countdown.

Johnnie kisses Lisa. She sits on the golf buggy cart clutching a book.

Cut back to the house where Johnnie hugs a weeping Jemma, Blair and Ben are hugging and Chrissie looks happy.

Ad break

Gretel greets Lisa and leads her down the mirrored hall to the roaring crowd. There's some chanting from the audience, 'Lisa! Lisa!'

Lisa sees her two friends and runs over to greet them. Then she returns and sits next to Gretel. Gretel tells her that everyone in the house is upset, especially Jemma. Cross to house, where Pete is hugging Jemma (who is still crying).

Lisa says that she liked Jemma and that she developed a strong bond with Johnnie. Boos from the audience. Lisa is stunned by the response to Johnnie.

Gretel tells her not to worry and shows the voting: 50 per cent for Lisa, 21 per cent for Sara-Marie and Chrissie, and 8 per cent for Blair. Lisa says, 'Gee, so everyone wanted me gone.' Gretel says, 'No, 50 per cent of the people wanted you to stay.' Lisa is visibly cheered by this remark.

Full footage of Ben's, Blair's and Peter's nominations of Lisa. Gretel asks about Ben, and says that people thought a romance might have blossomed between Lisa and Ben. Lisa laughs; she said she thought Blair was okay (shouts of approval from audience).

Shots of Lisa in the house — all happy shots: in the shower, dancing, doing the circus task.

Lisa's friends join her on the couch.

Ad break

Gretel and Lisa on the couch. Lisa nominates as her charity the Lost Dogs Home; her legacy item is *A Guide for the Advanced Soul*. She is asked the eleven *Big Brother* questions:

1. What did you miss the most?
   A: Friends and family
2. Who did you like the most?
   A: Jemma
3. Who did you like the least?
   A: Christina
4. Who has the most annoying habit?
   A: Sara-Marie — she was so boisterous

The contestants on the first night (courtesy Channel 10)

Gretel Killeen, sassy host (courtesy News Ltd)

The *Big Brother* House at Dreamworld (courtesy News Ltd)

The well-lit dining room

The open-plan living area

The pool and gazebo

The contemplative herb garden

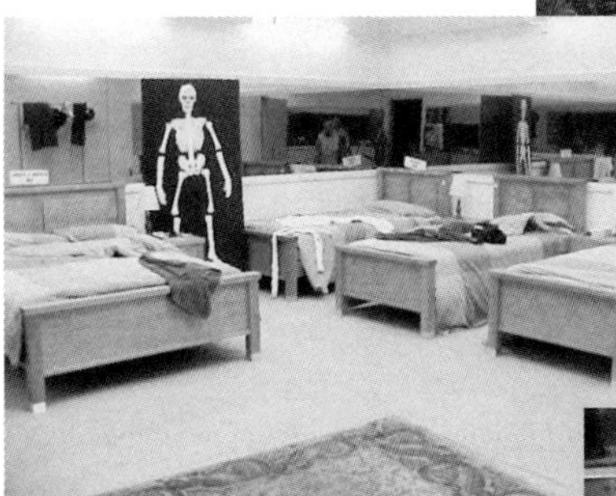

The blue/grey bedroom with $100,000 challenge skeleton

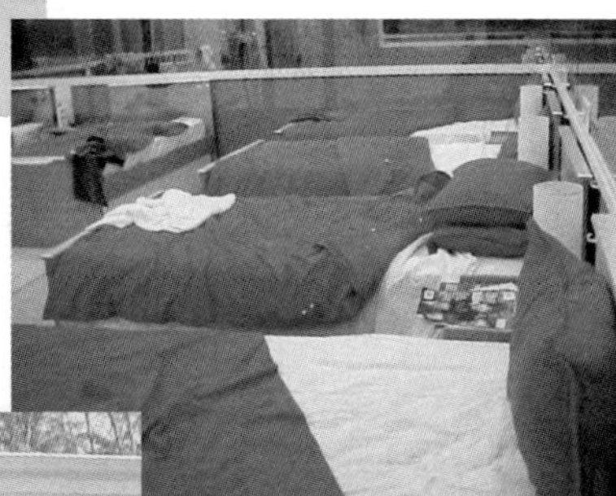

The orange bedroom

The portal back to the real world

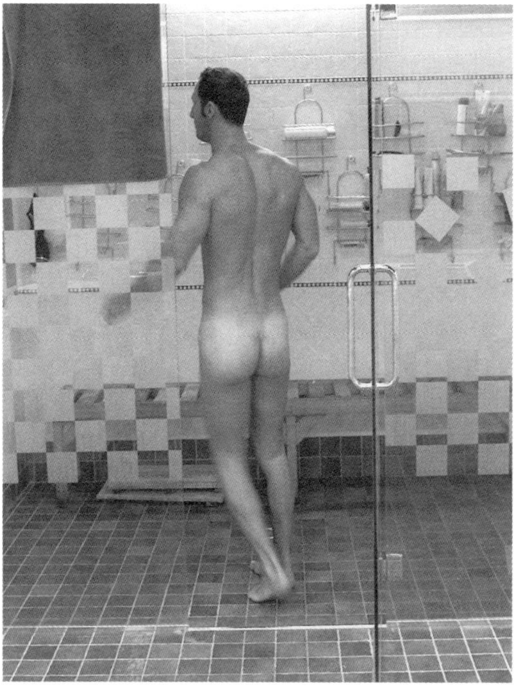

Johnnie in the share-shower

Ben relaxing on one of the comfortable couches

Big Brother, Southern Star Endemol's Peter Abbott (courtesy News Ltd)

Popular runner-up Sara-Marie (courtesy News Ltd)

The Heineken TV Bunny

Christmas in June transformed the backyard (courtesy News Ltd)

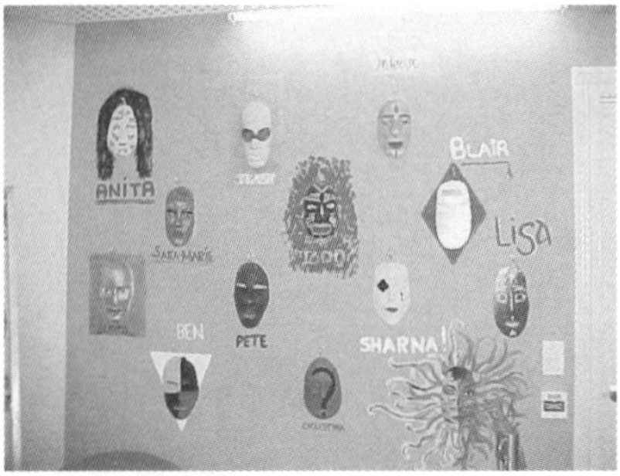

The wall of masks

Andy's Sunburst

Sharna's Kiss

Tribal Todd

Flash Gordon

Square-eyed Lisa

Hairy Anita

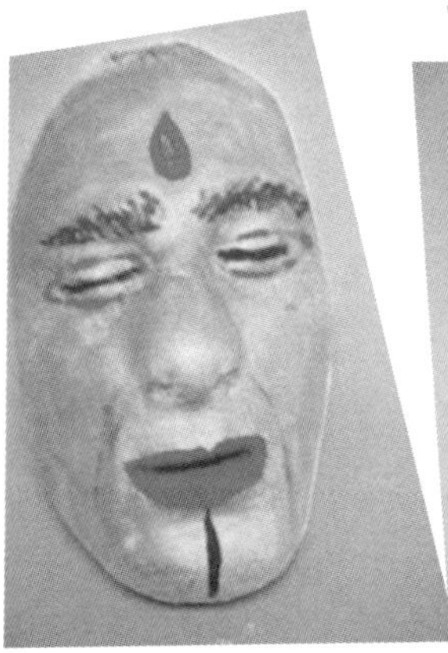

Contemplative Johnnie

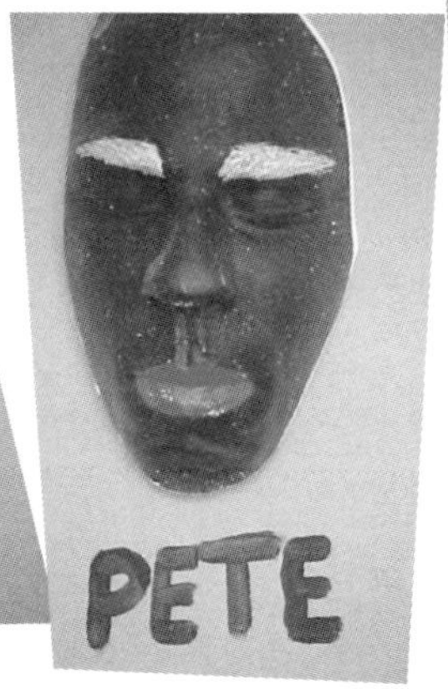

Blue Peter

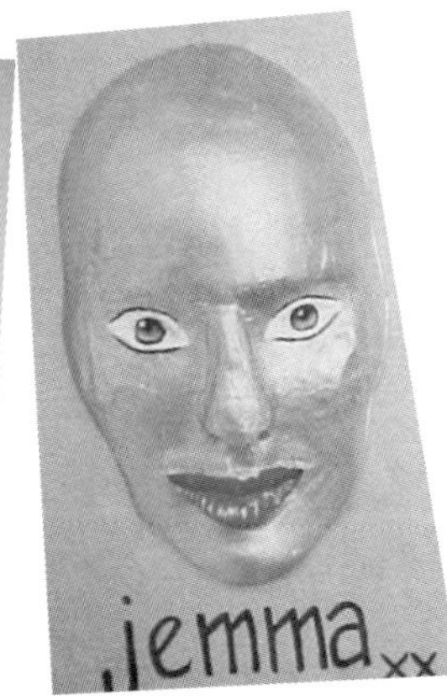

All-seeing Jemma

Glittery Sara-Marie

Enigmatic Blair

Ben's Jersey

The mirrored hall to the Dreamworld stage

The Dreamworld auditorium

An intimate room for Big Brother Uncut

The interview couch on stage at Dreamworld

Long-Johnnies, *Juice*, September 2001

PVC Andy, *Juice*, September 2001

The Chook's Revenge, *Juice*, September 2001

Rent Boys with Girl, *Juice*, September 2001

From the coathanger to bunny ears (courtesy News Ltd)

The finalists preferred the floor on the last night

Blair bathing outdoors, but he's wearing undies

Sara-Marie, Gretel, Ben and Blair making their way to the Dreamworld stage on the final night (courtesy News Ltd)

Ben's a Big Brother

5. Who could you most fall in love with?
   A: I'd say Johnny (shrieks from crowd)
6. Who is the funniest housemate?
   A: Lisa agrees with audience who shout 'Ben'
7. Who is the laziest housemate?
   A: Sara-Marie
8. Who is the cleanest housemate?
   A: Jemma
9. What is your greatest regret about leaving the house?
   A: Not getting to know Christina better
10. Who will go next week?
    A: Sara-Marie — 'She's getting on a few people's nerves'
11. Who will win?
    A: I hope it's Jemma

Blair hugging Lisa — a voice-over says that Blair voted for Lisa but he is the first to comfort her. Cross to the house and clips of the other housemates' reactions: Jemma weeping; Sara-Marie looking shocked, her hands to her mouth; a long hug between Sara-Marie and Chrissie; Johnnie shaking Blair's hand; Anita talking to Blair and referring to the jinxed room; the cure — 'sprinkle ashes or something' on the sheets.

Ad break

Jemma in the bathroom talking about Blair and his apology. Shots of the contestants in the yard listening to the noise from the crowd. 'Lisa! Lisa!' can be clearly heard. Pete puts his arm round Jemma. The nominees return their suitcases to the bedrooms.

Sara-Marie in the Diary Room says she was bored and was prepared to go. She remembered that Gordon went on his third time and she thought she would too ... she's amazed that she hasn't. She says the last few days she's not been herself. 'I've been snappy not happy.'

Ad break

Sara-Marie consults the tarot cards in the bedroom. Johnnie in the Diary Room: he'll miss Lisa; she was grounded and could laugh at things and herself. He thinks she also learnt something about herself in the house and so got what she wanted.

Jemma is in the bedroom still talking to Sara-Marie about Blair and the apology.

Ben, Blair, Johnnie and Chrissie are on the couches. Blair thought he was a goner when Gretel mentioned the apology. He thinks the whole argument would have looked very bad for him.

Sara-Marie asks Peter whether he and Chrissie will be together after the show. She is happy with his answer because it is more positive than a few weeks ago.

Chrissie is chatting with the guys. Johnnie says that Chrissie has changed since she came into the house. Chrissie says she's just got more comfortable; when Andy had got her whips out, she'd wondered what she was doing there.

Jemma, Pete and Sara-Marie are in the bedroom talking about exercise.

Pete and Chrissie are shown in bed cuddling. Johnny is sitting pensively outside. Cut to Chrissie hopping back into her bed; Sara-Marie's arm stretches out to her. Johnnie walks about slowly, then says, 'Goodnight Lisa'.

Gretel on the couch gives a quick wrap-up, reminds viewers that 'Big Brother is watching' and introduces the musical act.

Final sequence is the band, with Lisa and her friends dancing.

Behind the scenes at an eviction

(Modified from Whit4you posting on The ClubHouse website)

It's 7:30 pm and the contestants have been sitting on the couch for half an hour chatting. Big Brother warns them not to drink alcohol while on the show, not to look up at the ceiling, not to call Big Brother 'Peter', and not to swear.

They are 'assuming' their positions … which is how they've been sitting for ages. They are bored. The live show is starting and someone suggests that as soon as it goes live they hide behind the couch.

Finally, 'This is Big Brother, please stand by'.

Gretel says: 'Nominees, give five good reasons why you should stay in the house.'

Gordon: 'Volleyball, volleyball, volleyball, volleyball, volleyball.'

Sara-Marie: 'Volleyball, volleyball, sunbaking, jocky watching, chickens.'

Todd says: 'Volleyball, pool, chess, volleyball, jumping in the pool.'

Johnnie is asked to go to the Diary Room, again; this is the third time in the past hour-and-a-half. Gordon wants to wager $100 on who goes, but nobody's up for it. They are just all talking at once … waiting … waiting … waiting. Someone suggests a *Big Brother* dumb quote of the week. Someone tells Todd to take off his ring because it's bad luck. He asks why — and receives the answer 'because Bianca won't marry you'. Todd says he doesn't want her to marry him. Sara-Marie asks why. He says he was joking, that she should know that by now (or something to that effect). Todd reckons, 'I'm not a man, I'm an adventure.'

Silence.

Sara-Marie asks Big Brother if she can go to the toilet, and says she'll take off her mike. There is no response. Someone says, 'I can see it now, Gretel comes back, where's Sara-Marie? She's taking a piss.' Todd says she shouldn't go, as they could cross back at any moment. Sara-Marie asks Big Brother again, but there is still no response. Todd and Gordon both look extremely tense.

Big Brother warns them that they have five minutes. Sara-Marie runs to the toilet. Gordon takes off for somewhere. A female Big Brother says: 'This is Big Brother. Please remain in your seats, and don't communicate with Big Brother in *any* way.' One of the contestants responds 'Okay'. Another says, 'YOU just did.' They all crack-up laughing.

Todd is voted out. They are all upset inside the house. Gordon says he feels like he'd rather it have been him. Sara-Marie says that it feels so weird because it was their second time and only his first. 'Oh my god, I can't believe it wasn't me. I feel terrible.' Someone observes that, because everyone adds to the group, every time someone goes from now on it's going to be worse. Jemma's hugging Chrissie and wiping away tears.

They toast, 'Here's to Todd.' Someone comments that it's harder staying, in some ways. Someone else (possibly Gordon) says that's how he was feeling last week. Someone comments that suddenly it's a lonelier place, without Todd. Jemma is still crying.

Johnnie gathers them around to listen to a poem he's written:

The Worst Poem Ever
So from twelve we are down to nine
So far it's all been pretty fine
We are getting used to Sundays
When someone leaves this place
All we are left with is an empty bed space
We've got Chrissie and Pete who are hanging
And who knows maybe they will start banging
The whole world is looking
To see what's cooking.

They all like his poem and there is total silence for a moment. Sara-Marie goes to the Diary Room. Peter sits next to Chrissie. There is still silence in the room. Someone says, 'Should we turn on the stereo, or the television or something.'

Total silence.

Chapter Six

The Young and the Restless: The Contestants

O brave new world
That has such people in't.
(*The Tempest*, Act 5, Scene 1)

They became manufactured celebrities in a matter of weeks: from obscurity to the best-known faces in Australia. *Big Brother* proved that you don't have to have talent to be a 'star' — which is something that most people suspected anyway.

For a variety of reasons thousands of hopefuls responded to the media appeals for applications. Not surprisingly, the applicants were screened by health professionals.

The selection process was a vigorous one. The application form asked how the applicant would spend the money if he or she won, what they would bring into the house, and their sexuality. Potential contestants did all manner of things in their three-minute videos, such as the famed nude dash through a shopping centre, but if the ones shown on the pre-*Big Brother* television special[1] were anything to go by, they were generally more embarrassing than original. It took more than outrageous behaviour to make the final cut.

Mass auditions were held. There were more questionnaires and lots of group tasks, done under the watchful eyes of producers and psychologists. There was psychological testing before the final cull was made. The producers cut and pasted, realising that the right mix of contestants was essential. They had to select those who could provide good television. The *Survivor* producers have the casting gene. Did the *Big Brother* producers have it?

Fourteen strangers, one house, 85 days, a shower cam, a toilet cam, one winner. What *were* they thinking? Fame. They got fame in buckets. Since the contestants were introduced to (or thrust upon) the Australian public, they were rarely out of the media. They were in the press, on the television, on the radio; there were stories, songs and photos of them. Sara-Marie was mentioned in over 350 newspaper articles, and Gordon received 100 mentions.[2] Even people who didn't watch the show heard the name Sara-Marie.

The public's first introduction to the contestants wasn't auspicious. The Sunday before *Big Brother* went to air, News Limited newspapers contained an eight-page Armchair Guide to the show (22 April). Accompanying the awkwardly posed photos were equally awkwardly written biographies:

> Peter, 28, Dubbed Wine Buff. Wine is Peter's thing. He has studied viticulture, worked in wineries and now works in sales for top Sydney bottle shop. But before the grape called, Peter's most unusual job was as a mortuary transferer — moving dead bodies for police and funeral parlours. He hails from NSW.

Was it the mixed metaphor, the bad grammar or the ambiguous sentences which grated? As well as Peter the Wine Buff there was Jemma the Gorgeous Blonde, Ben the Beefcake, Blair the Spunky Teen, Andy the Discipline Therapist, Gordon the Animator, Christina the Dancer, John (not Johnnie) the Gay Personal Trainer, Sharna the Hostie with the Mostie, Sara-Marie the Stripper Manager, Todd the Musical Brickie and Lisa the Meat and Potatoes Kind of Girl. So some contestants were defined by their looks, the majority by their occupations, and, well, they obviously didn't know what to do with Lisa.

By the time the Armchair Guide was released, contestants were in the house and had no idea about the media feeding frenzy that was to grip Australia. Which was lucky for them, for the first responses were none too flattering. Jonathan Green called them 'whining, self absorbed, trailer trash'.[3] Amanda Meade didn't hold back; to her they were 'narcissistic, exhibitionistic dysfunctional ... idiots'.[4] One writer felt that they were the 'least interesting bunch of young Australians'.[5] For another, the banality of the contestants made him 'appreciate ... truly talented people'.[6] David Dale called them 'half-crazed ... sadists'.[7] Sadists because they were torturing viewers or did he mean masochists? But you can't keep a good sadist down. The contestants wondered about the sanity of the people watching them; Ben couldn't believe that people would watch 'fourteen idiots like us' (final show).

Many wrote of the potential physical and psychological harm that could befall the contestants. Andrew Dodd predicted there would be 'punch-ups and cat fights'.[8] Others wondered about the potential for violence: 'no amount of screening by the Australian producers ... can guarantee a tragedy will not happen here';[9] and only a few weeks later an American contestant held a knife to the throat of another contestant. In the final weeks, Ian Oshlack felt that *Big Brother* had gone from 'being fun to being deadly serious',[10] which was a bit of an overstatement. He felt that the house was a 'prison ... [which] is slowly descending into a kind of hell'. In part he blamed the tasks which he believed inflicted a type of mental torture:

> *Big Brother* introduced dolls [the mechanical babies] and asked the group to become parents. These pseudo babies were programmed to cry at inopportune times, usually during the night, recalling the common brainwashing technique of sleep deprivation.

Most new parents would agree with him. The contestants must have derived some comfort from knowing that (unlike real parents) theirs was a temporary state, and perhaps it was a valuable life lesson for them. Oshlack concluded that Sara-Marie was showing signs of stress by talking gibberish, Blair had all the symptoms of withdrawal and Chrissie was close to being a basket case. Clearly he hadn't been watching the show for long; Sara-Marie had always talked 'gibberish'. There are plenty of examples when adults use nonsensical language. Sara-Marie's chicken chat is similar to 'motherese' (the simplistic talk that mothers adopt when talking to young children and recently parodied on a television commercial); twins often use secret languages to communicate with each other; lovers call each other silly names. Those who feared that the contestants would suffer emotional scarring underestimated their robust psyches. As one media critic noted:

> Many of my fears subsided when the truly awful dominatrix Andy and the coarse Sharna were evicted from the house. They weren't upset at all, I thought. Maybe these people won't be devastated by the experience after all ... Turns out the only anguish Andy suffered was her failure to 'shag' five men in the house before being evicted.[11]

In fact, Andy has celebrated her press coverage; on her website is a collection of press clippings — even negative ones such as:

> The first outcast, Andy, turned up on the red carpet at the Australian premiere of blockbuster war flick *Pearl Harbor* last week ... a sign the movie's promoters had clearly reached new depths for a star attraction ... when a former Heidi Fleiss escort and card-carrying dominatrix like Andy is the biggest name on the bill around town, things must be looking grim for our social survival.[12]

Overseas contestants could have warned the Australian contestants that fame can backfire. In South Africa, a teacher (Janine) was censured for swearing, for voicing strong political opinions, and for demonstrating oral sex on a cucumber; she is currently undergoing investigation by the South African Council of Educators who believe that 'educators must behave in a proper way, so as not to bring the profession into disrepute'.[13] Bubble (UK *Big Brother* 2) complained that his confessions about drug consumption have hampered his career since he left the house. In the United Kingdom, tabloids paid big money for kiss-and-tell tales; subsequently some ex-lovers with axes to grind have stepped forward and told all. Contestants found their love lives plastered across the front pages. In Australia the *Daily Telegraph* invited people who knew the contestants to contact the paper; but nothing surfaced. Whether this reflects the integrity of the Australian press or the integrity of the Australian public remains to be seen.

Stories about *Big Brother* contestants can increase newspaper circulation. In the United Kingdom, the *Sun* reported that sales increased by 90,000 copies every time it included a story about *Big Brother*'s Helen Adams. In 2000 stories about 'Nasty Nick' (Bateman) boosted sales by up to 30,000 copies. In Australia, magazines in particular (the newspaper blitz was a given) capitalised on the interest in the contestants. There were even newspaper articles about stories about contestants in magazines (e.g. Sara-Marie's *Cosmopolitan* appearance).[14] The industry became quite cannibalistic.

Magazines couldn't resist the temptation of fourteen new celebrities.

A magazine's cover is its promise. Who is on the cover reflects the magazine's belief in what appeals to potential buyers:

- Sara-Marie as model on *Cosmopolitan*
- Blair as *Neighbours*' star on *Who Weekly*
- Christina and Jemma as eye candy on *Ralph*
- Christina as almost-wife on *Bride.*

Naturally there were plenty of group cover shots. Several *Who Weekly*s had groups of contestants and sometimes magazines selected certain contestants:

- *NW* selected Blair, Jemma and Sara-Marie for their 'Hot Bodies' issue.
- *New Idea* had glamorous Christina, Andy and Sara-Marie.
- *Juice* preferred controversial Andy, Johnnie and Peter.

Inside, the stories reflected the magazine's personality. *Woman's Day* might have titled their article 'Randy Andy's Happy Hubby', but it described their marriage in typically romantic mode: 'Despite the couple's non-conformist views, how they met sounds like an old-fashioned love story'. *New Idea* focused on Andy's education and Catholic upbringing but didn't mention her husband.[15] The *Sunday Telegraph*'s 'Body + Soul' section concentrated on her healthy lifestyle:

> Q: How do you stay in such good physical shape?
> A: I've been doing a lot of exercise since I was quite young. I did a lot of jazz and ballet until was 13, and then I started doing hip-hop aerobics and became a gym junkie for a few years in Brazil ... I began to ride a bike everywhere and it kept me fit. I still do that now. I tend to go dancing quite a lot and I go pretty hardcore.
> Q: Are you health conscious in your daily life?
> A: Yes. I eat a lot of fresh vegetables and fruit and everything organic. It was difficult for me being in the house for two weeks not having organic food. The food tasted like plastic to me. I have normal cereal, with muesli and sultanas for breakfast and some fruit. I'll have a sandwich on rye bread for lunch ... I don't eat a lot of yeast and I barely ever drink alcohol. I hate beer and usually don't drink wine either, so I stick with water and fresh fruit juice. If I drink it's vodka and orange ... I don't smoke much either, maybe two or three cigarettes a week when I'm out. For dinner I have a mountain of steamed vegetables with sour cream and spices. I eat free-range chicken and organic meat, and I barely eat pasta.[16]

Much of the material about the contestants in *New Idea*, *Who* and *NW* was standard celebrity fare: bios, who they were dating, what they did before the show, interviews with anyone who knew them, what they were going to do after the show. Many promised exclusives, exposés and secrets:

- 'Secrets of *Big Brother*' (*Who*)
- '*Big Brother* Exclusive: Gordon's Amazing Secret' (*New Idea*)
- 'Secrets the Camera Missed' (*New Idea*).

And the secrets? Recycled information readily available from many other sources. Some were quite deceptive: *NW* promised 'the 14 Housemates Bare All' in their 'Hot Bodies' issue — but they didn't.[17]

Some of the photo shoots were as unimaginative as the stories. For 'Hot Bodies' Ben wore footy gear, Gordon was draped in a sheet, Christina posed in ballet gear, Sara-Marie wore bunny ears,

Todd had his djembe, Jemma applied lip liner and Andy knelt on a bed and waved her whip. The photographers didn't seem to know what to do with Peter and Blair so they shot them topless: Blair in a towel and Peter in jeans. Lisa, Johnnie, Rachel, Anita and Sharna were more subtle. One tongue-in-cheek aspect was the grouping of the contestants: Jemma and Gordon, Peter and Christina, the intruders, and diplomats Johnnie and Lisa.

Juice's threesome cover (of Peter, Johnnie and Andy) is a visual metaphor of the sexual hopes and voyeurism of *Big Brother*. Inside, the pictures are rich in subtext. The straight guy (Peter) wears nail polish and jewellery. The three wear tee-shirts which referenced 'the human wholesale that is *Big Brother*',[18] but they also contained other subtexts: 'For Lease' (possibly gesturing to Peter's attempts to get out of his contract), 'Terms Negotiated' (also reflecting Johnnie's reputation as a mediator), and 'Make an Offer' (another reference to Andy's occupation?). The accompanying article was the most media savvy. Its examination of the *Big Brother* phenomenon included commentaries from media specialist Dr Jane Rosco, Simon Thatcher, psychologist to *Big Brother*, and Channel 10's Tim Clucas. Its interviews were insightful.

Female magazines went to some trouble to align the contestants with their readers. *New Idea* gave glam makeovers (a perennial favourite) to Sara-Marie, Christina and Andy. The contestants were reinvented as screen sirens; it was a clever collapsing of television and movies. Clearly though, the article is about fantasy (the word is used four times), fairytale, Hollywood, and the 'stuff dreams are made of'. The inference is that this can happen to anyone, even 'you', the magazine reader. Sara-Marie's *Cosmopolitan* shoot highlighted her ordinariness. Her section included photos of her hugging the editor and two fashion designers; rival cover girl Britney Spears is not hugging anyone. In the accompanying story, the writer stresses, 'She's so real, so genuine, so down to earth'.[19] Sara-Marie did the shoot in her own shoes rather than the high heels provided because she wanted to be comfortable. (Comfort and fashion are rare bedmates.) Even her makeup is accessible: Sara-Marie wears Avon; Britney wears Clarins. 'Real' celebrities aren't photographed embracing those on the other side of the lens; Sara-Marie was one of 'us' not one of 'them'.

Contestants were generally perceived as approachable. Because Johnnie and Sara-Marie's compassionate natures came through on *Big Brother*, the two of them were 'agony aunts' for a short while. Johnnie had a 'Dear Johnnie' on Triple M's Club Veg. *Sydney Confidential* signed Sara-Marie for a five-week period as 'Big Sister' to dispense advice such as:

> Q: I am renting a property with two other guys, and recently one of them has gone off his rocker. Over the past few months he has become more and more crazy — buying a speargun and shooting windows and couches, writing on the walls, smashing his stereo and other appliances, swearing, spitting on the floor and talking jibberish all the time. He has also lost his job. My fear is he may turn on us at any moment. What can I do to help him through this and also save my sane housemate and myself?
> Dazed and Confused
> Blacktown NSW
> A: You should be worrying about your own health and safety. You have to leave the house now! It appears that no matter what anyone would do to help your friend, he probably wouldn't listen. Obviously there are reasons for his behaviour that neither you nor I can control. Let him know that you are moving out, but make sure you have somebody else around when you do it. Your friend needs a lot of professional help.[20]

The columns provided Sara-Marie with enough material to produce a book, *Sara-Marie's Guide to Life*, which was released at the end of 2001.

It was reassuring for viewers to see a collection of ordinary people. This was the democratic nature of *Big Brother*. It was their 'ordinary' quality which attracted fans and praise. Jane Fraser felt that Ben Williams was a better role model than many sports heroes, and considered that 'Mr Nice Guy [was] the new, quintessentially Australian hero'. Kate De Brito called them 'Twelve

Good Sports'.[21] Viewers saw their Anzac Day remembrance, their participation in the 40-Hour Famine, their unequivocal acceptance of Johnnie, Sara-Marie's compassionate nature, Jemma's thoughtfulness, Blair's ability to apologise, and generally their caring attitude towards each other.

Basically, the contestants looked and acted 'just like we would in front of the camera'.[22] Sometimes they got lax about the cameras (Peter admitted this in an interview), but they didn't forget them entirely; they couldn't. Sometimes the cameras made a noise, or the contestants saw them behind the mirrors.

So the contestants were performing — not in a theatrical sense, but they were acting out their ordinariness on television. Some of the contestants realised this and commented on it. Ben recognised that they weren't being themselves and observed that he would like to meet up with the contestants (even Anita) to see 'how they are away from the cameras' (Week 12). Some were even aware of their re-presentation by *Big Brother*. Ben asked Rachel how she thought *Big Brother* would stereotype her. She didn't understand the question and he explained: 'Todd the hippie, Jemma the fashion designer' (Week 6). Gordon went further and felt they were all 'characters'.

The contestants reacted to the constant camera surveillance in different ways. Some played up to the cameras: Ben tried to make the wipers move, Blair talked to the camera, and Johnnie did his sock-puppet show. Some mimicked television shows: Sara-Marie staged bread aerobics in the kitchen; Johnnie conducted exercise classes in the living room; they even did a news bulletin. They had their favourite performance spaces: Sara-Marie in the herb garden, Andy in the shower, Anita on the couch. And they adopted different techniques: Gordon exercised and brooded; Johnnie meditated and mediated; Anita was stressed; Andy was theatrical; Christina loved. Sharna swore and fumed; Lisa observed and thought; Sara-Marie laughed and performed tricks. Sometimes they adopted different roles; for the virtual babies challenge Johnnie was a devoted father, Sara-Marie was a doting parent and

Jemma was a disinterested mother. They were aware they were being filmed but unaware of being broadcast.

A common performance space was the Diary Room. The first indication of this was Sara-Marie's question 'Is this going to be televised?'. Each contestant struck a pose; only a few sat comfortably. Sara-Marie draped herself casually across the chair, Johnnie crossed his legs but his body remained open, Jemma perched eagerly on the edge of the chair, Ben and Blair leaned forward with their arms on their knees. Rarely did they look directly at the camera for other than quick glimpses.

Several conversations reflected contestants' awareness of how *Big Brother* worked. Jemma remarked that the website and show were time delayed, so swearing, talking about drugs and references to friends would be bleeped out … and that she'd be angry if they weren't (Week 4). She explained to Blair the voting process: 'People could be voting you out because they feel sorry for you in the house, or they feel empathy for you, or think you'd be better off leaving', or "I want Blair to stay in", so they vote for another nominee to keep Blair in' (Week 6). One day Christina was thinking about a birthday present for Peter and another contestant suggested that the website should have a poll: 'What present Christina should get for Peter' (Week 4). Andy decided that circumlocutory talk would be difficult to edit, so using long sentences and taking forever to make a point would be edited out (Week 1). Peter adopted a different system and decided that swearing was the better alternative:

> If there was something we didn't want *Big Brother* to screen we would swear every second or third word because we thought they couldn't screen it on television, but then we heard it was screening uncut on the internet and we just stopped.[23]

The editing process

Roughly 70 television hours came from 182,570 hours of filmed material (25 cameras 24 hours, 85 days). Each day 23 minutes were edited from 36,000 minutes. Obviously, the material was severely culled.

The *Big Brother* production team never hid the editing process; they even reminded viewers by showing images of the editing suite in the opening sequence. Contestants in the United Kingdom reported that, after a week in the house, Big Brother called them in and asked them 'What role do you feel you play?' This apparently helped the producers to construct their narratives by recreating contestants in digestible personas. Ben Elton describes the process in *Dead Famous*:

> 'It's built in the edit.'
> 'You manipulate the housemates' images?'
> 'Well obviously. We're not scientists, we make television programmes. People are basically dull. We have to make them interesting ... [in] order to create a nightly half-hour of broadcasting we have at our disposal the accumulated images of thirty television cameras running for twenty-four hours. That's seven hundred and twenty hours of footage to make one half-hour of television. We couldn't avoid making subjective decisions even if we wanted to.'[24]

In Australia, the most obvious casualty of editing was Johnnie. His construction as the villain of the piece was clearly a desperate attempt to add drama. The Sara-Marie love stories with Ben/Blair rang pretty hollow. As did the 'Is Peter gay?' narrative. When Rachel entered the house, she had the advantage of having known the contestants as on-screen personas and then as real people. The disparity between the two shows some of the editing biases:

> *Rachel*: Before I met Blair I thought we wouldn't get along at all! Granted, I hadn't watched much of the show but I thought he was really quiet and (here goes) arrogant. When I got into the house I found that my perception of him was COMPLETELY wrong! ... Also Chrissy was a bit of a shock. She seemed very quiet and unconfident on camera but in reality she is a really awesome chick. She's definitely one of the nicest people I've ever met. As is Jem! I thought that someone that applies that much lip-gloss would be an absolute tosser but I couldn't have been further from the truth. In all

honesty I don't think I've met a more genuinely nice person in my life! She was so welcoming and just the best![25]

When they saw themselves on television, how did the contestants feel about their portrayal? Andy said that it was 'pretty accurate'. Sharna felt that, although the footage wasn't doctored, the material wasn't presented in truly chronological order. Splicing shots together to create narrative is a basic film production technique. For example, a shot of someone blowing a kiss is juxtaposed with a shot of someone's cheek; the two incidents might be totally unrelated, but it creates a story for the viewer.

Just as important as construction in film production is omission. Material that ended up on the cutting-room floor included Sara-Marie's dummy spit over the synchronised swimming costumes her middle-of-the-night antics which kept housemates awake, Jemma's talk to Sharna about apologising, and Ben's sense of humour ('He's really funny but you don't see it on the television', said the cameramen).[26] Internet viewers told of the many incidents that were not aired, fuelling conspiracy theories and cries of 'unfair'. In spite of the contrived editing, 'there's something touching and true about the people in the *Big Brother* household'.[27] Suzanne Carbone summarised it succinctly: 'It's real people on TV doing real things, but it's not reality TV.'[28]

As many fans were watching the live feeds, it didn't take long for them to create fansites of their favourite contestants. Jemma's and Blair's were the first to appear; Ben's was one of the last. Andy is her own webmistress. The only contestant without a fansite was Sharna. A fansite usually contains photos, articles, and any information which may be of interest (i.e. appearances on television, live appearances etc.). However, a visit to the fansites at the end of 2001 revealed exactly how fleeting fame is — many of them had not been updated in months. 'Just Jemma' was for sale. More had closed down completely. 'Christina's Web' and 'Blaircentral' were still being updated. Johnnie's and Sara-Marie's fansites are webmastered by others (in Sara-Marie's case, Harry M. Miller). In addition to the fansites, there are about 20 internet fan clubs on Yahoo devoted to online discussions of contestants (from the 'Rachel *Big Brother* Fan Club' to 'Johnnie's Private Mardi Gras').

After the show finished, the contestants appeared on other television shows. They competed on Channel 9's *Sale of the Century*. and Channel 7's *The Weakest Link*. They returned to Channel 10 for the 'Starlight Challenge', a combined telethon and pantomime. The panto opened with Ben phoning the contestants and trying to convince them to do the panto.

- Blair was on the phone on the set of *Neighbours*, saying 'No Flick, no sex okay'.
- Andy was relaxing by a pool in skimpy swimmers.
- Anita was crying ... 'No, no, I'm just slicing onions,' she says ... she was on the phone in the kitchen.
- Johnnie was doing one-armed push-ups.
- Todd was begging on a street corner, wearing a tee-shirt which reads 'Remember me ... I was on Big Brother!'
- Gordon was playing play station.
- Chrissie was saying 'No, it's not a good time.'
- Jemma was in front of a mirror.
- Rachael says, 'Can I be in more than one scene this time?'
- Pete was driving the Alfa Romeo he won on *Sale of the Century*!

The contestants were still being typecast by their *Big Brother* personas.

This is Australia!

Most viewers and critics felt that *Big Brother* held a mirror up to Australian society; they felt they were watching 'Aussies at their most raw'.[29] Channel 10's Tim Clucas 'sees himself as the scientist, casting the show with housemates who were "representative of the public" '[30]. So what did the 'representatives' of the Australian public tell us about ourselves?

Well, it seems that Australia is a young nation — when they entered the house the oldest contestant was 34 and the youngest was 19; the average age was 25. This reflected the demographic

Channel 10 aimed for, but it contrasts with the overseas shows which were also aimed at a young audience but had older contestants. In the United Kingdom the minimum age was 21, because producers 'wanted people who would have stories to tell the others … people who had done a few things';[31] the average age was 30. In the United States the contestants' average age was 29. South Africa was closest to Australia with an average age of 26 years. The Polish winner was a 47-year-old male.

There were some natural selection processes that ensured younger contestants would apply. The call for applications went out on youth media: Channel 10 and on Triple M. The whole process took around four months, from December 2000 to April 2001, and not many people can afford to put their lives on hold for that amount of time. Australia is the only country that didn't have someone drop out at the last minute. The contestants had to put aside at least 85 days plus time after the show for publicity purposes. Many post-show activities were gratis. The contestants were paid a per deim, one which enabled them to meet their financial commitments outside the house; it was approximately $500 per week, which may not suffice for some. It was thought that there was some room to manoeuvre, and there were rumours suggesting that Jemma had negotiated a better deal. Of course, this was the first time round; a wider range of people will probably apply for the second series.

One of the most obvious cultural differences between the Australian and the European *Big Brother* shows was the communication style. Italian, French and Greek contestants were given to wild gesticulating; their speech *sounded* dramatic. Our contestants relied on the raised eyebrow, the smirk. The Australians were generally more laconic, the notable exceptions being Sharna's outburst and Anita's confrontation. One viewer described the differences she observed between the Greek and Australian shows:

> I don't speak Greek, but I understand in a general way what is going on. It's interesting that even though I don't understand a thing, it's still very translatable. They [the Greek contestants] are very friendly

> toward each other. The guys touch each other a lot, not sexual, but affectionately, but they can also get short-tempered; that's probably the most different thing I noticed; they don't have the patience our *Big Brother* housemates had towards each other. For example, this week's challenge is to learn all the flag signals in soccer. Dinos was trying to test Christos and he kept getting it wrong, so he threw the flags at the wall and went and sat in the kitchen ... They are very loud ...[32]

There was a 'sense of tolerance ... remarkably little conflict', observed Big Brother Peter Abbott. This tolerance was expressed in many ways. There were no obvious factions; although some contestants formed friendships, the house rarely divided over an issue. They didn't have house meetings to discuss problems such as sharing the household tasks or shower schedules. Given the state of the house, though, maybe they should have. Other households often divided along gender lines. The Australian house was the first to have mixed bedrooms, which may account for the more harmonious male/female relationships. Tolerance even extended to family members and supporters of contestants. Overseas *Big Brothers* have had to keep the contestants' families apart. However, in Australia it seems that the families and friends didn't need this. There actually seemed to be some bonding between families, especially those who came back for several times for eviction nights.

In other households, contestants exhibited bizarre hoarding behaviours (Leigh in South Africa buried spoons; Mel in the United Kingdom gathered discarded batteries). Such behaviour demonstrates the contestant's level of anxiety. The fact that the Australian contestants didn't do anything particularly strange indicates that they were more comfortable with their surroundings. Is it possible that Australians have more experience with shared accommodation? Even the youngest had lived and travelled overseas.

Generally, they were a caring lot, if Andy's eye 'injury' and Jemma's sprained wrist were anything to go by. Viewers who were watching the live feeds noticed how they supported each other. One American commented:

> The guys are all now coaching Sara-Marie to how to look for the camera … it's really cute. She's got her hand on Blair's thigh, and one of the guys … Peter I think … goes over and fixes her top for her ... one of the other guys says, looking good, chin up! (The ClubHouse)

Another agreed:

> One thing I noticed, these guys are all very very nice and gentlemanly to the ladies … watching how tender and helpful and totally patient they were with them as they were trying to learn the stilts was impressive. They were also very patient with each other (the other guys) as they were working on it [the circus challenge]. (The ClubHouse)

Viewers saw Ben asking for favours for others and thanking Big Brother when he gave them a special treat. Anzac Day was commemorated with biscuits and silence. Their succinct discussion of the Anzac heroes and the futility of war examined one of Australia's most important myths. And probably said it all, the swearing included.[33] Perhaps one of the attractions of the show is watching ordinary people discussing important issues naturalistically; the lack of scripting is a big plus in these instances.

For many, the most flattering portrait of Australians was the contestants' lack of homophobia. As Jon Hart noted: 'We're no longer the strongly homophobic society we're portrayed to be … they were curious about Johnnie's experiences in a positive way.'[34] American viewers were particularly entranced with the boys' attitude to Johnnie. Two viewers were surprised:

> What surprises me about this is the way the one guy is laying on the other guy and they've been doing this for the past half hour — perhaps things are just different there, but here I just don't see a lot of guys laying together like that on a bed … not saying there is anything WRONG with it, it's just sooo different than what I'm accustomed to. (The ClubHouse)

Another wrote:

> They are so non-homophobic it impresses me (non-homophobic guys in the US are usually not this NON homophobic. I mean they are

breathing heavy and ... pumping push-ups and Johnnie's really enjoying this. (The ClubHouse)

No wonder they were impressed. Less than one month later a US *Big Brother* contestant unleashed his homophobia:

Kent leans into the camera and says that homosexuality is 'deviant, it's perverse and it's the kind of lifestyle that 90 per cent of Americans don't want near their family ... Yeah! Don't push it on me. It used to be sickos, weirdos and freaks. Now it's "alternative lifestyles". Don't come into my face and tell me it's normal.'[35]

The lack of censorship on the Australian live webfeeds was particularly noticeable. In South Africa the station bleeped out the word 'God'. Americans were surprised that many of the conversations were aired:

1st it was talk of levitation, now it's talk of orgasms. Now the guys and women are talking about penis size. 'Have you got a big schlong?' My, this is NOT BB US — lol.

Holy cow! This group is sure a lot more XXX than the American BB was. Been listening to them the past hour as they prepare to go to sleep, and half of what they are saying I don't think I could say here without getting censored. Basically a lot of chat about BDSM/ affairs/ cheating / 3somes / and so on.

Definitely more explicit then the American BB was ... not that I am complaining. They could not shock me LOL. But I am sure it will shock some 'vanilla' folks out there. (The ClubHouse)

The nudity and shower cams also raised a few American eyebrows.

Language is an obvious cultural marker. Ben Elton parodies this in *Dead Famous*; his contestants endlessly repeat 'bigged', 'up' and 'respect' (which are also hallmarks of that other British cultural observer Ali G). What is the current state of linguistic play in Australia? As this was language in a naturalistic setting, most of the utterances are incomplete, grammatically incorrect and characterised by the vernacular. Editing doesn't help either. However, their sexual vocabulary was quite extensive. Some familiar words were used in new ways; for example, 'goon', originally short for flagon wine, was used as shorthand for any wine. And some terms were added to the Australian vernacular: bum dancing, doona dancing, and an alternative meaning for greyhound racing. The contestants were called housemates in Australia, whereas in the United States they were 'houseguests' ... a subtle but telling difference. As is often the case with language, it takes an outsider to point out idiosyncratic use of language. United States viewers were particularly confused by some of the contestants' lingo and the following were posted on a discussion board:

> Legend: Johnnie enjoying lunch says, 'Whoever made this bread is a legend'
> Filth: Sharna doing well on the stilts exclaims, 'This is FILTH!'
> The Shits: used for very good or very bad ... Lisa's laugh is the shits!'
> Sunbaking: Used in place of suntanning and sunbathing.
> Milo: A delicious chocolate drink which is the shits. (The ClubHouse)

Another defining element of a culture is the food. Standard Australian items include Vegemite, cordial, golden syrup, Milo, tinned beetroot and pumpkin. However, there were a number of Pacific Rim items: soy sauce (specifically Ketjap Manis), sweet chilli sauce and coconut milk. Mediterranean items included arborio rice (or is this just another form of Rice-a-Riso?), couscous, and various pestos. If the *Big Brother* household is anything to go by, many Australians are eating less meat. Vegetarian dishes were popular; the only meat on the first shopping list was a kilo of sliced ham. (Because of the high consumption of vegetables, in Week 3 *Big Brother* added them to the staples.)

The group also exhibited casual eating patterns. They often ate around the smaller coffee table rather than at the table in the formal dining room. Breakfasts were often eaten outdoors: on the patio steps and in the gazebo. Naturally there were the Saturday afternoon barbecues. Recognising the central place of the barbecue in Australian culture, one of the first tasks was to build one.

The strict exercise regime of the household (one to two hours each morning; Gordon's sit-up challenge) was noted by a number of American viewers who thought they'd tuned into an exercise channel. Because smoking wasn't allowed on a 7 pm timeslot, some contestants gave up smoking (Sara-Marie, Peter and Anita). And drinking was fairly minimal, though it might not have appeared that way on television. Peter observed that the house was 'almost like a health farm. You give up smoking and you cut down on your drinking. We hardly got anything to drink in the house to be honest.'[36] Peter used to drink every day before *Big Brother* and has since kicked his pack-a-day cigarette habit. In fact, the house was a positive influence on many contestants.

Tim Pegler summed up what Australian *Big Brother* showed about the Australian psyche:

> *Big Brother* says nice things about us ... the disparate personalities didn't resort to sniping or violence ... but concentrated on coexistence. Factionalism didn't evolve and tactics didn't come into play. If there was a theme to be gleaned, it was how the contestants learnt to respect each other.[37]

Appearances

Appearances can be decoded. Fashion can have political (brown shirts), cultural (national costume) and personal (dress for success) significance. Even hair has meaning. As the contestants were the most visible group of 'ordinary' Australians, what did their appearances tell us about them and about our culture? What did the audience adopt as signifiers for the contestants?

The most obvious fashion-horse was Jemma. Her trademark off-the-shoulder outfits, wide belts and hipsters reminded the fashion conscious that the 1980s were back and added fuel to the rumours that she was sponsored by a clothing company. Her careful grooming and lack of nudity were, as she herself admitted, part of something she was deliberately controlling: her image and her future. Although Jemma might conform to society's imposed images of femininity, the control she exercised over her image indicated a shrewd business mind.

Andy opted for fantasy outfits. Many of her costumes reflected her reported lifestyle: the corsets, the soft-bondage wear, the jungle bikini. Her outfits screamed 'look-at-me'. Although both Sara-Marie and Andy had no problem with nudity, Andy's attention to her body was more narcissistic. Sara-Marie became known for her Winnie-the-Pooh pyjamas, which were carefree and comfortable. The bunny ears, originally Andy's were playful and kittenish but also gestured to a sexuality — as in a *Playboy* bunny. Generally, the other female contestants kept their appearances low-key. Casual and comfortable attire was favoured by Christina, Lisa, Sharna, Anita and Rachel.

The males appearance was also casual. Blair and Ben often wore football jerseys. Football with its conservative masculinist values reflected their blokey companionship. Gordon's hip sports gear reflected his high-energy approach to life. Johnnie's sleeveless shirts showed off his physique and reinforced the image of the body-conscious gay man. Todd's look might have been 'alternative' but he was as self-conscious as Jemma. According to his girlfriend: 'He likes to wear the right labels and stuff and the right street wear and jeans. It costs a lot of money to be alternative.'[38] Peter's tousled appearance attracted a lot of female fans and earned him a modelling contract with Just Jeans. His penchant for Jemma's clothes remains a house enigma but reinforced his sexual ambiguity.

The contestants' hair attracted inordinate attention. But that is not surprising, as hair is one of the greatest signifiers of all: tonsured monks, Mohicaned punks, dumb blondes and fiery redheads. Hair is emblematic of many things: political ideology (punk, roundheads), ethnicity (Afros, cornrows), occupation (shorn United States marines, business-style hair), even sexuality (think Village people here). Since time began, people have adorned, cut, coloured and tortured their hair into numerous styles. In the last century we had the 1920s bob which professed women's liberation, the conservative 1950s high-maintenance bouffant with its teasing and lacquer (a lá Jacki Onassis and Marilyn Monroe), the 1960s asymmetrical bob and longer locks that rejected conservative values (Mary Quant and the Beatles), the 1970s long, unkempt hair that signified anti-draft sentiment (*Easy Rider*); by the 1980s the Me Generation had returned to hair care and complicated styles (Farrah Fawcett's mullet and the coiffed disco look). The triviality of hair and its central role in romance was parodied in Alexander Pope's *Rape of the Lock.*[39]

Gordon's asymmetrical hairstyles attracted the most criticism. Less-than-kind people said his outrageous hairstyles made up for his beige personality. During the first show it was mentioned several times, and in interviews his friends and teachers responded to questions about his hair. Gordon wanted a look that had 'texture'.

Speaking of texture, Todd's dreads had texture. Todd's hair screamed alternative, hippy, dole-bludger even. He admitted to Gretel on the first night that he hadn't brought any shampoo with him. From then on his hair (and by default Todd himself) was 'dirty' and 'smelly' — narrative editors were only too happy to exploit. But Todd succumbed to conformity. He realised that to avoid typecasting (he wanted to be an actor), the dreads had to go. So Todd played Sampson to Jemma's Delilah.

Blair, Ben, Peter and Johnnie sported more functional locks. Blair's Dennis the Menace lick reinforced his 'little brother' look. Ben wisely lost his blonde buzz before he entered the house. Peter's hair echoed 'Peter Brady' and its mussiness reflected his casual attitude to grooming.

Lisa, Sharna and Sara-Marie all maintained short, easy-to-care-for styles. Sara-Marie's bouncing blonde hair reflected her personality, and since she has left the house her new look includes a more groomed (and therefore professional) attitude. Her hair is not naturally blonde but it's a colour which works well with the whole Marilyn Monroe thing. Christina's hair was frequently pulled back in a style typical of many ex-ballerinas. Jemma's hair was as carefully tended as the rest of her image and as conventional. Anita obviously felt that her hair was an important feature as it figured prominently in her mask. *Who* ethnically cleansed Lisa by 'straightening' her hair for the fence-sitting shot. Andy preferred adornment and paraded a range of hair accessories, including a tiara.

Surviving in the house

As can be imagined, the isolation and confinement inherent in the *Big Brother* format can lead to bizarre behaviours. This reinforces the need for psychological evaluation before contestants are accepted. Not only are contestants thoroughly evaluated before they go into the house, but while in the house they have 24-hour access to a psychologist or other health-care professional. These sessions are private and are not taped. Furthermore, after the contestants leave the house, they are debriefed before they are reunited with their families and friends.

One of the side effects of living in a *Big Brother* house was a change in sleeping patterns. Contestants around the world tended to stay up later and to sleep in later. Often contestants slept for more hours than normal. In Australia Johnnie called out Pete's name in his sleep, and Ben's chatted about chooks. ('Where's the chook?', 'Are there any left?' and 'Where's the chicken?'). Unusually vivid dreams were recorded: Todd recalled dreaming that he was in prison where he shared a cell with females; Sara-Marie dreamed of an underwater restaurant; Lisa and Johnnie also reported strange dreams.

The contestants utilised some traditional house spaces in different ways. Contestants Ben, Blair and Sara-Marie dragged their mattresses onto the floor and slept on the floor for the final few nights. Two contestants slept on the 'dance floor' just in case Big Brother was going to be particularly sneaky one morning. Gordon stood on the coffee table and did chin-ups on the door frames. But that wasn't as strange as Blair bathing in the laundry tub, clothed. Did he forget he'd been seen nude for weeks on the show? When Andy showered outside, she didn't bother with clothes; but then perhaps it was because she peed in the shower stall. Is this use of space indicative of a confusion between private and public space?

For Ben and Blair, living with females was quite an experience. As Ben told Christina, Sara-Marie and Johnnie:

> Let me tell you guys what being here has meant to me ... since I've lived with my dad since I was 8, living here has made me understand women a lot better ... made me appreciate them more, not that I didn't appreciate them before, but now I understand them better. It's always been me and my dad. I've never had a live-in girlfriend before. (Week 4)

This reminds us that the house-sharing experience for Ben was limited. Blair too hadn't been away from home for this long before. Todd was an old hand at house-sharing; Johnnie, Peter, Sara-Marie, Andy, Sharna, Jemma and Christina had all lived away from home. Sharna recognised that she was missing the 'freedom' of being able to do what she wanted. She didn't have terribly long to miss her freedom because she was the second housemate to be evicted.

Nominations and evictions

Nominations were done on Tuesdays and contestants went to the Diary Room and told Big Brother who their choices for the week were. Each person gave their first choice two points and their second choice one point. Observed across the series, a nomination and eviction pattern emerged; people were nominated and voted out because of group dynamics, then relationship dynamics and finally individual dynamics.

In the first half of the series, the housemates nominated those who didn't fit in with the group as a whole: Andy, Sara-Marie, Sharna, Todd and Gordon. From week two to six, the 'relationship' phase, Peter and Christina attracted nominations because they had broken away from the group. By week five, the halfway mark, the most 'annoying' had gone and the group were clearly at a bit of a loss — hence the even spread of nominations which resulted in four potential evictees (Sara-Marie, Christina, Blair and Lisa). And in the final weeks, the contestants retained their nomination holding patterns: Christina and Sara-Marie hadn't voted for each other and neither had Ben and Blair.

During the 'group dynamics' phase, in the first three weeks, the audience voted off the most outrageous. During the 'relationship' phase, the audience protected Peter and Christina. Then the audience evicted those they didn't like — the 'best-in-show' phase.

Typically, a female goes first (in Australia Andy, in United States 2 Sheryl, in South Africa Nina , in United Kingdom 1 Sada, in United Kingdom 2 Penny). Sharna was next not because she was a female but more likely because of her unsporting behaviour (76%). Todd was a bit of a surprise (38%); surely it wasn't because of the 'smelly' label? Gordon (41%) seemed to lose footing because of his inability to read non-verbal signals. Lisa (59%) didn't appear to contribute much, but maybe people just didn't want to split the couple. Peter (42%) hadn't been nice to Christina or the chooks. Anita (79%) had to go as we don't like people who whine, nor do we particularly like intruders (in other countries intruders tended to be voted off early). Johnnie (70%) was the victim of a hatchet editing job and was evicted in his first nomination. Jemma's eviction (61%) was probably because of her constant grooming. And by the time Christina went (41%), voters were starting to run out of choices.

Sara-Marie was the most nominated, and although it looked like she was a goner in the first week, her popularity taught the public a very valuable lesson: first impressions are not necessarily lasting ones. (Of course, there were others who believed that first impressions of her were correct.) While she drove her fellow contestants crazy, it slowly dawned on them that it would be better to sit on the nomination couch with anyone but her. She attracted 40 per cent of the votes in the first round, but by Week 6 only 21 per cent voted for her. One could almost hear Jemma's mind-wheels spinning when she told Sara-Marie, 'They [the audience] must love you, girl'. And Jemma quickly changed to a nominate-anyone-but-Sara-Marie strategy.

Despite her popularity, Sara-Marie didn't win. Why? Despite rumours of vote-rigging (every country has these rumours), often the most popular contestant doesn't win. The first series winners are almost always male. And in a blokey society such as Australia it would have been quite a surprise if Sara-Marie had won. Could it be that voting is gender-related; as the show rushed to its closure were more men motivated to pick up the phone because there would be an outcome? So it came down to Ben and Blair. Todd might have been a contender if he'd lasted longer and audiences had been able to get to know him better. Was he too alternative? Johnnie? Well, the next best thing to a bloke is a gay bloke (the second UK winner was a gay male), so better luck next time. Peter? Could he have been too cultured? Gordon was too superior and he was a New Zealander. Blair was a possibility but he was too young and, besides, he didn't have that wicked sense of humour.

In a game show that has no real contest, there was no way for the audience to decide who had 'won', but it seems that people voted for the person who they liked the most. And that person was likely to embody certain ideals: a sense of humour, someone who wouldn't 'waste' the money, a nice guy, someone who had a need for the money (Ben's eyes), someone who didn't irritate. And someone, of course, who was male.

Whose charity items attracted the most money? Not Ben's, not even Sara-Marie's or Blair's. Johnnie's boardshorts topped the list (pink dollar rules, okay); even Anita's bat beat Ben's ball. Thus popularity does not automatically translate into dollars.

Johnnie's boardshorts	$5500
Sara-Marie's bunny ears	$5270
Blair's footy jersey	$3100
Jemma's tee-shirt	$3050
Anita's cricket bat and yoyo ball	$2830
Ben's soccer ball	$2800

You know you're a celebrity when you're replaced with another celebrity. And when there was talk of a *Celebrity Big Brother*, one journalist trotted out the equivalents for each contestant:

Andy: Angelina Jolie. Has unconventional marriage and is fascinated with S & M.

Gordon: David Duchovny. Believes the truth is out there … and only he knows what it is.
Sharna: Courtney Love. Can be unkempt and uncouth, and can crack glass with her voice.
Blair: Chris Klein. Was the youngest (and arguably the spunkiest) in the house.
Lisa: Emma Bunton. Appears to be a sweet, shy, single gal with an infectious giggle.
Todd: Matthew McConaughey. Has been labelled the great unwashed. Good with bongos.
Johnnie: Rupert Everett. Is debonair, dashing, has a six-pack to die for and, well, he's gay.
Jemma: Gwyneth Paltrow. Aka Little Miss Perfect with never a hair out of place or lips unglossed.
Peter: Russell Crowe. Is dark, handsome and possesses a wicked way with the ladies.
Sara-Marie: Anna Nicole Smith. Is big, brash, busty, blonde and works with strippers.
Ben: Eric Bana. A lovable larrikin: the house clown and all-round good guy.
Christina: Kylie Minogue. May seem shy, but she's a big hit with the boys in the house.[41]

For those who didn't win the money and for those who didn't gain fame, what did the experience give them? Johnnie noted that, ironically, within the confines of the house he broadened his horizons. Another reality-tv contestant described his experience thus:

> It [*Survivor*] has changed my life in every respect … my relationship with God and everyone else, myself, the world … Everything was taken away from me. Without all the distractions [of modern life] you have to look inside yourself … I value things like time, friendships, food a lot more. It made me realize all of us spend so much time focusing our energies on things that really don't matter … There is nothing worth hurting another person for.[42]

The pantheon of *Big Brother* winners is not too diverse. By and large it consists of white males under 30 years of age. But we all know who the real Australian winner was.

Individual contestants

Andy

Andy was the perfect *Big Brother* contestant: an educated, attractive, environmentally aware dominatrix eager to have sex on television.

Andy may not have been in the house long, but she certainly made an impression. She grabbed the double bed and spent the first few days (or so it seemed from the promotional clips) asking people to share it with her. Who was the first taker? Johnnie. Andy confessed that she wanted to have sex with five people; she particularly fancied Gordon, Todd, Blair and Christina. It seemed that nearly every shot of her was sexual, whether it was chatting with Gordon or building a barbecue while wearing only a towel.

In the desire to show Andy at her most outrageous, the editing made her sexual antics look amusing rather than shocking. Put a dominatrix in a suburban home and, well, it just loses something in the translation. Bondage and serious S & M are for dungeons and British politicians. Strapping a man to a post during a dinner party and giving lessons in whipping provides much laughter but little in the way of titillation. Tongue-kiss a female by all means, but at a barbie? Her performances (whipping Todd, casting a spell, anointing Gordon) lacked authenticity, and provided much laughter for contestants and viewers alike. But it was all in good fun. She just tried too hard and was hampered by some tragic dialogue: 'I'm gonna shag five people, baby'. Andy's activities were constructed into a range of sexy female clichés: dominant mistress, predatory nymphomaniac, sexy witch.

Johnnie considered her 'out of control'. But Andy was very much in control. What she couldn't control was Gordon, so she slipped outside for a little fireside voodoo spell.

Andy's theatricality was mediated through her costumes. She wore beads, bangles and baubles. There were jungle prints, pvc corsets and dominatrix gear, wigs and tiaras and bunny ears. Her eviction outfit was a black corset over an animal-print bikini, fishnet stockings and high heels, sequined cat ears, a black 'feather' boa and a studded choker. Though generally associated with soft bondage clothing, her signifiers were her tiara and her sequined ears — the haughty princess and the sex kitten. Why? Her website explains that a mistress is 'a woman ... in charge [who] has power [and] nobility'.

Though she buddied up with Gordon and Sara-Marie, Andy tended to be a loner; or at least that's how the editors represented her. When Jemma was injured, the cameras juxtaposed shots of Andy alone in the pool with shots of the other contestants who were helping Jemma. It made Andy look as if she didn't care. Similarly, when the contestants received the instructions for the barbecue, they all had to go to the bathroom to include her because she was in the shower. This editing made it look like she wasn't part of the group.

Male viewers didn't seem to care if she was part of the team: she was their eye candy. A number of newspapers reported that women voters wanted Andy out because she was a flirt, and male voters wanted her to remain because they could perve on her. The 'Save Andy' campaign launched by Triple M targeted male viewers.

On her eviction night, the boys carried her to the door on their shoulders. This never happened again — Sara-Marie insisted she didn't want it and everyone else agreed. But for Andy it was a fitting farewell — to be carried, like a princess, on the shoulders of a number of men.

Magazines were divided about Andy. Some persisted with the sexy imagery: a whip-wielding dominatrix for *NW*'s 'Hot Bodies' and the tousled waitress in *Juice*. Others such as *New Idea* presented her more elegantly (Rita Hayworth in 'Screen Sirens'). *Who Weekly* dressed her in feather boa and tiara for 'Castout'[43] and demure in a long green dress for the 'Who Will Win?' issue.[44]

Andy's website is provocatively addressed www.mistressandy.com, but there is no sexual material on the site. There isn't even a nude or semi-nude shot. The sexiest photos are on her 'official' fansite.[45]

On the cutting-room floor: her environmental concerns, her healthy food choices, just about anything not sexual.
Fashion: linked with Nicole Kidman as responsible for the return of the corset.
Quote: 'I want to get down and dirty and go out with a bomb, baby.'
Pantomime character: Puss (get it?) in Boots.
Her face mask: vibrant: half blue and half red/orange; she winks back at the onlooker; hair/mane or sunburst frame; her name is written vertically in purple; her mask is the most outstanding one on the wall.

Anita

Anita was contestant number thirteen. Viewers who carefully watched the *Big Brother* prequel would have seen Anita arguing her point in a role-play situation. And arguing it well.

She came to the house equipped with a number of games to amuse the bored contestants. But no matter what she did to entertain them, she was never going to last to the end. Blair indicated this when he said that she would have to 'prove herself'. Simiarly, viewers didn't think the introduction of the two intruders was 'fair'.

Anita's confrontation with Johnnie and Blair over *Man Down* might have been a dramatic moment, but it did not endear her to viewers. She was voted out at the first opportunity.

She will be remembered as the whingeing, crying intruder who almost split the house along gender lines.

Since she left the house she and Rachel have appeared with the other contestants on a number of television shows. The two were photographed together for the *NW* 'Hot Bodies' issue; they are armed with flashlights, crowbars and builders' pouches ready to break in. In the article Anita had one more swipe at Blair: What is her biggest turn-off? 'A guy who bites his nails. Blair was always chewing his nails — yuck!'

Her face mask: white, no eyes, red lips, Hebrew words, framed by long black hair, her name in bold red print.
Audience's costume: the large hat she wore in *Man Down*; others brandished oversized packets of chewing gum.

Ben

Prophetically the last to arrive, Ben, was the last to leave. His introductory footage showed him at home with his father — they shared a hug. He was filmed in working-man's clobber — an orange safety jacket, shorts and heavy work boots. In short, he was 'a labourer'. He sat on the couch with a bunch of males watching football on television — here is a blokey guy. His cousin thought that Ben could sit in a house for three months and do nothing because 'he's done it before'. On the first night, Ben was greeted by a member of the Australian Rugby Union team who presented him with a Wallabies' football jersey for luck.

Ben went on the show because it was a 'bizarre challenge' and 'to have a laugh and enjoy myself'.

In the beginning, his questions made Christina suspect he was a plant from a men's magazine. (And she should know — she'd been in *Ralph*). By learning more about each contestant, Ben acquired a storehouse of knowledge which helped him to win, as sociologist Peter Groffman explains:

> When an individual enters the presence of others, they commonly seek to acquire information about him or to bring into play information about him already possessed. They will be interested in his general socioeconomic status, his conception of self, his attitude toward them, his competence, his trustworthiness, etc. Although some of this information seems to be sought almost as an end in itself, there are usually quite practical reasons for acquiring it. Information about the individual helps to define the situation, enabling others to know in advance what he will expect of them and what they can expect of him. Informed in these ways, the others will know how best to act in order to call forth a desired response from him.[46]

'Gentle' Ben was the house nice guy. He thanked Big Brother

for Blair's and Sharna's party, he asked Big Brother to turn off the lights when Christina had a migraine and to excuse Sara-Marie from the task when she had a sore back. His concerns about the dog, Ebony, gave his good-guy image a boost. Ben brought hand cream into the house even though he didn't use it, because he figured the girls would run out and he'd have some to share (Week 4). Even the cameramen liked him the best of all the contestants; he made their job a 'delight'.[47] And when he confessed that he had an incurable eye disease, you could almost hear the viewers' oohs and aahs.

He wasn't afraid to call a spade a spade, but he didn't call it a shovel as Sara-Marie did. He might have asked Big Brother to make allowances for Sara-Marie's bad back, but when she said she didn't need it he quickly told her to 'get on with the f … ing task then!'

From the second week Ben was tipped to win; he was a 'leader', claimed a story that appeared in most News Limited Sunday papers,[48] even though Blair had been leading the official *Big Brother* popularity polls for weeks. Ben's relationship with Blair helped to garner him support. The two never nominated each other. But they did practically everything else together, including the notorious greyhound race. When Ben was declared the winner, he told Blair that he wouldn't forget him. He promised to buy him his heart's desire: an XM Ford, a 1964 model that belonged to Blair's father and that he had wanted to buy from him for years. 'I owe Blair so much,' Ben said. 'I wouldn't have lasted if it wasn't for him.'

Ben's sense of humour made him the house favourite and somehow this transferred to the audience's consciousness. Little of his humour translated into air time; apparently it was mostly in-house humour. Not everyone was amused by him, though. Anita bemoaned his penchant for flogging a dead joke. But then she hadn't heard Jemma's first-night 'wide-mouth frog' joke. Viewers did get to see his mock interviews at the 'premiere' of *Man Down*, when he asked Anita if she had had to prepare for the role of 'neurotic'.

Since the show ended, Ben has been involved with charity work. He organised the *Big Brother* pantomime for the Starlight Foundation and did a television special for World Vision. He had his own television show, *Personal Best*, and he has written a sports column for the *Australian*. He (like Sara-Marie) was swooped up by Harry M. Miller.

It seems that Ben is condemned to be remembered as the footy guy. In the *NW* 'Hot Bodies' issue, his Wallabies football jersey screams 'vodaphone' and dollar bills peep out from his socks and shorts and litter the floor in a clever juxtaposition of Ben, football, money and sponsorship.

At one stage Ben was the only housemate without a website; finally a (female) fan constructed a 'Legend' fansite.[49]

Best exchange: Blair said that his mother loves doing the laundry for his three brothers and her husband. Ben's sardonic reply was, 'Has she actually said that, mate?'
Audience costume: Hawaiian shirt he wore in *Man Down*.
Sayings: Jota!
Pantomime character: one of the elves, Boofy.
Ben's favourite joke (according to Blair): Two birds were sitting on a perch; one looks at the other and says, 'Do you smell fish?'
Memorable non-verbal communication: the look on his face when Anita was arguing with Johnnie and Blair.
His face mask: quartered like a football jersey: red eyebrows, blue lips.
Why did he win? Because he was a 'big brother'.

Blair

Even before the first half-hour episode was screened Blair was the most popular contestant on the official *Big Brother* website. His popularity rarely wavered. Though many thought he would win *Big Brother*, he was really 'kid brother'.

Throughout the course of the show his kid-brother image was reinforced. Viewers saw him cry over his brother's birthday message. His family figured prominently in various shows: his brothers Gavin and Ryan often appeared on the live shows. In the house his relationship with Ben (who was only a year older) placed Blair in the position of 'little' brother. When the two of them ganged up on Sara-Marie, it was as if the two brothers were picking on their sister. Blair commented at various times about how this was the longest period of time he had been away from home and how he was not used to living with females.

Blair was the heart throb — someone for the younger girls to tune in and watch, as Kidgalore noted in his poem:

> Me, unpopular? HA! Please now, don't make me laugh,
> The average age of my fanclub is eight and a half.[50]

Blair didn't have a romance in the house even though Big Brother tried to construct a 'lurve' narrative with Sara-Marie. It was an unconvincing narrative undermined by their performances: they were clearly kidding around. When the intruders came, there seemed to be the potential for romance, especially when viewers saw Ben and Blair's joking, quasi-animal drooling. Their attempts to impress Anita and Rachel — the spitting contest, Blair helping Anita to unpack — seemed promising. But even the best editing in the world could not disguise Blair's mateship with Rachel and his animosity towards Anita.

Blair might have been popular with some viewers, but his popularity was not universal:

> I like footy and rugby and guzzling goon,
> If you don't think I'm hot then I'll fly to the moon!
> * * *
> I feel horny, Sara-Marie, get your bum over here
> And I'll grope at your chest and talk crap in your ear.
> * * *
>
> Oh, shut up Anita, I'll smirk all I like,
> If you don't like it, you wench, you can jump on your bike.
> And I 'date stupid girls', huh? Well now that's a bit rough,
> I don't date them, you moron, I just feel them up.
> * * *

As for Sara-Marie? Wow her breasts sure are BIG!
Aren't I a stereotypical chauvinist pig?
I'm boyishly handsome from my head to my toes,
And I'm so far up myself I can blink through my nose.
Yes, good-looking chicks deserve keen, close inspection,
But why, for Pete's sake, should I have to respect them?

Blair's drunken activities clearly didn't amuse everyone.

Blair, like Christina, will probably be best remembered for maturing while in the house. This was mainly seen though his interaction with Johnnie. Blair grew from the 'raging heterosexual' (as he said in the first few minutes of his video) into a person who considered that a gay man could be a 'legend' too. He cried when Johnnie left, because Johnnie 'taught me to be proud of myself' (final show). Blair's maturation was one of the longest-running narratives on the show. In the final eviction show, he wore a tee-shirt Johnnie had given him and called him a legend several times.

Blair has been the most obviously successful contestant to date; so far he is the only one who has realised his dream of becoming an actor. After the show finished, Morrissey Management signed up Blair because he seemed to be 'the stand-out personality who has a career of longevity in the media'. Soon a bit part in *Neighbours* followed. No wonder, he had had 85 days in front of a camera, and he found time to perform a scene from *Good Will Hunting*. His was the standout performance in the *Best Ever Panto*.

The magazine media made Blair the poster child for *Big Brother*: he was on the cover of *Who Weekly* for 'Secrets of Big Brother', he shared the front cover with Ben and Sara-Marie for the *NW*'s 'Final Countdown', and he was with Jemma and Sara-Marie for *NW*'s 'Hot Bodies' issue (pushing Ben to the back cover). *NW*'s article on *Big Brother* promised 'Hot *Neighbours* Pics' on the front cover; inside Blair's story came first and occupied more space than the other contestants' stories.[51]

He nabbed a six-page spread ('Blair's Big Break') in *Who Weekly*. On the cover, a James Bondish Blair is flanked by two female co-stars as he smirks at the camera. Inside, the first photo places him symbolically on top of a television. And guess who's on the television screen? The shot contrasts Blair as a 'real' urbanboy and the screen shot as a *Neighbours* cowboy. His lack of footwear tells you that he might have donned a suit but deep down he is the same 'country' boy. The 'Boy Next Door' photo/story recalls teenage heart-throb magazines. His biography juxtaposes a number of images to remind readers that Blair is basically a working-class boy who made good. After recounting his brief university career, readers are told that he worked as a labourer and has a 'good work ethic': 'he … dug holes, fixed the taps'. The article finishes with an appropriate home metaphor: Blair has 'outgrown his nursery'.[52]

Blair has the most internet fansites and fanclubs. His 'official' fansite (www.blaircentral.com) is one of the best organised and most informative. Blair contributes to it frequently. He clearly understands the value of keeping his fans happy.

Memorable quotes: 'It's like feeding a nation' (whatever that meant) while fondling Sara-Marie's breasts.

On the *Sale of the Century* quiz:

Glen Ridge: Who am I …

Blair buzzes: Glen Ridge

Q: Were you really smirking at Anita?

A: Yes yes yes yes yes yes yes yes yes yes yes yes yes yes yes yes yes yes yes yes yes yes yes yes yes yes yes yes yes yes yes yes yes yes yes yes yes yes yes yes yes yes yes yes yes yes yes yes yes yes yes yes yes yes yes yes yes yes yes yes yes yes yes yes yes yes yes

On the cutting-room floor: picking his nose.
Audience costume: Heidelberg football jersey (black with gold diagonal stripe).
Pantomime character: the handsome prince.
His face mask: divided into three parts: yellow forehead, blue mid-face, yellow chin; set in a black diamond frame; red markings include a horizontal stripe on the forehead, and red 'eyebrows'

which meet in the middle and run down the nose over the mouth to the chin; one of the most enigmatic masks.

Christina

Christina was the first contestant to arrive at the house. She told Gretel that she wouldn't mind winning the money *and* a bloke. Unfortunately, she didn't get either. However, she did provide the house with its only 'romance'.

By the end of the first week, Christina had forged an alliance with Peter and had created Australian television history in the form of what was to become known euphemistically as 'doona dancing', or 'fiddledy diddledy' as Gretel called it. Their romance was to become synonymous with sexual relief and angst. Even though she was the only woman to be involved in sexual activity in the house, Christina was not given the same sexy image that Andy had. Although Christina showered nude, she was not subject to the same camera scrutiny. Why? It's not as if she was not comfortable with her body. She had appeared nude in *Ralph*.

The camera gleefully followed Peter and Christina, and viewers were treated to various examples of Christina's humiliation at Peter's hands: his dismissive and condemnatory response, 'Never say that to a boy', when she asked if they could have a chat later, and his sulking when she refused to let him into her bed for 'cuddles'.

Her time in the house is divided in two periods: pre-Peter and post-Peter. The first could be considered her 'invisible' stage and she seemed to be mediated only as part of a couple. During this phase she was seen trying to sort out her relationship with Peter, talking to others about Peter. The scenes were of her and Peter on the couch, in bed, doing the body doubles task.

After Peter was evicted, Christina aligned herself with Sara-Maria and this is considered her 'blossoming' stage. She attracted more air time and viewers were treated to images of her in *Man Down*, in the herb garden, dancing with Sara-Marie, and just generally interacting with the other contestants.

She mightn't have been as loud as Sara-Marie, but Christina provided the most cliff-hanging material: her on again/off again romance, catching Jemma and Johnnie betting on the nominations, the 'doona dancing' episode, her 'confession' that she had been in *Ralph* magazine, and her 'secret' wish to meet her brother.

Christina's dialogue was liberally sprinkled with deprecating self-analysis. She considered herself 'weak'; she didn't speak up enough; she wasn't 'bold' enough to disagree. She tried to excuse her weeping: 'I'm just working on my Gwyneth Paltrow impersonation'; and she was frustrated that her crying made her like one of 'those girls on a reality-tv show'. On the night of the $100,000 Challenge, Gretel commented that she seemed nervous; Chrissie replied, 'I want to do well and not let the others down'. Gretel tried to reassure her that 'we' would love her anyway.

Viewers were allowed many glimpses of Christina: her insecurities, her adoption, how Peter treated her. By showing all her awkward moments, confessions and crying jags, Christina was cast as the 'damaged' woman — the fragile girl/woman. Yet she survived six eviction nominations, and prior to the show had had a great deal of public appearance experience.

Of all the contestants Christina had led the most sophisticated life: she had performed in front of thousands, travelled the world, lived in Europe, even dined with royalty. One would have thought that these experiences would have given her confidence in herself. However, she seemed the least confident of the female contestants. As her alter ego, Sara-Marie, said, 'I could never stand up in a crowd and tell jokes — I'd have wee running down my leg.' Yet Sara-Marie was clearly the mentor in this relationship.

Since the show Christina has appeared in a wider variety of magazines than the other female contestants: she has been the elegant Grace Kelly (*New Idea*), the demure bride (*Bride*), the girly dancer (*NW*'s 'Hot Bodies') and the steamy siren (*Ralph*). Her appearance on the cover of *Bride* is heavily ironic — she is *sans* groom. However, she shares her page with Peter in 'Hot Bodies'.

Her fansite is very-Christina.[53] It is elegant, crisply written and well planned.

Quotes: 'I hope to get a high-profile waitressing job; ' … as soon as I cash in my One.Tel shares … what do you mean it's gone under?'
On the cutting-room floor: her sense of humour.
Pantomime character: Bella Ballerina.
Audience costume: ballerina tutu.
Her face mask: dull blue with a large black question mark, blurred features.

Gordon

Gordon entered *Big Brother* to 'reference his TV self against the self he thinks he is' ('Armchair Guide'). He is best referenced against his nicknames: Flesh/Flash Gordon.

Presumably he was dubbed 'Flash Gordon' because he was a fast-paced dynamo. His introductory video showed him in a helmet and on a racing bike, with background techno music. Most of his air time showed him sitting on an exercise ball executing his famed 800 sit-ups. His costuming was appropriately hip, sporty, leisure clothing. He kept saying he found the house 'boring'.

The 'Flesh Gordon' referred to his 'relationships' with Andy and Jemma. When Andy expressed her desire for Gordon, the camera spliced together a Gordon/Andy narrative. There were shots of the two of them talking about group sex and him strapped to a table while Andy and Sara-Marie dribbled wax and icecubes over him. After he deftly avoided Andy's clutches, he was then paired with Jemma. The audience saw him hugging Jemma, dancing with Jemma, and aimlessly wandering around her. It seemed as if he did little else. The press didn't help when they reported that 'the slippery hair weirdo hasn't done himself any favours by sleazing all over BB babe Jemma'.[54]

The viewers didn't see any of his intellectual discussions with the other contestants. He and Todd spent many hours debating a range of issues (including Pauline Hanson). Gordon's self-deprecating remark that the 'dumbest guy always wins' (*The Weakest Link*) indicates his awareness of strategies and game shows.

The flash of his penis on *Big Brother Uncut* earned him the name 'donkey boy', a fact that was revisited in the *Best Ever Panto* and various photo shoots. Even though it earned him a potential endorsement for underwear, Gordon realised that he didn't want to be commodified as a penis. However, it seems likely that he will be remembered for his penis and his hair.

His press personality was largely negotiated around his flashy hairdo. Articles inevitably include comments from friends who remarked on his ever-evolving hairstyles; a past teacher remembered that he frequently changed his hair colour. It is a focus point in his photos and most photo shoots include at least one shot of the back of his head. His other outstanding feature was not forgotten but not explicitly displayed. In the 'Hot Bodies' spread, he poses in front of a mirror, with his back to the camera and a sheet draped around his buttocks. His hair (a kaleidoscope of textures, patterns and colours) competes with his body for the viewer's attention.

Gordon's website no longer contains material about him. It has been revamped since he left the house. There is a fansite but none of its images load and many of the links are broken.[55]

Quote: 'I'm not sure if I like threesomes or foursomes.'
On the cutting-room floor: his conversations about politics and the relativity of time.
Audience costume: his hairstyle.
Pantomime character: an elf, Donkey.
His face mask: white mask in blue square frame, black eyebrows; the outstanding features are the blue swimming goggles with reddish eyes; his name is visually metaphoric.

Jemma

Jemma was too easy a target for stereotyping: the shallow dumb blonde. In the prequel show one of the producers commented about a contestant lugging around a large makeup bag; no names were mentioned, but it seems a small jump to conclude that they were talking about Jemma. Unfortunately, it didn't take too much editing to turn her into a primping, vain woman. Unbeknown to her she fed them more material than necessary: her lip-gloss applications, her extensive collection of off-the-shoulder tops, and her time-consuming grooming routines. What failed to make such great television was her generosity (everyone borrowed her clothes), her thoughtfulness (which was commented on quite often by the other contestants), her mediating abilities (she got Sharna to apologise to the group), and her intelligence (which was more apparent in the quiz shows).

Her primping was not simply an end in itself; she explained that her grooming was her attempt to maintain a sense of normality while in the house. She tried to act as if she was going to work. And she was. She was really auditioning for an opportunity outside the house. If she wanted a job as a television presenter, Jemma had to demonstrate a professional attitude (i.e. no swearing) and an impeccable appearance. As a poem by Kidgalore explained:

> It's me again, Jemma, the one you adore,
> I'm a surefire winner, I'm sure you'll agree,
> Good looks are what counts when you're on the TV,
> So what if I offend with my dumb, mindless chatter,
> I'm stunningly gorgeous, that's all that should matter!

Although the ode satirises Jemma, it also takes a swipe at television, and the contemporary preoccupation with looks. She wasn't the only one who groomed herself — Sara-Marie also plucked away — but the editors made personal grooming Jemma's particular domain.

When Gordon sought Jemma's company, the editors reinforced this by splicing in clips of her saying that he made her feel uncomfortable. It was amusing to watch her body language: her stiffening when Gordon hugged her, or her glancing at her feet while they danced together. Their pairing up in 'Hot Bodies' ironically harks back to their 'relationship'. In their photos, Jemma tends to her lips and Gordon admires his body. He gets a full-length mirror for his body and Jemma has a hand mirror which she focuses on her face. Her robe has (naturally) slipped off and exposes one shoulder; his sheet barely covers his bottom. It is an interesting juxtaposition of images and meaning: Gordon's narcissistic gaze and Jemma's business preparation.

After spraining her wrist on the first day, the *Daily Telegraph* asked its readers if she should be allowed back in the house; 94 per cent said yes. When she was caught betting with Johnnie about the other contestants, she was not so popular. In fact this was not her first slip-up; webviewers had heard her almost tell Lisa and Johnnie that she was going to vote for Gordon two weeks earlier. By the time she and Johnnie had their chat, her popularity had slipped considerably (she had been ranked second to Blair but was now polling around fifth). Kidgalore felt:

> If I get into trouble, I cry and I pout,
> Big Brother fancies me bigtime, he won't kick ME out.
> Three times so far, I've been warned by Big Brother,
> But it goes into one ear and straight out the other,
> Can I help it if my brain's the size of a bean?
> Collusion's such a big word, what the hell does it mean?

Unfortunately, instead of apologising to Christina, who had overheard their conversation and who, as one of the most frequently nominated contestants, felt hurt by the conversation, Jemma decided that attack was the best form of defence. She blamed Big Brother for making her look bad; Big Brother responded with a laconic 'It is you who are making yourself look bad'.

Her no-nudity policy earned her both criticism and congratulations. But she was not a prude. In several *Big Brother Uncut* incidents, Jemma joined in the group discussions about sex and she swore with the best of them. But she realised that swearing on live television was inappropriate and censored herself on her eviction night. Also, by wearing underwear in the shower, she gained the attention of underwear manufacturer Hey Sister!, who offered her a modelling contract for six months. Ironically, Gordon was offered an underwear contract for the opposite reason.

Jemma also achieved another of her goals: to appear on television. After the show finished, Channel 10 signed her to act as Big Sister to the young hopefuls in *Search for a Supermodel*.

Jemma's fansites reflect her girly image. 'Princess Jemma' uses tiara and makeup icons; 'Just Jemma' has a recipe for lip gloss. Neither site has been updated since October 2001; 'Just Jemma' was for sale in January 2002.[56]

Quote: 'You're ruining my life' (to Big Brother).
Lowlight: On the night of Johnnie's eviction she's bereft but still managed the one-armed sweep to adjust her top.
Pantomime character: Goldiocks.
Audience costume: off-the-shoulder tops, lip gloss.
Her face mask: As was to be expected, Jemma's eyes and lips are the most prominent features; both are coloured, but the overall effect is of slightly UFOish eyes. The rest of the face is silvery and is set in a square silver frame. Her name is written in tidy and clear lower-case letters and is accompanied by two kisses. It is, perhaps, the most stylish mask.

Johnnie

Johnnie probably suffered from the effects of representation more than any of the other housemates. He will always be remembered for two things: being gay and being 'rotten'.

His biography in the 'Armchair Guide' told us that he was a 'gay personal trainer' and tended to focus on his grooming. It told us that Johnnie planned to take care of his skin: he would 'cleanse, tone and moisturise every day'. And he was the runner-up of Mr Gay Sydney in 1999. Andy obviously hadn't read the papers and she seemed surprised at his lack of interest in her when they shared a bed on the first night.

Despite what *Big Brother* had written, Johnnie didn't prance around the house covered in night cream or spend hours tending to himself in the mirror. His house personality was markedly different from his press one. He was as blokey as any of the males and participated in all the sports. As Todd explained, 'I don't believe for a second Johnnie's gay … he kicks a footy better than anyone else! He's a mean-ass volleyball player, and he's always in bed with the girls!' In fact, Johnnie's role was to be that of house 'father'.

Johnnie's role as mentor started from the first day when he led the contestants in morning exercise/yoga classes. During the course of the show, viewers saw him responding patiently as the other contestants questioned him about his path to gaydom. Judge Johnnie presided over the intruder court (he was nominated by them to mediate when they had to select which intruder would stay). He was also selected to direct their movie, *Man Down*.

If conflict arose in the house, it was often Johnnie who stepped in and soothed things. After Anita exploded, he allowed her to vent and listened to her concerns. He apologised to Christina for hurting her feelings after she walked in on him and Jemma discussing nominations.

The misrepresentation started after clips of Johnnie hugging the people he had nominated were aired. The serial hugger became the serial stabber in the eyes of the media. Jennifer Dudley nicknamed him 'Johnnie Rotten', radio station Triple M took up the cause with a song with a catchy tune and damaging lyrics ('and then he says I love you'), and the transmogrification seemed complete. Triple M's smear campaign contrasted with their heterosexual 'Save Andy' campaign.

The *Daily Telegraph* did a complete turnaround. In the first week Johnnie had been stereotyped as a 'queen' who 'loves a good bit of bitching'; a few days later he had progressed to being a 'backstabbing bitch … [with] the treachery of Judas and … Shakespeare's Iago'; then the paper tut-tutted at *Big Brother* who was 'creating villains and heroes at his whim, effectively manipulating the voting of the public' and claimed that 'Johnnie was portrayed as a dastardly traitor, nominating evictees and then later cuddling them. Seen as a treacherous backstabber, he was given the temporary moniker of Johnnie Rotten by Ten'. There was no mention of their own contribution to the demonising process! After he was evicted, the *Daily Telegraph* was almost misty-eyed in its headline, 'Johnnie's Exit a Crying Shame', and it told how his fellow contestants would miss him: 'His soul-mate Jemma will likely crumble without him. Baby Blair could struggle without his gentle advice and kind support. Sara-Marie has lost a supporter.'[57]

The contestants saw Johnnie the peacemaker, Johnnie the house-father and Johnnie the all-round nice gay. From the teen-who-used-to-be-known-as-homophobic Blair to never-one-to-speak-out-of-turn Lisa, they all sang Johnnie's praises. Peter was 'shocked' at Johnnie's reputation and reminded people that it was 'the way it's been edited and the way it's been cut'.[58] In an online chat Jemma said, 'He's the most wonderful, caring, unselfish person you could ever wish to meet, and every house member loves him!' On the Saturday night show following Johnnie's eviction, Ian Roberts (the gay footballer) also took a swipe at the show for its unfair portrayal of Johnnie.

So if Johnnie was so popular, how come he was nominated by some of the other contestants? It seems to have been one of those coincidences — he hadn't received any nominations until that week and a few people decided it was time that he experienced what it was like to be nominated. The contestants were surprised that the audience didn't love him as they did and his eviction shook them up.

While on the show Johnnie was the cover boy for a number of gay papers and since then he has appeared with the contestants in the usual photo shoots. He donned boxing gloves and trunks for the 'Hot Bodies' shoot; he is the active contender to Lisa's fence-sitting diplomacy. His *Juice* shoot with Peter and Andy plays up the 'bisexuality' of the three of them. His individual shot poses him meditating in long-johns (a nice visual pun). For the *Best Ever Panto*, his pseudo-gladiatorial gear recalls the sword-and-sandal flicks of the 1950s and their visual appeal for many gays of the time.

Johnnie's fansite had over 20,000 hits in 2001.[59]

Audience costume: gangsta rap outfit (beanie, dark wraparound sunglasses).
On the cutting-room floor: contestants choosing him to be Judge Johnnie.
Memorable quotes: 'I know'; 'I love you'.
Hammiest moment: 'Goodnight Lisa' after her eviction.
Pantomime character: Sporty Spice; over-the-top pseudo-gladiator.
His face mask: gold, eyes lined with red, eyebrows accentuated, black line from lip to chin, the tilaka (the teardrop-shaped bindi).

Lisa

Lisa was the most enigmatic contestant. Shy from the moment she stepped out of the limousine, she was so laid-back that Gretel asked her what she had taken. It was as if the producers needed a foil for the exuberance and sophistication of the others.

Her introductory video positions her as 'family' girl in the same way that Blair was the kid brother. She was the 'middle' sister. In the popularity polls at the website, she always remained in the middle of the crowd. She arrived after Blair (in ninth position) and before Johnnie, sandwiched between the teen heart-throb and the gay icon.

There was the potential for romance; her friends claimed that boys loved her. But she did not have the same sexual promise of Andy, nor was she as 'single' as Christina or Jemma. There were glimpses of her in a red wig, sitting on a number of boys' laps, and participating in sexual discussions. She wasn't a prude or a wowser; she liked a bet (she wanted to risk 100 per cent of the week's budget on one challenge) and a beer. She wanted to learn how to lap dance. During the pantomime, her entrance was punctuated with stripper-like music.

While in the house she was perceived by some of the viewers and contestants as not being particularly interesting — she got up early, she cleaned the house, she didn't fight or get drunk.

Lisa's presence was an absence. If there were any discussions about her ethnicity, these were not aired. She and Johnnie were considered diplomatic, but she was dubbed a fence-sitter whereas he was a mediator. She was portrayed as passive and he as more active.

What *was* aired was her confrontation with Gordon. When she told him he bulldozed people, it showed that she could hold her own in a discussion without becoming emotional. She also pointed out to him (accurately) that, though he complained about people not doing anything, he was doing little himself.

In a conversation that television viewers didn't see, Ben, Blair, Peter and Johnnie claimed that she had the largest vocabulary (Week 7) — perhaps this hampered her television presence. She was nominated because she hadn't formed strong alliances. It's no wonder she sobbed that she felt 'so alone', as even the cameras ignored her. The second time she was nominated she was competing against Blair, Sara-Marie and Christina — the toughest opponents.

The audience had picked off the outrageous ones and were starting on the 'boring' ones.

Magazines tended to recall her negative moments, such as her irritating laugh, and *Who Weekly* reported that she had 'no memorable moments'. Even Lisa's perception of herself was tinged with negativity. *New Idea* reported that she was 'amazed by her sudden notoriety'.[60] Surprisingly, she showed the most cleavage in the 'Hot Bodies' issue: perched on a fence (a good visual metaphor) she is dressed in pseudo-country white denim. But the midriff top is unbuttoned revealing a white bra and she wears white high-heeled boots. During the pantomime, as the good witch Harmony from the Eastern Suburbs, she asked the girls to settle down and maintain decorum.

Still Lisa had her fans. At her fansites, they refer to her integrity and intelligence, and consequently are rather dismissive of the show.[61]

Quote: 'I get more interesting than this.'

Most memorable non-verbal communication: practising a sexy look in the mirror/camera.

On the cutting-room floor: almost anything she did and said.

Her face mask: black tribal mask with incredibly detailed eyes, square pupils; white markings divide the face horizontally; her name is stylish and printed in clear red.

Peter

In his introductory tape, filmed in the 'fine wine department' of a Glebe bottle-shop, Peter explains a little about wine. While in the house, Peter had discussions about art history and talked knowledgeably about a number of topics; after the show he won *Sale of the Century*. However, for the purposes of the *Big Brother* narrative he was the bad-boy charmer — in the style of celebrities such as Sean Penn.

During his romance with Christina, Peter was not presented in the most flattering of lights. He chided her when she wanted to talk and gave her short shrift a couple of times. The shot of him cleaning the mascara from his shirt after she had cried on his shoulder was a particularly nice piece of editing. And when he did not talk for a number of days, it looked as if it was pure cussedness. It was only later that viewers learned about his Crohn's Disease, and the fact that he was hospitalised after he left the house. (Peter has brought the disease to the public's attention and is currently their hippest spokesperson; at the Australia Crohn's and Colitis Association website there is a photo and letter from him.)[62]

Peter snapped at Sara-Marie when she stepped out of the demarcation line around the fire drum. The chook-'kicking' incident, though trivial in itself, didn't help his image. He tended to correct other's grammar (Sara-Marie and Jemma). He joined Blair in their pointless debate with Jemma over her no-nudity policy. He even physically distanced himself from the others and ate at the formal dining-room table.

His don't-give-a-damn attitude was reflected in his *Juice* shots — the two-to-the-valley, defiant gesture. In his individual photoshoot he holds a chicken and bears the scars of an encounter.

Positioned as sexually ambiguous, he and Johnnie were the focus of an 'is he?' *Big Brother Uncut* narrative. When asked about this outside the house, he explained that he felt it encumbent upon him as the older and wiser male to show the younger ones how to behave:

> I've had many, many gay friends over the years, and I've also had them as flatmates, so the gay thing has never been an issue with me. Thinking back at it, it was more to let Blair and Ben relax around Johnnie and let them see that gay people are normal. They breathe the same air and think the same things — if you know what I mean. The young guys were a little bit standoffish at the start because it was obvious it was the first time they'd ever had a gay friend. So I tried to show that you can muck around with them just like any other mate.[63]

His propensity for wearing nailpolish, Jemma's clothes and jewellery didn't help. And, *voila,* in the September issue of *Juice* Peter is in bed with Johnnie. On the reverse side of the fold-out cover, he tries to put his tongue in Johnnie's ear. And he's still wearing nail polish. The boyish grin as he cups Andy's right breast shows the cheeky Peter. The reporter feels he is a 'no-bullshit average guy' and this appeals to the interviewer who paints him in a more flattering light than he did Andy.

One of the first things Peter did when he left the house was to wriggle out of the *Big Brother* contract with Haven Management. The press also reported that he was going to sell photos of him and Christina; Christina was supposed to be furious about it. He won an Alpha Spider on *Sale of the Century* (and $5,000 donated to the Surf Life Saving Association). He has modelled for Bonds and Just Jeans. Appropriately he's wearing a pair of jeans in his 'Hot Bodies' photo — and little else. He and Christina face the camera; his steady what-are-you-looking-at? stare contrasts with Christina's welcoming smile. It is rumoured that he will be hosting the Saturday night *Big Brother* 2 shows.

It seems that Peter is not as net savvy as Christina, Johnnie or the other contestants who have written to their fans and thanked them for their support. He hasn't contacted Peter Lovers Anon website. Nevertheless, the devoted webmistress keeps the site up-to-date and scours the media for the latest about Peter.

Memorable moment: when he tried to kick the door jamb and slipped — it was replayed often, as if people wanted to see him fall on his behind.
Memorable quote: 'Never say that to a boy' to Christina when she said they needed to have a chat.
Pantomime character: one of the elves.
His face mask: midnight blue, red lips and yellow eyebrows.

Rachel

As the intruder who spent only three days in the house, there is little to relate about Rachael, though she said she felt 'like I've known them [the other contestants] my whole life'. How could Ben and Blair resist someone who greeted them with 'Good morning, dickhead'? Despite her short stay she still managed to attract press attention. After the show she was 'looking to work on radio' and worked with Sydney's Triple M Rock Patrol and Melbourne's morning show.[64] She also appeared on *Sale of the Century* and *The Weakest Link* and joined other evictees for a *Who Weekly* cover shoot and *NW*'s 'Hot Bodies'. She says, 'A few people have recognised me but mostly if they do they say, "Have we met before?" '

Sara-Marie

Sara-Marie was the unofficial winner of *Big Brother*. Yet she was up for eviction more times than any other contestant. She was lucky not to be voted out in the first week, but viewers found Andy's sexuality too much. It seems that, because Sara-Marie was part of the sex-industry ('stripper-manager' was the most popular term in the newspapers), the public feared she was another predatory female. It didn't help that she aligned herself with the reportedly loudest and most unpopular contestants.

She made a few mistakes in her first weeks: viewers saw her unrepentant after almost losing the housemates the fire-sitting task. This near-mistake earned her the reputation of not being a team player (like Andy). Though Sara-Marie laughed it off and challenged Peter, she went to the Diary Room clearly worried about her mistake. Her remorse was somewhat endearing. Big Brother tried to edit her as a non-team player for the body doubles challenge, but she completed the challenge. When she was singled out as the person who failed the movie task for the group, the viewers empathised when she sulked.

If there was a moment, Sara-Marie was there. Consistently nominated, no doubt because of her loud behaviour, she was the housemate viewers loved to watch but would probably hate to live with. Over the weeks, she grew from annoying to refreshing. She also dropped much of her sexual display after Andy left. The domesticated Sara-Marie appealed more to the public. In the first week she frolicked in the nude with Andy, but in her final week the nude dips in the pool were much more decorous.

It was the same with her language. Sara-Marie talked the language of the people. She liked to sing and hum and make a noise of any kind. By the end of the show she had toned down the swearing and was even censoring herself. Her made-up words reflected her childlike demeanour which jarred with her sexual sophistication. As Kidgalore wrote:

> I swear like a trooper, and act like a fool,
> Using phrases I learnt in pre-primary school.
> When I talk about poo-holes and doodles and wee
> You'd never believe I'm almost twenty-three.

The public seemed to be divided about her: you either loved her or hated her. Those who liked her believed that her refreshing approach to her body and her refusal to back down were signs of a strong, independent woman. Those who found her annoying felt that her loud voice and over-the-top behaviour covered up an inferiority complex and that she was really emotionally stunted. Women particularly seemed to warm to her and to defend her because of her no-nonsense stance with the males in the house; it was men who found her loudness irritating.

Sara-Marie combined a little-girlish appeal with sensuality. Her bunny ears and later photo shoots capitalise on this imagery. Her trademark Pooh Bear pyjamas underscore her childlike attitude. Her job, her g-string and her frequent nudity gestured to her sexuality. Even her repertoire of adult party tricks — her bum dancing and her breast pouring — were funny rather than naughty. Well, they amused some.

She had a number of memorable moments that endeared her to viewers. She writhed on the Diary Room floor in embarrassment when she thought that her trip to the toilet had been filmed on the night of Jemma's eviction. There's the classic shot of her with an empty Heineken carton on her head, the shot collapsing television, advertising and drunkenness in an exquisitely post-modern moment. And there was her compassionate nature, when she comforted Christina and explained how 'older' parents sometimes followed the rules 'too much'.

She wasn't always popular. In the first weeks she was at the bottom of the popularity polls on the *Big Brother* website. In the first round of voting she received 40 per cent of the vote; by her fifth nomination only 15 per cent of viewers wanted her off: she had become a 'cult figure'. After she survived a number of nominations, the other contestants realised that she was a potential winner.

Part of her appeal is her extraordinary ability to say the right thing and something incredibly clever and insightful without realising it. She's almost the wise fool, the naïve *savant*, as some of the following quotes from a web-chat demonstrate:

Kaz asks: How does it feel to have the number 12 single in Australia?
Sara-Marie: Bit freaky but exciting! Can you please keep buying it till it reaches number one!
Jane Gould asks: What was it like writing your book?
Sara-Marie: It was fun because all I did was speak into a dictaphone for hours and then I got someone else to type it out for me.
Bum-Dancing Chick asks: I get teased at school by one girl, even

when I'm nice to her. What advice do you have for me?
Sara-Marie: Don't waste your time, you've done your best. People who tease others are just insecure.
HELLen asks: What is the toughest question you've been asked since leaving the house?
Sara-Marie: I don't know ...[65]

She doesn't like computers or exercise, but she loves chocolate; she can't do quizzes but is a speed reader. She kissed men *and* women in the house, but she didn't have a romance. She flashed her body and let people play with her breasts but she wasn't sexualised. She loved animals and slept with Ebony (the dog) on the couch. She was loud and lazy and no one seemed to care.

It didn't take long for Australia to adopt her mannerisms and sayings. She started a bum-dancing craze which became a national occupation: there were bum-dancing contests, *Big Brother* contestants did it, and even Bert Newton did it. Some viewers insist that the Whiskas cartoon mouse is bum dancing. The ubiquitous bunny ears were seen everywhere from Dreamworld to the opera (Ghillian Sullivan took a bow in a pair after a matinee performance of *The Elixir of Love*).

Over the course of the series, nearly 400 articles about Sara-Marie appeared in the press. The stories evolved from 'Sad Sack Sara' to admiration. Jane Mulkerrins of the *Australian* was so impressed that she thought Sara-Marie should replace Gretel for the next series.[66]

Magazines loved her too. *NW* started a 'Save Sara-Marie' campaign and at the end of the show claimed, 'We have only one true winner in our hearts'. *New Idea* transformed her into a barefooted Marilyn/Madonna complete with pink strapless evening gown, long pink gloves and 'diamond' accessories. The Australian Material Girl played up to the camera. The photographs collapse Marilyn's sexuality with Madonna's commodification — Sara-Marie melds two of the most potent female images of the 20th century. In the same week she appeared in *NW* as another idealised female form: the Playboy bunny. Then it was back to pink for the *Cosmopolitan* 'Body Love' issue.[67]

The 'Body Love' issue caused some controversy. The divine miss SM was on 'one' of the front covers in a pink dress. She poses defiantly: hands on hips, thrusting out her body, the slip dress accentuating her body and defying the fashion magazine browser/buyer not to consider her body as acceptable. Inside, Sara-Marie recounts her journey to loving her body but reminds readers that health is more important than image. The irony that glossies such as *Cosmo* have built empires on diet and size 8 fashion seemed to have been missed. The 'Body Love' section fills 25 of 197 pages. Her eight-page fashion spread includes shots of her in a number of pink outfits and in one, gasp, she wears a bikini.

Of all the contestants, Sara-Marie has become the best known. Since leaving the house she's endorsed pyjamas, 'written' a book, released a single, and produced the almost inevitable Bum Dancing Album. She hasn't take part in all of the group *Big Brother* appearances, avoiding *The Sale of the Century* and *The Weakest Link*. She seems to have been on every list for 2001: Roy Morgan's Top 10 Women, Personality of the Year, Best New Talent, and so on.

Numerous 'Save Sara-Marie' websites appeared when it looked as if she would be ousted. Did they understand the irony of a website devoted to such a publicly confessed technophobe?

Memorable quotes: 'Well, we have the same body — mine's just bigger', in response to Gretel Killeen's comment about sunbaking next to Jemma; 'and then' and 'Hercules';[68] 'big bums are good for something'.
Best non-verbal communication: her purr.
Pantomime character: Cinderfella (without shoes, naturally).
On the cutting-room floor: her 'God Songs': 'This Is My First Communion Day', 'God Is Dwelling in My Heart', 'The Lord Is My Shepherd'.
Audience costume: bunny ears and pyjamas.

Her face mask: mid-blue (like Christina's), covered in silver glitter; detailed eyes (like Lisa's); very girlie looking; red lips (pursed), pink eyebrows, blush; her stud is there; hair red and black curls; her name has a heart which dots the 'i'; very flamboyant but not as outstanding as Andy's.

Sharna

'The Hostie with the Mostie' is probably going to be forever remembered for her dummy spit, or for 'doing a Sharna', as it has become known colloquially.

In her introductory video she wouldn't let the cameras film her in her apartment, because it was a 'mess'. The heavy hint was that she'd just had a big night. She told viewers that she spends three nights a week at the pub. She said she's been single 'forever' and needs a man (if only to pump her petrol). She lived alone. The cityscape was her backdrop. She was packaged as the *Sex in the City* sophisticate.

Her 'whisky' voice became a vocal metaphor for her: it gestured to her loudness and her hard-drinking, late-night lifestyle. She described herself as loud and she was. When she talked to people she often talked over them: her turn-taking skills were not good and it made her look rude. As Andy was anchored to her sexuality, Sharna was bound to her loudness.

Her famed dummy spit came after being nominated. Andy reacted badly to nomination, but sensibly she spoke to the psychologist and worked out her frustration in the pool. Viewers were given a full airing of Sharna's volatile reaction, her 'spraying' of the contestants.[69] She told them she hated them ('youse') and she wasn't going to bother learning the circus tasks. She greeted fellow nominees Christina and Peter with 'Hello losers'. She sulked. These unflattering clips were shown several times during the course of the week, even on *Big Brother Uncut*. Even though her swearing was beeped out, the beeping only served to accentuate its frequency. Gordon parodied Sharna's behaviour when he was nominated, jokingly storming off to the bedroom and slamming the door. Her spit was written into the *Best Ever Panto* and after the show she had a 'Dummy Spit' column in *Jackpot!*, (a reality-tv magazine). The following poem by Kidgalore summarises how she was perceived:

Hi, it's me, Sharna, the dummy spit queen,
I'm sure you dumb @#$*'s know the %&*# what I mean.
* * *
When I feel I'm hard done by, I swear and I sulk,
I wear orange so much I could lead my own cult.
I've a mannish, cracked voice you can feel through the floor,
And I get myself off at the Liquorland store.
* * *
Big Brother painted me as a wizened old hag
With a mouth like a leaky colostemy bag.

It may not have been flattering moment, but it was certainly a truthful one. It seemed that the viewers didn't appreciate such raw emotion. Certainly her abject apologies to the other contestants were given hardly any air time and too late to prevent her eviction. When they did appear, they were positioned as a secondary issue to her outbursts.

Sharna has joined the housemates for their various appearances. She gave Peter a run for his money on *Sale of the Century*, and also did quite well on *The Weakest Link*. In the *Best Ever Panto* she was dressed in a black evening gown and sported a French roll hairstyle, both of which reinforced her as the bitchy older woman; she was the stereotypical stepmonster.

Her jetsetting image in 'Hot Bodies' relied on a strange travel ensemble. With the quasi-sailor cap and nautical colours one would think she was going on a shipping holiday; however, her airline bag and dark suit gesture to air travel.

Sharna was the only housemate who didn't have a fansite.

On the cutting-room floor: Her apologies to the other contestants were delayed until Saturday night.

Best non-verbal communication: her fist-in-hand description of what she would like to do to Peter.

Pantomime character: the swearing, evil stepmother.
Quotes: 'Oh you are sooo not gay' to Johnnie;
'I'm 90 per cent sure I'll stay in.' (She had the highest eviction percentage until Anita.)
Audience costume: her orange top.
Her face mask: white, elegant, one eye a black diamond, the other eye black tears; red lips; it mimics a harlequin's mask or a member of 'Kiss'; her name has an exclamation mark.

Todd

Todd was so obviously the alternative person. His introductory tape showed him at work labouring (well, using a nailgun anyway). This helped to dispel any suggestion that he was a hippie dole bludger. He was the 'musical brickie'.

To complement his musical hippie image he bought along his djembe, which provided music for the aerobics class. He hung his microphone from a pierced nipple. Of course there were the tattoos and the dreadlocks. But although he was 'alternative', he was Australian alternative. He worked in a typical aussie job. He might be a vegetarian, but he liked a drink (in Week 3 he suggested they spend more money on alcohol). He didn't preach messages of spirituality or understanding. When Sara-Marie told him he smelled, he dismissed her with 'You're out of control'. And of course there was his much-loved dog.

The dreads prompted Gretel to inquire if he'd brought shampoo; he hadn't. She quipped about live things in his hair, collapsing hippie/alternative with unclean. This was later picked up by the unsubstantiated remarks of Sara-Marie about his anointing oils and their smell.

Todd came from the exhibitionist school of reality-tv contestants. He said he had 'no shame'. His girlfriend admitted that he liked people to look at him. Within a few hours of arriving, Andy was whipping him.

Todd was never going to provide romance; his girlfriend featured prominently in his clips and during his filmed conversations.

And though he was Andy's whipping boy, he was generally removed from any sexual activity. He didn't even seem to participate in the sexual conversations on the couch. His sneaky note asking his girlfriend to marry him was spotted by a number of people. Gretel prompted him to propose on the night of his eviction and provide *Big Brother* with a viewing highlight, but he didn't.

Todd romped around the house like a big disruptive puppy dog. He was the first in the pool, he threw things around the room, he play-acted with Andy. The other contestants seemed to take his practical jokes and stunts in good spirit. He played with the boys, he boxed with Gordon and he carved chess pieces (and explained to Johnnie what the pieces meant). Despite his rather frenetic energy, he bonded with everyone, and his eviction was the most emotional up to that time. At heart a conservative, he tried to 'marry' Christina and Peter. He had his locks lopped at the Jemma school of grooming. A more conservative image was necessary if he wanted to pursue an acting career.

After his eviction Todd showed how good he was at vox popping. And the public at Dreamworld seemed to love him. He has snagged a Harley Davidson endorsement. Todd's cowboy hat hides his shorn locks in his 'Hot Bodies' shot. Typically his drums are there. His nipple ring and tattoos are visible, and he wears tan cords.

Todd's was the most thoughtful of all the charities nominated by contestants — an organisation aimed at preventing male teen suicide.

Memorable contribution: the chess pieces.
Audience costume: His dreads.
Pantomime character: Stinky Toddy, one of the elves.
Memorable quote: 'I'm not sure if Johnnie's aware he's being two-faced, but if he is, I like him more for it.'
His face mask: set in a red frame his tribal mask is incredibly detailed; the red lips were outlined in blue and white; his was the only face to have facial hair.

Chapter Seven

Daze of Our Lives: The Audience

It was the show that everyone was talking about but no one was watching. It was no wonder that viewers of *Big Brother* remained in the closet for so long. Even before the show had started, critics despaired about the warped personalities of the potential audience — people who (they believed) wanted to watch others undress, have sex and fight. It was a game person who would admit to being a peeping tom with a penchant for a 'perve-fest'.[1]

Luckily, all the negative hype did not discourage viewers. Viewers translate into ratings. Ratings, of course, are about providing information for advertisers and not about how many people watch television.

'Audiences', 'ratings' and 'share' are television industry terms bandied about but little understood by the people being 'measured'. For the majority of viewers, 'ratings' is a blanket term that describes the number of people who watch a television show. The television industry uses more specific statistical data:

- Ratings: the percentage of the potential audience that is tuned to a particular station at a particular time; that is, if 25 of 100 households on Monday night at 6 pm are watching a particular show, the rating for that show is 25 per cent.
- Target Audience Rating Points (TARPs): measure a specific demographic audience; for example, if 25 women (under 25 years of age) of 100 women (of all ages) were tuned to *The Panel*, the TARP per cent is 25 per cent.
- Share: the percentage of the total viewing audience at a particular

> time watching a particular program; for example, if of 100 households with the television turned on, 25 are viewing *The Panel*, the share is 25 per cent.[2]

You may have spotted the flaw already: turning on a television set does not guarantee 'viewing' — people may not even be in the room (the familiar dash to the toilet in the ad breaks) or they may watch only intermittently (while talking on the phone).

And of course not every household in Australia contributes data. Currently OzTAM has 3000 households.[3] These households are described as a 'true representation of the population'.[4] Each household has 'peoplemeters' installed on every television set in that house. Peoplemeters record the time, whether the set is on or off, the channel and the number of people viewing (though how this is ascertained is unclear).

Despite the proliferation of statistical information, thinking exists about viewers: all soap opera viewers are thought to be lonely housewives, and all *Big Brother* viewers are young (teenage) females. Television producers are particularly cynical about their audiences. Yet audience researchers (especially academic ones) generally agree that viewers 'read' shows in complex and sophisticated ways.

Television is watched in a myriad of ways and for a variety of reasons. A program might be viewed in its entirety as it is screened to air, it might be taped and viewed later, or it might be viewed piecemeal as the viewer does the ironing or reads. Some viewers watch every show of a series; others might watch the show intermittently. Extrapolating information from audience data is not precise nor fullsome, but it can provide some general information about how a show was viewed.

Big Brother rated well. It occupied six of the 'top twenty programs' for 2001; the two 'final' shows ranked in the top three. Throughout the 11 weeks of the show's run, it rated in the 'top twenty' thirteen times. Generally, *Big Brother* is regarded as putting Channel 10 back into the free-to-air competition. But *Big Brother* was more than just a ratings winner; it became part of

Australian culture for a while — it filled columns in the press, people who didn't watch it talked about it, and friends would gather to watch episodes.

Methodology

All of the data for this chapter was derived from written survey forms. The data came from two sources: people who attended talks and lectures about *Big Brother* and people who participated in an internet *Big Brother* discussion group. The surveys were distributed three times — at the beginning, middle and end of the series. The quoted comments come from these surveys.

In all, 119 people completed surveys. Sixty responses came from high-school students and university students who attended talks given at Dreamworld. The questionnaires were distributed and collected at the beginning of the talks. Another 30 Media Studies students completed the surveys before a lecture on *Big Brother* at the University of Queensland in the middle of the show's run. A survey posted on the author's website after the show had finished received 19 responses; 18 responses came from *Big Brother* bulletin board participants (who responded to a request); and one came from a web surfer. Not every person answered every question.

Information from such a small and limited population yields, at best, speculative data, but it does give some indicators as to how a number of people viewed *Big Brother*.

The samples have two biases — age (many of the participants are students) and gender (there were more female than male participants).

The questionnaires contained both open questions (such as 'What words would you use to describe *Big Brother*') and closed questions ('Have you visited the *Big Brother* website?').

The responses have (in some cases) been standardised for grammar, repetition and spelling.

The author has had no contact with those who completed the surveys. The personal essay at the end of the chapter comes from a *Big Brother* forum participant who volunteered after a request was posted on a bulletin board.

Who watched Big Brother?

Nearly 90 per cent of those who completed the surveys (107/119) watched *Big Brother* at least once. In January 2001 another group of students completed a 'six months later' follow-up survey and 89.9 per cent of them had watched *Big Brother* too.

The data indicates that the majority of viewers were under the age of 30: 76 per cent were in the 15–29 age group (81/107); 17 per cent were in the 29–39 age group (18/107); and 6 per cent were older than 39 (7/107). But they weren't necessarily teenagers: the average age (of those who gave an exact age) was 22 (N=30). Internet viewers were older; their average age was 33 (N=19).

Of the 114 viewers who nominated their gender, the majority (68 per cent) were female (85/114) and 31 per cent were male (39/114). Internet viewers demonstrated the same gender breakdown. Of course, the sample could be further biased by the predisposition of women to complete surveys. In one *Big Brother* internet discussion forum, women posted requests for male contributors to complete the surveys. Some of these women prompted their husbands to complete the survey. Many of the males who contributed to the internet discussion group did not complete the survey.

Anecdotal information indicates that the range of viewers of *Big Brother* is more diverse than the results of the survey indicate. One viewer watched 'with my partner who wasn't particularly interested' (he didn't complete a form); a male viewer confessed that his wife's addiction to *Big Brother* intrigued him and so he watched with her because he 'needed to find out what [makes] my wife tick (and still ticks)'. In at least one family, *Big Brother* had three generations of viewers: 'We confessed early to family [that we watched *Big Brother*], as generally we visit parents on Sunday nights, so we made them watch *Big Brother* as a condition of them seeing their baby grandson' (33-year-old female). Others commented that they watched with friends but didn't nominate their friends' ages or their gender: one watched 'whilst visiting friends that couldn't interrupt their life to pay attention to me instead of the TV while it was on'.

Obviously not all of those sitting in front of the television are going to watch the show with the same degree of intensity; the tolerant viewer's attention will be less engaged than the fan's. Nor will they 'read' the show the same way; the disgruntled viewer quoted above was more critical.

Watching *Big Brother* was often combined with other activities such as eating dinner, preparing dinner or socialising (e.g. in a pub or with a number of friends). Such detached viewing can enhance the perception of the show as real.

Males and females watched the show for approximately the same length of time: males for 3 hours and females for 3.2 hours per week.

Why?

When asked what prompted them to start watching the show, nearly one-third of viewers responded that they had been introduced to the show by mothers, friends, flatmates, wives (11/35): 'My mother watched it, then I got hooked', 'Friends [sic] encouragement' and 'My flatmates'. This mirrors the soap-opera experience; soap fans reported that they started watching soaps with friends and relatives.[6] Five watched to be part of their peer group; 'everyone else was' and so they wondered 'what everyone else was talking about'; some even felt isolated: 'I felt left out of the conversation at work and among friends'. Many of these casual viewers watched only 'when friends who were fans were over'. Others were motivated by 'curiosity' (4/35). There were those who viewed the show as a television experience, because it was an 'interesting concept' or it 'would be interesting to watch'. Some people tuned in because they usually watched Channel 10 (3/35): 'It took over *Seinfeld* and I had nothing else to watch so I got hooked!'; another watched it a couple of times because it was after *The X-Files* and when *The X-Files* finished so did their *Big Brother* viewing. Three students watched it because they were Media Studies students and it was part of their coursework. For one viewer it was an opportunity to see a show they 'didn't think would be screened in Singapore'. For others it was serendipitous: 'I just happened to come across an episode halfway through and was intrigued by the show so I kept on watching'. Some viewed it to avoid studying. Often there was a multitude of reasons:

> I had heard about the English show in 2000 as my parents were in the UK, and then I heard someone from Southern Star Endomol [sic] interviewed and calling for contestants on the radio. We [family] generally watch the first episode of any new show that may be interesting, then decide after that. We watched the early show where they explained the concept and showed some audition tape footage, and it still looked interesting. And we are not big *Home and Away* or *Sale of the Century* fans, so 7 pm didn't disrupt our life too much.

The second most common response was the publicity; the 'pre-production campaign' and 'support/promotion from *Rove*' prompted them to tune in. Two respondents had heard of the overseas *Big Brothers*. The importance of the publicity cannot be overlooked. In January 2001 (four months before the show started) a group of Year Twelve students indicated by a show of hands that most of them had heard of *Big Brother* and were anxious to see it.

The variety of reasons for watching *Big Brother* underscores the multiplicity of viewing positions. The respondents' motivation for tuning in were reflected in the number of times and the intensity with which they viewed the show. As was to be expected, the three who tuned in for research purposes watched twice as many hours as the others and their engagement with the material *should* have been more intense; fans knew more about the contestants and the show in general.

But once people had tuned in, what prompted them to keep watching the show? Thirteen people responded to an open question about whether they were attracted to the show or to the contestants.

Five claimed that both the show *and* the contestants kept them viewing; four said the show was the drawcard and four said it was the contestants. One felt that the two were inexorably linked, but his/her lengthy answer indicates that the contestants were the primary motivator:

> Probably … the contestants more than the show. The TV show frustrated me at times with its manipulations and biases (as they appeared to me). The contestants engaged me in different ways. Some of their reactions to comments and situations reminded me so much of my friends, and also got me thinking about how I would react in a certain situation. And then I got enveloped in the whole *Big Brother* online world where you could discuss things as you watched them live, sharing the moment, but also with the benefit of others' perceptions of the same event, so you could re-evaluate you own opinions as a dialogue was being played out on the screen. And then reconsider them when you saw it later on TV. Each week I would barrack for who I wanted out, either because of personal likes and dislikes, or because of the interactions and relationships. I wanted some of the unpopular ones to stay in the house and continue to cause conflict, and contestants have to find ways of coping in this situation, and alliances to be split if possible, so people were out of their comfort zones. I suppose I was keen to see other sides of the contestants, and more personal growth and challenges to stereotypes.

In an article on shame and television viewing, Pertti Alasuutari found that people who watched 'professional' wrestling and soaps were ashamed to admit it.[8] Having admitted on paper that they watched the show, did Australian fans of *Big Brother* tell others that they watched it? Participants' responses (26) ranged from vague denials to brazen outing:

- '[I] quite proudly admitted to watching it — right from the start. I did not submit to the highbrow/lowbrow attitude it incurred.'
- 'At first I was a bit embarrassed and I didn't like to admit I watched it but once it became a bit of a phenomenon, I had no problems admitting I loved the show.'
- 'Eventually. I entered a competition, won a *Big Brother* T-shirt

> and so basically had to "come out of the closet" if I was going to wear it.'

One person couldn't 'reveal just how much I watched it' and others qualified their responses. Men had fewer problems about admitting to watching *Big Brother*; 90 per cent admitted to watching it without qualification, whereas only 70 per cent of females did. Females often added disclaimers such as 'but I don't watch it every night!'

Two males who watched *Big Brother* described it in work terms: 'as I was running a commentary on the Web, I didn't have much choice'; the respondent didn't indicate what prompted him to start the web commentary. Another was more enigmatic: 'because it got me the info I needed to keep up to date'. None of the females turned *Big Brother* into a work activity.

Eventually the peepers came out of the closet. The words used to describe the show tended to reflect the negative images constructed in the press:

- '[I] wasn't interested in the beginning but became hooked at the end.'
- 'My flatmates were obsessed, so I jumped on the bandwagon.'

The words 'obsessed' and 'hooked' gesture to the stalker and the drug addict. Words commonly used in the media evoked the same negative image of fans. Others invoked the repulsive but compelling viewing which incites people to rubber-neck at traffic accidents, crime scenes and train wrecks.

Fan-atic

Fans have been instrumental in the longevity and success of some shows. There are the famed *Star Trek* and *Cagney and Lacey* fan-bases whose support saved the shows from being axed.

But generally fans have a bad reputation, especially if the fan-base has negative connotations (e.g. trekkies). This was parodied on *Saturday Night Live* some years ago. A group of trekkies wearing Spock ears kept asking William Shatner in-depth (and clearly stupid) questions and he told them to 'get over it'.

One of the most obvious definitions of a fan is self-identification — admitting that you are a fan. Of the 119 surveys, 104 identified themselves as 'fans'. This reflects the bias of the sample — a non-fan would hardly be likely to attend a lecture on *Big Brother*. Only one internet participant was not a 'fan' — the person had visited the author's homepage and decided to complete the survey.

Did fans spend more time watching the show? Yes. Fans spent approximately 3.8 hours per week watching *Big Brother*. The internet fans watched it more because they were viewing the live feeds. These hours are approximate because some participants selected from a given list of times (e.g. 0–2 hours), whereas fans nominated more precise figures.

Of the 39 people who identified themselves as fans, eleven did not change their normal social behaviour to watch *Big Brother*. One viewer 'still went out every Thursday, Saturday and Sunday night'; another 'only watched it if I was at home doing nothing else'. Some people did alter their usual routine; some ate dinner earlier; one mother commented that 'the child's bath-time became 6:45 instead of 7 pm [and I] tried to have dinner cooked before the show so I wasn't in the kitchen during the show'.

While 'watching' television we are working, eating, talking, and we don't give it our undivided attention. Because of *Big Brother*'s timeslot, it comes as no surprise that the most mentioned activity that accompanied *Big Brother* viewing was eating and/or preparing the meal (9/38):

> If we were having a normal night at home (what's that!) we have a TV in our dining/family room and we would watch it whilst eating/preparing dinner. It was nice to have something so realistic to watch as a family and everybody enjoyed it (4 of us). I taped every program, not to archive but to ensure that if I missed it or any member of the family did we were able to see it the next day. I personally always watched my BB videos on the day it was shown, no matter

how late, so that when I got on the Internet the next day I knew what had happened.

Some turned *Big Brother* viewing into a social occasion: 'All my friends watched it; we would get together to watch it; esp on big nights.' One university student reported that it became a cult show: 'I live at college and we used to sit around watching; BB was quite big at college; you could hear it — on every floor.' Those who watched the show alone often discussed the show with others; one woman 'watched BB on tv, usually whilst eating dinner, alone, and then would call a friend after or during the commercial break to discuss it'.

The fan does more than watch the show every night. Fans translate their viewing into cultural activities. These activities can vary from taping shows to joining fan clubs to buying items connected with the show. Two people reported spending 73.5 hours per week in fan-related activities. Others spent considerable amounts of time in fan activity but wouldn't classify themselves as fans (the author for example).

The taping of shows is a primary fan activity. First, a fan need never miss an episode because of other commitments; one person 'taped it whenever I was out and watched it the minute I got home' and another 'taped shows for [my] sister who was overseas'. Obviously taping shows requires forethought. Two months after the show ended one fan was still annoyed that she had missed one vital episode because she 'was out for the first show and this was not taped for some reason (GRRR!)'. Second, fans keep those videos that contain noteworthy episodes: 'I videotaped the final episode and watched it over and over again; [I] will keep [it] for as long as possible.' Third, tapes have cultural currency because they can be sold, lent, given to friends or relatives and so on. At the end of 2001 a British *Big Brother* fan posted a request for tapes of the Australian *Big Brother* — and was willing to pay for them.

Having taped the show, people related different experiences in viewing it; one viewer 'watch[ed] it in the early hours of the morning when I got home as I work shift work'. Two less-dedicated viewers taped episodes but 'never got round to watching them'. Three fans taped a few episodes but did not keep them, because 'the footage is out of date, not relevant now'. In all, thirteen viewers of *Big Brother* admitted that they taped the show.

Really dedicated fans (soap fans particularly) will tape shows and make compilation tapes (e.g. clips that follow a romance, or clips of weddings only); no *Big Brother* fans admitted to this, but they probably suspected that a 'best of' tape would be released after the show had finished. Typical fan behaviour combines more than just taping and watching the show: 'One friend had taped an eviction show and watched it the next day without knowing what happened, and then had to ring me to discuss it as she did not know anyone else that watched *Big Brother*.'

One of the most defining aspects of *Big Brother* was the widespread discussion of the show. People talked about the show with friends (3), flatmates (2), family (2), work colleagues (1) and even university tutors (1) (N=9). In the press *Juice* noted that everyone in the *Juice* office was talking about the show; people heard it discussed in pubs or at work. The fan community has thrived recently, due to the internet, and the most active *Big Brother* fan community was the virtual one.

For the online *Big Brother* fan there was the official *Big Brother* website which had forums and live chat rooms. In the chat rooms fans could talk with each other, but many found posters at the official site too offensive and thus it became known as the 'cesspit'.

Fansites such as the Big Brother Television site[9] had information about the show and the contestants. Many fans simply created an online shrine to their favourite contestant. However, the most dedicated fans logged into the discussion forums. These forums provided an alternative to the institutionalised official wesbite. In Australia, the Ozupdates.com forum was one of the first and most popular. Dedicated fans spent hours viewing the live feeds and typing up the action for others to read. A regular updater guesstimated that he spent up to 70 hours a week on the internet. Fans who couldn't access the webfeeds could log in and read about what was happening in the house. From these 'objective' statements, discussions grew as contestants' behaviours were analysed. People posted the latest information, photos, articles and gossip about the contestants and the show. Six months after *Big Brother* finished, the Ozupdates site was still active. In January 2002 the following was posted:

> *Nat*
> Peter co-hosting on Channel V today
> Part of the Channel V and Nova join broadcast today Peter was co-hosting Channel V's Music Bus, he didn't say much, just smiled and stood there a lot, but he did an ok job at what he was doing. [sic]

In other words, the forum had become a rich (if not the richest) repository for information about all things *Big Brother*.

The forums were used in a variety of ways: for some they substituted for the television show; a female fan found that as 'a regular on Ozupdates.com [I] don't need to watch it on the internet or even the tele sometimes'. Others found that belonging to a fan community made them eager for more information: 'I don't think I would have become so completely hooked without the live feeds updated board, where others were just as addicted.' Others thought it enhanced their viewing pleasure: 'Once I found out about ozupdates.com [I] could get a more well-rounded view of what was happening 24/7 in the house and found by using ozupdates.com I generally knew before it was on tv.' Often the forums provided a more 'real' experience; as there was limited editing 'it was very interesting to see what the producers would keep out — like Ben vomiting (just going from the evidence) and Jemma's flash.'

The bulletin boards provided a safe community in which aficionados could discuss the show without feeling 'guilty'. One fan felt that 'I like to see what isn't being shown on TV, and because, in conjunction with a fan forum, I feel as though I'm sharing the ''secret stuff'' with a group of like-minded friends'. The 'secret stuff' is the gossip which is essential to fandom and gestures to the isolation many fans feel. As any anthropologist knows, gossip plays an important role in creating a cohesive group; it sorts out the inner from the outer circles and works actively to bond 'like-minded friends'.

One fan commented that though he watched the show alone, he felt he 'had most [of] the BB updaters with me' (47-year-old male). This feeling of community provided more 'isolated' *Big Brother* viewers with additional information.

Gossip and rumour allowed fans to speculate on the potential outcomes of voting, if romances existed and the contestants' behaviour. Although gossip is generally trivialised as a feminine activity, it is quite a powerful tool. There was more to these internet discussions that just idle chatter.

A special language ('DH' for dear husband; and 'n/t' for no text) and netiquette developed; the Ozupdaters forum frowned on vilification of the contestants and anything spurious. At the official website the tone was puerile, abusive and overly sexual; at Ozupdaters.com the tone was lighthearted, insightful and informed. Studies have shown that fan commentary is 'more detailed, complex, analytical and nuanced'.[10] The discussions centred on contestants, the show and general gossip.

Some of the most active participants on the forum were not even Australians. What was the attraction for overseas viewers? One Canadian fan summarised her reasons for watching:

1. I was an avid watcher of the first Big Brother in the US and was curious to see how the Australian version would be.
2. Once I started to watch the live feeds I really enjoyed getting to know each of the houseguests.
3. Loved the interaction and different relationships between the houseguests, especially Peter and Christina.
4. Really enjoyed learning about Australian culture and really got a kick out of the accents.
5. Loved the weekly challenges! Some of these challenges brought back a lot of great memories from last year's US version of the show.
6. The format of the show allowed us to relate to others in another

country and it also shed a lot of light on not pre-judging people but getting to know and love them for who they are on the inside.

7. Became very attached to the houseguests and was very sad when it was over and even more sad after I watched the new US version of BB which had changed the format completely!
8. It made me laugh and cry![11]

Overseas *Big Brother* fans who watched the live feeds started their own discussion site, called The ClubHouse. One American viewer translated her viewing experiences into the first (and still most comprehensive) fansite for her favourite Australian contestant, Peter Timbs.[12] The postings of overseas fans reflected some of the cultural differences between Australia and North America. As one viewer put it, 'I've learned more about Aussie watching the past two weeks than I've learned my whole life about the country.'[13] Often the North American viewers would ask the Australian viewers at Ozupdaters for clarification about language etc. As one fan explained:

> The BB community [online discussion group] was a major reason to tune in! ... the majority of the people I came in contact with have been so friendly and helpful! The people who come here [Ozupdaters] are one of the major contributing factors to the success of the program in my opinion! The whole concept of *Big Brother* allows people from different walks of life and countries to come together and share in an amazing experience! So I guess that should be my number 1 reason for tuning in and keeping up to date with *Big Brother* Australia! Thank you to all of you who have made this into an amazing experience!

Thus the forums encapsulated a wide variety of social, psychological and cultural experiences.

Believe it or not, people found the fan communities not a waste of time but an educational experience. At the most basic level, using the forums taught many people about using the internet. Old hands could guide new ones through the difficulties of software etc. In the earliest days, people turned to the forums for technical help — especially as there were considerable problems at the official site (e.g. downloading and using RealPlay — the software program necessary for the live feeds). One male fan (in the 15–23 age group) stated that the one thing he had learned from *Big Brother* was 'technology'.

Many of the topics helped people come to some understanding of their own prejudices and to even question their own belief systems. In entering a discussion about why a contestant's behaviour was offensive, viewers learned more about themselves. The bulletin board provided a space where textual interpretations were negotiated and evaluations shared.

The economics of fandom cannot be underestimated, and Southern Star certainly didn't underestimate it. As reported in the press, the voting process generated considerable income; in the first week over 250,000 votes were registered. Then online voting was introduced, and it was even more expensive. Nearly all of the female fans voted (9/13) and half of the male fans (3/6). Some voted nearly every week, but the majority voted only when motivated. Voting, like all fan activity, was done with considerable forethought. One female fan didn't vote because she 'didn't want to contribute to any of them [contestants] having to leave; another voted to protect her favourite contestants, 'to keep Christina in'. One fan explains her voting pattern:

> I got to the Sunday afternoon, several hours before votes closed, and started to think that Ben would stay and we would lose Sara-Marie, so I started to vote for Ben to be evicted. Most of the other votes I had not really cared about, or felt that my vote would not make a difference. Each week however I would barrack for who I wanted out, either because of personal likes and dislikes, or because of the interactions and relationships.

The use of the inclusive pronoun 'we' in the first sentence is telling. Clearly, the fan had developed a sense of community, a community that had similar views (not wanting to lose Sara-Marie). And they took action to avoid the loss of another valued 'member'/contestant.

There was considerable discussion about voting, and quite sophisticated calculations going on. Consider this example:

> Now, of course, I have to decide who to vote for. It's definitely not Gordon, because he was the only nominee who admitted that he might not get on with some people. Both Andy and Sara-Marie just whined and said the house would be boring without them. I don't think that's true of Sara-Marie, so she might get my vote, but I'll wait a couple of days. I suspect Andy's stocks with viewers will go up after the adults-only special on Thursday.[14]

The Australian *Big Brother* consortium was the first to capitalise on the popularity of the eviction nights. Dreamworld increased the entry fee as the live evictions became more and more popular. People turned up in the hundreds not just to witness the show but to be part of the *Big Brother* 'experience'.

In another form of textual poaching, people adopted contestants' hair, dress styles and accessories and wore them to the eviction nights. Audiences were filled with obvious signifiers such as Sara-Marie's bunny ears. Christina tutus appeared on many fans, even though she did not ever wear one in the house. It also demonstrated the fans' ability to 'deconstruct' contestants; one Jemma lookalike dressed in a bikini complete with shower curtain. Some fans had different signifiers: Anita fans wore hats and carried oversized packets of Juicy Fruit chewing gum. The public display increased with each successive show. This was of course encouraged by the producers of the show, who offered prizes for the best costume as an incentive.

Fans also spent their money on secondary fan material. The 'official' merchandise (videos, tee-shirts, mugs) was not available to some fans because of the geographical location (e.g. one fan who lived in Adelaide reported that a friend had purchased a coffee mug for her when visiting Dreamworld). One fan bought the compilation video but found its material unsatisfactory.

> *Nat*
> BB Video and CD
> I brought the BB Video and CD, was disappointed in both actually!

> The video left out way too much fun stuff and there were a lot of really boring bits, and I would have rathered been able to get it on DVD.
> The CD was ok, I love the video for the BB Theme song, but some of the music that I wanted wasn't on it — 'Doctor of Love' (aka Peter's song) and that song that went '... maybe moving in together wasn't such a great idea'.
> Having said that I **had** to buy both, no matter what ;-)

Fans can be highly critical; several complained about the predictability of the compilation video. They are also selective: 'I couldn't bring myself to buy *Ralph* — there are limits and it was only Jemma.'

Fourteen per cent of the fans bought magazines which they would not normally buy 'to read about the contestants'. Others donated money to charity during the Starlight Challenge; and 5,000 people contacted World Vision after Ben's documentary (half have signed up, which translates into A$1.5 million per year).

Big Brother canon

In order to form a collection of core material which viewers felt typified the *Big Brother* experience, viewers were asked to nominate the most memorable *Big Brother* moments. There was a general consensus about this. The majority of memorable moments came from the challenges: the dance marathon (especially the interruptions to Johnnie's meditation), the '$100,000 challenge', and the babies task ('Jemma was sitting on the couch and the baby was crying and she was just daydreaming away, until someone said "Hey, that's your baby!" '). Sharna's 'dummy spit' was also a favourite. Honourable mentions went to Ben's sleep-talking, Anita's 'smirk' remark, Blair's apology to Jemma, Lisa telling Gordon off, Sara-Marie and Johnnie under the doona, Ben and Blair on the couch on the last night and Sara-Marie and fish fingers. Memorable moments tended to be dramatic events.

Defining moments also were solicited; defining moments were

those that summed up 'what the show was about'. The majority nominated moments that related to the unfolding of relationships; the three responses below were typical:

- 'I liked watching the close friendship/bonds that were formed and displayed during the last five weeks (especially when it got down to Johnnie, Jemma, Christina, Sara-Marie, Blair and Ben). From that point on evictions were especially hard (especially Johnnie's) and *Big Brother* became almost compulsive viewing
- The arguments, such as the one with Jemma and Blair. And also Anita and Blair. I think the whole idea of the show was to really get into the minds of these people and see how they interacted, and the arguments and debates were part of that. Another thing, although it wasn't an actual moment, but I loved to see the way friendships developed, i.e. Sara-Marie and Christina and Ben and Blair.
- The overall theme I took from *Big Brother* is a story of mateship. At the start they were strangers who had to get along for the sake of the game. As they got to know each other better, they began to genuinely care. The level of tolerance and understanding displayed by most members of the household was astounding, given that many of these individuals wouldn't choose to say g'day to each other in the street.

The choices reflect the development of narratives and feelings.

Viewers could not resist the opportunity to have some linguistic fun of their own. Like topical jokes (dingo jokes, Lady Di jokes, *Challenger* jokes), this reflects how the show/contestants had captured the popular imagination. The internet was a rich source for this kind of linguistic play:

Buying a Jemma: The purchase of an expensive item for its authenticity which turns out to be a cheap fake.
Benning: The mindless repetition of witicisms while maintaining just one facial expression.
Coming the Blair: sulking and smirking simultaneously.
Copping a Christina: masturbating quickly under the covers knowing that your parents could burst in at any minute;
Having a Sara-Marie: Being unable to sleep due to the constant screeching of car alarms.[15]

The widespread appeal of the show is demonstrated in the following anecdote:

> I was fascinated while travelling in 4 wd across the Simpson Desert to find how much Big Brother is a part of the language of everyday Aussies. We had UHF radio to communicate with other cars on the track (to avoid a head-on collision when crossing sand dunes) and it's sort of like a banter that people in cars keep up with other members of the group they're driving with (like truckies' talk but less obscene). All these groups I overheard were using *Big Brother* lingo. When cars went over a soft sandhill and nearly got bogged they called that a bum dance — the new technical term for the car waggling its rear as it grinds its way up over the sand. Sara-Marie was a popular code name for persons on the radio.[16]

So from the Gold Coast to the Simpson Desert, *Big Brother* lingo created a common and understood language.

TV or not TV?

Of the 13 internet fans who watched the webfeeds, the majority (6) preferred television viewing, mainly because of technical problems ('the picture is useless on my internet!') and access problems ('at work I couldn't take advantage of the internet'). Yet they were not totally against the internet feeds: 'I enjoyed the new viewing a LOT and would have loved to watch it more — you saw so much more.' One viewer realised that the new medium required new skills and she/he was 'just used to tv I guess'. Six liked to view both, because they offered different viewing experiences: the live feeds 'were good to get the "true picture" of what was going on; however, the picture was very small and kept rebuffing; it was nice to sit back and watch it on the big screen and to then analyse the way it was portrayed by BB [the television show]'. For others, the half-hourly shows were more attractive because they offered a 'good summary of the day's activities' which staved off the 'boredom' of watching the live feeds. The live feed increased the viewers' awareness of the editing process and 'made me realise just how much we can be manipulated by television'.

The internet *Big Brother* audience often acted as docents. They claim to 'know' the *Big Brother* characters better because they have been privy to their most intimate secrets, secrets that the television show edits out. They are ahead of television audiences because they are seeing the events live; the television show is a day late. They are the doyens of gossip and rumour; they have read emails from people claiming to have dated *Big Brother* contestants and 'chatted' with people who claim to be family. They are in great demand at the water-cooler for they are the purveyors of the urban myths: the *Big Brother* house was originally used in *Paradise Beach*, Jemma is a 'plant' etc. Each day there is a new myth. Because of their encyclopaedic knowledge of the events in the house, their opinions are listened to with great reverence and their wildest claims are unquestioned. Generally, they are part of the MTV generation who grew up watching *Real World*; this is a natural progression in their viewing experiences. The paradox is that, because they have also been reared on quick takes, channel surfing and web surfing, their attention spans are supposed to be notoriously short and they are supposed to be excitement junkies. *Big Brother* to them is reality. They have seen the development of romances and witnessed the fights; they know the full 'story'. They have been watching since day one and the more they watch the more they want to watch. These viewers are more likely to be enthralled by *Big Brother* because it has become part of their lives.

Fine line between pleasure and pain

Survey participants were asked to list words that described the show. The most commonly used words were 'addictive' (11), 'interesting' (5) and 'boring' (4). Non-fans (N=9) used words with negative connotations: 'over-hyped', 'insignificant', 'fashion victims', 'annoying'. Surprisingly, fans used similar words, indicating the complexity of their readings: 'time-consuming', 'entertaining', 'clever', 'superficial', 'tedious', 'mindless entertainment', 'relaxing'.

A sense of wonder permeates the responses in the section that asked people to describe what pleasure the show had given them: 'I found myself genuinely excited when the evictions were on, which surprised me!' One fan described her range of emotions:

> Pleasure from the funny moments and the humorous comments of people online, and watching the contestants develop friendships. Outrage and annoyance and frustration over the unfairness of some incidents, biases of the editing or selection of items to go on the TV show. Fascination with some of the people involved and the situations they got themselves into. Anticipation watching live feeds about what would happen next, keeping me glued to the screen, e.g. Jemmagate, Christmas.

The most common pleasure was 'laughter'or 'happiness'.

When asked to comment on what they didn't like about *Big Brother*, more than half (8/13) complained about production issues, from voting to editing: 'the footage to the detriment of some housemates', and even wider television industry concerns: 'The production of a foreign concept in Australia doesn't constitute Australian-made shows.' Nine people felt manipulated by the editing process; one felt duped by 'editing and marketing'; and another realised 'how a show can be edited for the producers to create the effect they want (e.g. Johnnie Rotten)'.

Cynics noted the impact of economics on television: 'TV execs are always looking for more ways to make money'; just 'how much reality tv can make money for a network'; and 'branding can be very effective'. Another respondent was 'amazed' that the 'cross promotion — can turn something into a phenomenon'. Clearly the television producers have been constituted as the baddies, and this may stem from the negative press.

All of the positive comments concerned the contestants ('Great to see people just like the rest of us on TV!') and their personal relationships ('[I] liked the *camaraderie* between the HM'). Some were ambivalent about the show:

> I like the concept of the group house ... the group dynamics, I found it very interesting just how these normal Aussies could handle living in such a surreal situation. Disliked that we only saw what the producers wanted us to see and really feel they totally typecast people like Lisa and Johnnie Rotten ... it was very interesting to see what the producers would keep out — specially after seeing BB uncut with that literal porno of Andy and Sara-Marie playing nude volleyball — where you could see everything — thought that was very tasteless of channel 10 ... would be sueing [sic] if I were Andy! (31-year-old female)

The 'realness' of the housemates made viewers sympathise with their plight.

Even those who didn't watch the show regularly found themselves watching other television shows (*Rove Live*, *Sale of the Century* and *The Weakest Link*) in which the contestants appeared. Ten per cent of non-viewers said that they tuned to these shows even though they didn't normally watch them, just because of the *Big Brother* contestants.

Many might scoff, but some viewers felt that watching the house taught them about themselves, human behaviour and the contemporary media. Viewers learned, 'That I am pretty happy and content with my world without needing to be distracted by other people's goings on' and 'Not to judge anyone at first appearances ... I certainly did not like Sara-Marie in the first few episodes but she very quickly grew on you!'. 'Rizpect', by putting herself in a contestant's place, realised

> That I would have been thrown out very early in the piece, as I would not have been able to bite my tongue as they did; sometimes I thought they handled it better than I would have and it was nice to see how another person would handle a situation; other times I thought they were holding back just because they were on the show and, had the situation happened in their own home, they would have reacted different, e.g. the Jemma nominations situation.

On a personal level some viewers learned more about themselves: 'There really was a voyeur lurking beneath'; 'how easily

I am able to get totally addicted to a TV show'; and 'that I can get sucked into the hype of a tv show; don't think that's a good thing'.

> It sometimes made me wonder how I would have reacted in some of the personal situations that the housemates went through, and also made me feel like I was a bit of an obsessive person when I was on the internet every day catching up on other people's lives! We are all a little too voyeuristic.

For many, the experience of watching a show unfold over a period of time gave them pause to consider how they had changed their viewpoint:

> It's interesting to notice how much my attitude towards some of the housemates has changed over the past few weeks. When I first started trying to pick who should get voted off, Sara-Marie came quickly into view, largely because of her ongoing refusal to acknowledge any sort of culpability in the fire challenge. Jemma's superficial attitude also had me bugged. A few weeks later, I can't seem to muster up the same level of venom towards these two. I guess this is a consequence of shrinking numbers. With fewer people in the house, everyone gets more on-screen time, and thus has more chance of appearing like a decent human being.

Through their observation of the contestants, some fans felt that they learned more about human behaviour in general: 'First impressions are not always correct.' Some were more specific:

> 'The youth of Australia are not as homophobic as I thought they were.'
>
> 'That people can truly feel a bond with characters on a tv show.'
>
> 'I'm not the only one who dislikes attention-hungry people (Andy/Jemma).'

People learned more about television viewers in general: 'That generally people are interested in human relationships' and 'There are a hell of a lot of people out there [in Australia] that like watching someone else's life'; and the multiplicity of meanings generated by individual viewers 'that people's views are always different no matter which way things are portrayed'.

For many viewers *Big Brother* was like a siren's call; they could not resist it. The press was against them, as were their friends and family. True fans, however, found the show a rewarding venture; they watched, they discussed, they bought.

One viewer's story

(Ann Byrne)

The eyes. It was those eyes, the *Big Brother* eyes, that I first saw on the billboards near the Westgate Bridge in Melbourne. They sparked my curiosity and drew me in. What was this show going to be about? What was it going to *be*?

I had not heard of the *Big Brother* show before — didn't know there had been a series in England or in the US, or anywhere else. I hadn't watched *Survivor*, although I'd heard of it from the publicity around the first series and also because friends in the US were asking about the show taking place at the top end of down under. They wanted to know: what was this place in Australia that had both desert and jungle, sea and swamp, and was hot by day and cool by night? I finally watched a few tail-ends of the show, toward the end of that second series, hoping to see some tell-tale scenery. Instead I found myself caught up by the psychology of the tribal council voting — and wanting to find out more, to find out *why* they voted out her, or him. I even went to the website and read up on the past happenings and long-evicted participants, to try to get a sense of the interpersonal interactions.

Back in the 70s I'd watched the US reality show that filmed the day-to-day life of the Loud family, and in the early 90s I saw a tiny bit of *Sylvania Waters* in Australia, but I always found these 'deluxe home movies' rather boring after a few weeks. And while *Survivor*'s social dynamics intrigued me, the competitive 'game' part of it did not. So I was a tad curious about *Big Brother* and wanted to see what it would be like. Would it be something other than just a 'game' show? Would it be more than just filming a real-life house-sharing situation? I had to know, at least. Those eyes just really got to me.

Nonetheless, I somehow managed to miss the first couple of nights! I was only vaguely aware of when (and how often) the show was on, but at last I managed to catch it one evening, several days after it had begun. It took another week or so — closing in on Andy's eviction — before I was a more 'regular' watcher. If I was home, I'd make sure I turned the TV on to Channel 10 at 7 pm (much to the chagrin of my husband, who liked to watch the ABC news), but I must have missed many fragments as I also prepared dinner or talked to my husband (or, more accurately, as he talked to me, commenting on what nonsense this show seemed to him!).

So, to catch up on what had been happening, I began looking at the official *Big Brother* website. I signed up so I would receive regular updates by email and have access to live feeds. I tried many times to get the live feeds at work, but (probably luckily for my job status) the firewall wouldn't let me. Still, I read the daily news and summaries, looked at the background pictures and stories, and thus slowly began to be drawn further and further in.

I found I wanted to discuss my new interest with others. I tried the Chatroom on the official website, but found it full of what seemed to be immature 14-year-olds who were keener to try out all the bad words they knew on each other than to debate anything about the show. The forums, while they contained many mini-essays from the same crowd, were a bit more bearable and I occasionally joined in those. I found the frequency of news reports on the site frustrating, though — they were updated only once a day or so. This is not enough when you can't get the feeds and are dying to know what's going on! So I found myself looking everywhere I could find for 'more' — other sites about the show, fansites, and then even other *Big Brother* series — the UK one was already on, and the second US one was starting up soon and so had 'pre-view' hype on the website already.

By about the 2nd or 3rd week, my interest level had increased drastically. I still missed a show here and there, but I was definitely starting to become what I can only describe as obsessive. I started to tape the show any night I was in danger of missing it. Then I started taping every show even if I was there, just in case I was interrupted. I ate my dinner in front of the telly, although my husband refused to join me there after about three or four times, and so we ate separately. (I didn't mind this at all, since with him in the dining room while I was in the lounge room, he wasn't interrupting or making comments while I was trying to listen!)

I didn't mind at all admitting publicly that I watched the show, despite the snide remarks some people made. Quite a few people seemed to believe it was a very low-brow, silly, gossipy show aimed at teenage girls — and I'm 47. But I'd freely mention I watched it, and if anyone sneered 'Don't tell me you watch *that* nonsense!' I'd smile and say 'Yeah I do! I like it a lot!' Usually, they hadn't actually watched it, or had had only a glimpse — and when I would explain what it was about, they seemed a little less judgmental.

I started to want to discuss the show, and I would do so with anyone who showed even the slightest interest. Maybe five or six of my co-workers watched it, and I could usually get a few minutes' conversation about it each day with some of them, but none were nearly as engrossed as I was, and their willingness to discuss it would flag long before mine. Rebecca, a friend in my running group, was the only one who really indulged my single-minded conversation to any satisfactory extent, and we often spent the full hour of the once-a-week run chatting exclusively about *Big Brother* as we jogged or walked. Her husband and the other guys in the group knocked it — although, if she wasn't there on a given week, I could almost always get *them* going in a discussion on it for at least a short while! Of course, they claimed they only knew about it because their wives turned it on every night. My husband continued to ridicule the show too, and to act aggrieved whenever I mentioned it, but still I couldn't help myself telling him about things that were happening and my impressions of the housemates and events. I also watched the live feeds whenever I could, which was only occasionally — usually on evenings when my husband was working, so he wouldn't feel I was neglecting 'more important' things!

Although I wouldn't stay home or miss social events in order to watch the show, I was spending a lot of time watching it, and for me it took precedence over any other tv show. If we were going out on a Saturday night, my husband had to do without *his* all-time favourite, *The Bill*, unless he could get a friend to tape it, because it conflicted with the Saturday night *Big Brother*. He kindly yielded to me on this, because, as I argued, *The Bill* would 'always' be on, whereas *Big Brother* would run for only12 weeks. I also couldn't be counted on to pay attention to many other matters when 'my show' was on. This included cooking dinner, although sometimes I actually tried to accomplish this during the commercials — several burnt pans of risottos and casseroles were the result!

If any magazine featured an article on the housemates, I'd buy it, even if it were one I'd never otherwise purchase. I wanted to read up on each of the housemates, their backgrounds, family, what they'd done in the past, what made them tick. I'd watch any show the housemates were on, even (after the series was over) the horrible *Beauty and the Beast*. I wasn't 'Super-Fan' though, I guess, as I didn't buy bunny ears and I never made plans to try to get up to the Gold Coast to go to an eviction show.

Of course, I had my opinions, judgments and feelings about each of the housemates. From almost the start, Johnnie was my favourite. I'm not completely sure why, but he just seemed centred and fairly mature, fun-loving and sensitive yet able to laugh at himself. I wasn't surprised nor terribly unhappy that Andy was the first to go, nor Sharna soon after; though they brought in a bit of drama, they also somehow seemed threatening to the comfort of the group in the early days. I didn't want to see a *Survivor*-like game of upsets and conflict, or domineering personalities — I wanted to see a group of strangers working at sharing a house and meeting various challenges, basically in harmony.

Sara-Marie seemed a bit 'over the top' to me at first, but as the show progressed I came to like her more and more, as did so many others. I liked Todd and was surprised when he was voted off; I began to realise that the TV viewings were prejudicial in what they showed, whether or not they were intended to be. There simply wasn't enough time to show the complete picture — only the Internet could do that. The power of tagging — as Todd was tagged with being untidy and unwashed — was very influential on the fans who voted. I'd have loved to have been able to watch the live feeds much much more.

Gordon didn't make a very positive impression on me and I had actually hoped he'd be evicted sooner. I was disappointed in Christina's intense focus on Peter and felt it greatly diminished her interactions with the others, while *he* didn't seem to let the relationship affect him similarly. I thought the dog was a great idea, but unfortunately Ebony was just the wrong dog. Blair, Ben, Lisa and Jemma all had their moments. I had mixed feelings about the intruders' arrival, and then was surprised when the housemates chose to evict Rachel, who had appeared to fit in most easily. Still, I felt Anita could have provided a very positive element of stimulation and I was frustrated by what appeared to be her failure to even try to enjoy the housemates and the experience.

Overall, though, while I had favourites and opinions, I never really became a fan of the housemates, singularly or plurally (is that a word?), so much as of the show and of the group together. The interactions and dynamics were what kept me watching. At first I felt that the producers should have picked a more diverse group (in age and in background), but after seeing some of the other shows where there was a bigger mix (such as US *Big Brother 2*, although it admittedly was a cut-throat game), I came around to feeling they hadn't done so badly after all.

At some point I discovered the 'Australian Big Brother Updates' webpage (I don't even remember how I got there the first time!), and when I realised what it was, I was in heaven: it was a page where people who were watching the live feeds reported what was happening, and where people like me could read these reports to find out! And, they were people who liked *discussing* what was happening, too! Of course this didn't help my job performance — I was definitely falling behind from all the time I spent checking that site to see what was going on now — and now — and *now*. I was pleased when I was able to make contributions to the reporting, too, on the relatively rare occasions when I could watch the feeds for any length of time. I really began to worry about my obsession when I noticed I was enjoying watching the housemates on the net even if they were all asleep and doing nothing!

On the Updates page, regulars got to 'know' other regulars fairly well and people seemed genuine; they were similarly obsessed with the show and committed to sharing it all! Once, when I expressed a desire to have one of the *Big Brother* coffee mugs I saw Gretel with on the show, and which one could win in some of the website competitions, a girl in Sydney (Giulia, also known as 'Trailer Park Princess' as her nom-de-website) sent me her spare one! And we all immediately felt that Joey, who won a contest to attend the final two shows and take part in the celebrity challenge at the house the next day, was 'our' Joey, and we cheered him on as we watched.

So, when it was suggested that we have get-togethers in the major cities to watch the show's finale together, I wasn't at all worried about any axe-murderers showing up. The Melbourne group met at Planet Hollywood in the Casino, and it was terrific to put faces to names. In retrospect, a quieter pub probably would have been a better option; it was a bit noisy and with all the screens it was hard to pick which way to look for the best view, as well as to keep chatting about what was happening, but it was still terrific to be watching with a bunch of people who were as crazy about it as I was, instead of home by myself! We later posted the photos on websites, and also got to see photos of the housemates taken by Willow, a *really* big fan, who won tickets to an event where they were appearing.

Since the show has ended, I have slowly, slowly, been weaned off the obsession. There were so many 'follow-up' shows where the housemates were featured (like *Beauty and the Beast*, and *Sale of the Century*, etc.) that my husband was given to asking plaintively, 'Will this ever end?'. I bought a few more magazines that featured articles about the housemates, but now, as I write this several months later, I am less likely to do so; for instance, I looked at the issues of *Ralph* with Jemma and Christina in the newsagents', but I didn't buy them. I did watch the housemates on *The Weakest Link*, and taped the charity pantomime.

After *Big Brother* ended, for a while I turned to the UK and US *Big Brother* shows as substitutes, following them mainly via updates on websites and occasionally with live feeds, but they were very different from the Australian one and, I felt, not as enjoyable; the US one in particular was a really aggressive, unpleasant game. The South African series, which started in about September 2001, was most like the Aussie one in terms of what I guess might be called psychodynamics, and I kept up with that fairly faithfully, though not nearly to the degree I followed the Australian one. I realised recently that if Channel 10 ever ran the original series again in full I would watch it all! And I'd watch any sort of 'follow-up' show too, even though I no longer jump to catch the housemates' every appearance on a talk show or whatever.

I now only check the updates page (which has continued) *once* a day! Yes, I *can* stop if I want to! I am looking forward to the second Aussie *Big Brother* series, although I don't think it can ever be as 'pure' as the first one, wherein the housemates truly had no idea how the outside world was reacting. But you can bet I'll be watching it!

Chapter Eight

The Bold and the Beautiful: The Media

At the start of 2001 Big Brother meant George Orwell's *1984*, constant surveillance, totalitarian regimes and brainwashing techniques. By the end of the year, it meant bum dancing, Sara-Marie and greyhound racing. It all started innocuously enough: a prequel television show hosted by Rove McManus and a few newspaper articles introduced the *Big Brother* concept. Then came the deluge — for the next six months, the *Big Brother* media tsunami hit. Though Southern Star Endemol's media strategy involved an 'exclusive' rights agreement with News Limited newspapers[1] and radio station Triple M, it seems that every media outlet devoted space to *Big Brother*. The *Big Brother* spindoctors reinvented media saturation.

Print

Big Brother has sparked outrage and captured headlines in Europe, South Africa, Greece and almost every country in which it appeared. South Africa's newspapers were 'saturated' with *Big Brother* stories.[2] The British press, particularly the tabloid papers the *Sun* and the *Mirror*, covered their three *Big Brother* series in considerable detail. Front-page headlines pushed the British general elections to the inside pages. The broadsheets seemed bemused by the attention the shows attracted. The London *Times*, the *Financial Times*, the *Independent*, the *Guardian* and the *Spectator* ran hundreds of articles and printed essays by cultural gurus such as Germaine Greer, Salman Rushdie and Desmond Morris[3] (author of *The Naked Ape*). On the other side of the Atlantic, the home of trash tv, the United States press virtually ignored the shows, until one of the contestants in the second series threatened another with a knife.[4]

The *Big Brother* network ensures that all over the world fans know the latest *Big Brother* gossip. In Australia we read about *Big Brother* shows in South Africa, Russia, Greece and France. Optus aired the Greek *Big Brother* each day during its run in September 2001. Overseas countries took an interest in the Australian *Big Brother*. The BBC online news had a number of articles about it, as did the South African *Sunday Times*. *Variety* got into the act and reported that *Big Brother* down under was 'blah'.

Although Australian newspapers might not have devoted as much space to *Big Brother* as the British tabloids, nearly every newspaper reported on it. There was a flurry of *Big Brother* articles after the screening of Channel 10's *Big Brother Is Coming to Australia*; then there was a smattering of stories about the auditions and applications. Within hours of the show getting under way, the public debates about the show and its contestants began in earnest.

During the show's run, over 1000 newspaper articles throughout Australia mentioned either the show or its contestants.[5] Unsurprisingly, News Limited newspapers covered the show in detail: the *Herald-Sun* published 250 articles, the *Courier-Mail* 200, the *Daily Telegraph* 150 and the *Australian* 100. Other newspapers such as the *Sydney Morning Herald* published over 100 articles, *The Age* more than 40, and even the *Australian Financial Review* had around 10. As if that wasn't enough, some newspapers re-printed their *Big Brother* stories on their websites. For example, on Monday 14 May 2001, *The Age* had four *Big Brother* articles, one in print and three on the internet (one which had originally been in the *Sydney Morning Herald*). The number of articles positively correlated with the building momentum of the show: April 170; May 300; June 200; July 566.

For years 'Big Brother' has been shorthand for ubiquitous surveillance. Because it had regained cultural currency through the show, writers reinstituted the phrase. A documentary about Shane Warne was called 'Cricket's version of *Big Brother*'. Swimming star Ian Thorpe compared his goldfish-bowl lifestyle to that of being on the show: 'it's kind of like *Big Brother*, but *Big Brother* every day, and at the end of the day there's no big reward'. Even new car reviewers invoked the term: 'Holden's version of *Big Brother* can listen to you when you get behind the wheel'.[6]

Reaction to the show expressed concerns that ran the gamut from the show's sexual content to the impact on the television industry.

For many critics, *Big Brother* epitomised a decline in television programming. For some bizarre reason, most critics feared that *Big Brother* would lead to television shows in which contestants would kill each other for viewers' entertainment. Shows like *Big Brother* were 'raising the stakes [for] more sex, more violence, more humiliation, more cruelty'. This is a traditional moral panic. Years ago the same fears about the televised roller derbys culminated in the death-by-roller-game movie *Rollerball* (1975).

Many writers invoked talk shows when writing about *Big Brother*. The two genres are not synonymous, but critics felt that talk show's slide into sensationalism reflected decaying television standards. The reasoning usually goes along the lines: 'Talk shows, which started out innocently, have degenerated into ambush television'. Of course not all talk shows have taken that road, but writers chose to ignore shows such as *Oprah*. Talk-show 'ambushes' were responsible for

> at least two deaths. One, a man who shot an old friend after the friend admitted to admiring him homosexually on the *Jenny Jones Show*, and the other, a woman killed by her ex-husband, shortly after he vilified her on the *Jerry Springer* program.[7]

But what about the callous exploitation of shows such as *A Current Affair* (for example the Paxtons and the suicide of Benedicto Mendoza the television repairman)? The complex social issues surrounding the Jenny Jones and Jerry Springer 'murders' were ignored. It seemed a godsend to the *Big Brother* alarmists when the movie *Series 7* was released during *Big Brother* because it purportedly provided an exemplar of extreme reality tv. Interviews with writer/direct Daniel Minahan only exacerbated the perception:

> Far from rushing into production to take advantage of the present crop of shows, the former TV documentary-maker [Minahan] says he wrote the first draft six years ago — inspired by early reality shows such as *Cops* — and filmed it in 1999. He says he only heard about *Survivor* when he was on the set in Connecticut ... 'someone sent a fax that described the show and we thought, "It's just a joke". Six months later I'm sitting with my actors watching the season premiere of American *Survivor*'.[8]

Conversely, while some feared that too much reality was close to hand, others complained that *Big Brother* wasn't real enough. It was 'contrived, artificial — thinly disguised voyeurism dressed up as mass amusement'. It was not reality — 'it is manufactured beginning to end'. Some felt it was the 'ultimate cheat' and that viewers were being 'conned' because there were no grey areas; 'either it's "reality" or it's not'.[9]

The most common bedfellows were *Big Brother* and sex. Nearly fifty articles paired *Big Brother* with voyeurism. It was the 'epitome of voyeuristic television'.[10] Is there any other kind of television? All television is voyeuristic in the sense that people 'watch' it. Voyeurism is predicated upon the victim *not* knowing they are being watched; it is 'one of the paraphilias, characterised by marked distress over, or acting on, urges to observe unsuspecting people. Usually strangers, who are naked or in the process of disrobing, or who are engaged in sexual activity.' Clearly this was not the case in *Big Brother*; indeed Andy went to some length to exhibit her body. While there was nudity and sexual activity in some of the *Uncut* shows, most of it was sex talk. Still critics included peeping metaphors. It was a 'peep show watched by peeping toms'; Germaine Greer likened watching *Big Brother* to peering through the keyhole of a teenage child's room.[11] Allen Newton felt 'like a naughty schoolboy caught red-handed with

Playboy' when he visited the house and found that the most 'voyeuristic room' was not the shower room but one under the pool. It was 'like a scene from a pornographic movie with a cameraman [in a] damp and dark room [while] naked and semi-naked bodies frolick[ed] ... above him'. The cameramen resembled 'old men in raincoats ... waiting for something lurid to happen'.[12] In other words, it was regarded as televised 'pornography'.[13]

The press felt that the main thrust of the show was sex. One article claimed that the *Big Brother* producers had selected contestants based on their physical appearances, particularly their anatomy:

> So important was sex to this show, contestants were not only screened for psychological and physical defects, the size of their genitals (the boys' anyway) — and their willingness to expose them — were taken into account by the producers when casting the characters.[14]

But if the willingness to expose themselves was of primary concern to producers, one wonders why Jemma and Sharna were selected. The promise of sex whipped some into a lather: 'showering roommates, topless swimming and bedroom romps *are likely* to be aired', opined one writer.[15] *Big Brother* producers had to 'satisfy' viewers with a 'greater reliance on T & A'.[16] But the reality was, as others argued, that *ER* and *Dawson's Creek* were just as sexually focused.[17] Those who thought that the show would be titillating were disappointed. Danny Katz described his excitement when he

> heard my beloved yelling from the other room: 'HEY DANNY YOU'LL WANT TO SEE THIS. TWO GIRLS ARE KISSING'. That sequence of words — 'two girls are kissing' — is the most powerful in the male language; they could wake me from a coma.[18]

Instead of erotic, he found the sight 'puerile' and 'moronic' and not the least bit sexy. Another viewer agreed; he found the nudity too contrived to be titillating:

> when [Andy] casually dried herself off before two of the boys, letting the towel drop now and then, it didn't seem half so titillating. We

> weren't getting an unguarded peek at a breast (which turned out to be rigorously pixilated anyway) but in fact a bit of ham acting. Whether it was designed to please the boys or the viewers, I don't know, but either way it seemed a crude attempt to get people to vote for her to stay on the show, and not a bit sexy or charming.[19]

Obviously there was the opportunity for many to be offended by the 'sexual explicitness' of *Big Brother*. But viewers didn't seem to object to the *Uncut* version. The critics spluttered about public outrage, but the Australian Broadcasting Authority reported that it had received only about a dozen calls. Ten denied that it had been 'inundated with complaints about nudity'. In fact, it was reported that 16 viewers complained to Melbourne's Channel 10. Still, sex and *Big Brother* sell, and overseas news sources quickly picked up the controversy, even if they did overstate the case. A BBC news article remarked on the 'outrage over scenes of full-frontal nudity, bondage displays and tales of group sex'. The press speculated that the Thursday night content called for 'the ABA [Australian Broadcasting Authority] to hold a new inquiry' into present broadcasting codes.[20]

What really intrigued most people was the toilet cam. People shuddered to think about being filmed on it themselves. Filming people in the toilet was somehow 'worse' than being filmed nude or having sex. While Endemol tried to explain that the toilet camera was there to prevent collusion, reporters reminded readers that the contestants would still be watched by the camera operators, directors and producers. How did the crew feel? 'Camera work is camera work', said one cameraman; one director was 'embarrassed' and tended to avoid the toilet cam. And what about the contestants? Andy felt that as they had been told there would be no privacy that anyone who was 'overly worried — shouldn't have applied'.[21]

If the sex bogey man didn't faze adults, then the press preyed on parental fears by printing articles that focused on the negative effects of *Big Brother* on children. Reality-tv shows 'present aggression, bullying, cheating and lying as acceptable behaviour' they read. Another article warned that children could become emotionally distressed by the show. Dr Carr-Gregg felt that *Big Brother* was 'dangerous for children … They do identify closely … [and] start feeling the same sort of emotions as the housemates. [Children] could grieve … and that can lead to anger and depression'. However none of these statements were supported with evidence.[22]

It seems that everyone had a gripe against *Big Brother*. Industry professionals worried about the effect of using non-professional actors on television. ABC Chairman Johnathan Shier condemned *Big Brother* because he felt the show wasn't Australian. Some felt that the voting encouraged gambling; the RSPCA complained about the 'kicked' chook. Perhaps the strangest complaint was that it exposed viewers to 'the unsavoury antics' of everyday life such as 'showering, eating, sleeping, squabbling'![23] Showering, eating and sleeping — sound boring. Which was, perhaps, the most valid complaint of all.

Salman Rushdie, Richard Zachariah and Wendy Harmer thought *Big Brother* was boring. Kerrie Murphy was so bored she said so four times — in an article of only one hundred and twenty words. The *Australian* added 'inane', and *The Age* was even more expansive — 'boring, puerile, moronic'. Even *Variety* reported that the Australian *Big Brother* was boring.[24] Nearly fifty articles coupled *Big Brother* and boredom. Boredom and television are uneasy companions, and thus it would be imagined that viewers turned off in their thousands. But they didn't. Even those who found *Big Brother* inane and boring stayed tuned. It was 'disturbingly compelling'.[25]

Why did viewers who admitted they found it boring keep watching? 'It lets us pretend' that we can look into other dysfunctional lives and vote off the unpleasant people. It was a 'harmless' way to spend a half-hour. *Big Brother* offered a chance for a bit of a 'goss' about people; to view 'households more dysfunctional than our own'. And in the end, the contestants weren't all that dysfunctional; it said 'nice things about us'.[26]

In the scramble to fill columns with *Big Brother* material, anyone who could write on the topic did. News Limited had two writers: the *Courier-Mail*'s Jennifer Dudley was the dedicated *Big Brother* reporter who wrote over 100 articles and Kathy McCabe, another News Limited writer, wrote about 50 pieces. Specialty writers also contributed to the debate: comedian Danny Katz, veteran television producer Gerald Stone, counsellor/author Ian Oshlack.[27] Other 'celebrity' authors included Red Symons, who said he wouldn't do a *Celebrity Big Brother* — or did he? Andrew Denton, creator of the *House from Hell*, decided he had outgrown such shows; HG Nelson included Gordon and Sara-Marie in his mock race-to-fame racing piece.[28]

Columnists who followed the show from the start to the finish found that by the end of the series they had a change of heart. *The Age*'s Ross Warneke chalked up over twelve months of writing on *Big Brother*; his first article appeared after *Big Brother Is Coming* in November 2001. When it first started he was 'hooked', two weeks later he was bored, and by the show's end he realised that it was, after all, just a television program:

> My biggest complaint about *Big Brother* was not the show itself but the way so many people took it too seriously. At the start, I must confess I was one of them, although I was never as censorious as some of the puffed-up commentators who delighted in slamming it, using every adjective they could summon from a thesaurus. But it was all so much nonsense. *Big Brother* was a game-show-cum-reality-soapie that was played out for its entertainment value and nothing else. The players were consenting adults. No one was hurt. And as the series unfolded, the numbers in the house dwindled and honest, fun relationships began to develop, it became ever more watchable ... Roll on *Big Brother* II, and III and IV.[29]

His viewing experiences mirrored the slump that is the rhythm of *Big Brother*. At first the *Sydney Morning Herald*'s Miranda Devine was shocked by the shamelessness of the contestants; however, the viewing public wasn't the leering populace she expected and seemed surprised that audiences 'still want the good guys to win'.[30]

Academics provided more analyses. Graeme Turner noted that more harm had been done by investigative journalism than by *Big Brother.* Catharine Lumby saw little in the show to offend; indeed it exposed the artifice of television and the hypocrisy of the critics. On the other hand, Karen Brooks spiced her column with negative emotive words: 'inane', 'sadistic', 'raucous', 'self-destruct', 'bitch', 'whinger'.[31] Media Studies lecturer Lee Burton was clearly disgusted with the show; 'we're looking at new levels of crap'.[32]

Those reporters who did not blatantly state whether they were pro or anti *Big Brother* unwittingly revealed their feelings in the words they chose. In an article describing the house, Kathy McCabe used decorating terms: 'meticulously planned', 'salubrious', '90 mirrors', from the 'ornate teak doors' to the outside 'swimming pool, chicken coop, a vegetable and herb garden and a shady gazebo'. Others used decidedly more pointed language: the designer was a 'sadist' who gave a 'sinister chuckle' and cameramen 'prowl' the camera corridors.[33]

Once the show started, of course, the focus shifted from the format to the contestants. Sara-Marie drew the most media attention overall. But generally, the papers seemed more concerned with reminding the contestants that their fifteen minutes of fame wouldn't last; for over six months, the contestants were reminded about the fickle finger of fate. Miranda Devine failed to see the irony in her comment '*Big Brother* has been milked for all it's worth by the media'.[34] As did newspaper reporters and journalists who wrote article after article sneering at the longevity of the contestants' celebrity status. The fame was 'fleeting' and soon forgotten. In July, agent and celebrity maker Max Markson thought that 'in six months time it will be "Andy who? Peter who? Gordon who?".' Contestants were told they were 'tedious'; even the public's favourite, Sara-Marie, was 'fading'. In December one article stated that 'many media outlets [were] turned off covering events'.[35] Still, at the start of 2002, newspapers eagerly printed the smallest contestant gossip — Blair's new bachelor pad, Peter's love life, Ben's trip to Africa, and speculation about what Sara-Marie is planning next.

While the contestants captured most of the media attention, in the media feeding frenzy anyone associated with the show was allocated space. Host Gretel Killeen came in for her fair share of fame — she is mentioned in over 70 articles. Struggling singers and groups gained much needed exposure in closing performances on the Sunday night eviction shows. As one newspaper related, it translated into success for some:

> Singing star Lydia Denker has received a career boost from the strangest of places. The 20-year-old singer was fretting over which song to release when producers of the Channel 10 series *Big Brother* made the decision for her. They played a remix of Lydia's single 'Real to Me' on the show and sparked a new wave of interest in the song. 'I actually released it last year and it didn't do as well as we had hoped, but now it has re-emerged,' she said. 'It really grabbed the audience.' The song's popularity also scored the singer a place on the show's soundtrack.[36]

Even the most tangential staff received media attention. Security guard 'Phil' told how fame had affected his life![37]

Magazines

Reportage differed according to the publication's target audience. While the newspapers printed the latest gossip and debates, the *Australian Financial Review* analysed the fiscal rewards for Channel 10, Southern Star and Dreamworld. The *Bulletin* contained three essays — two of which examined reality tv. Deb Light gave reality tv the once-over; Catharine Lumby debunked the reality-tv myths; and Angus Kidman examined *Big Brother* and the internet.[38]

Because Australia lacks a tabloid press (such as the American *National Enquirer* or the British *Mirror* and *Sun*), magazines such as *Who Weekly* and *NW* are our celebrity watchers. It is clear from their content, layout and pricing that the magazines aim at the same readership. Their standard fare? The contestants as celebrities; the show as sensation.

New Idea straddles the celebrity/women's magazine boundary. Generally, it concentrates on human-interest stories and showing celebrities as mothers, fathers; in other words as reader-like. *New Idea*'s stories on Andy's marriage and Gordon's 'amazing secret' are typical; so too were the movie star makeovers for Sara-Marie, Andy and Christina. Fashion mag *Cosmopolitan* dressed Sara-Marie up and put her on the cover.

Men's lifestyle magazines have not embraced either the contestants or the show with the same zeal as other magazines. *Ralph* featured Christina and Jemma. Surprisingly, *Playboy* has not stepped forward and asked Andy to do a photoshoot, even though she made it clear that she wouldn't object. But though many overseas *Big Brother* contestants have appeared in *Playboy*, the magazine is shy of paying extra to reality-tv contestants (as Shannon from the second American series discovered).

The less gendered magazines made some telling choices. *Rolling Stone* made Sara-Marie its centrefold for its *2001 Rock and Roll Yearbook.* Sara-Marie's skills as a singer would hardly qualify her selection for a rock and roll magazine; clearly the magazine was exploiting her popularity with their audience demographic. *Juice* also gave Sara-Marie the thumbs up and mentioned her twice in its *2001 Yearbook*; in September it preferred an Andy, Johnnie and Peter threesome. Gretel Killeen managed to grab a few articles; not the least being named 'a good sort' in the launch issue of *S* (July 2001).

Television and Radio

It was part of the promotional package for evictees to appear on Channel 10 shows such as *Rove*, the *Panel* and *Good Morning Australia*. After the final *Big Brother* episode, viewers saw them on *Beauties and the Beast* and the *Starlight Challenge* (the combined telethon and pantomime). Jemma was Big Sister to wannabe models in *Search for a Supermodel*; Sara-Marie returned to *Rove* to launch her new music video; and Christina visited *GMA* to promote Planet Ark. Ben had his own show, *Personal Best* and his World Vision documentary *Big Brother, Little Brother.* Of course Blair started in *Neighbours* in December 2001.

After losing the bidding war for the first *Big Brother*, it was hardly surprising that Channel 9 ran a condemnatory segment in *A Current Affair* in which it showed humiliating clips from *Cheaters* (a new reality-tv show in which cameras catch and confront cheating spouses), mentioned the Jenny Jones murder case, and discussed 'Aftercare', the therapy for ex-talk show guests.[39] It was less damning in its *Sixty Minutes* segment on *Big Brother*, no doubt because the second *Big Brother* series was being planned and the contestants appeared on *Sale of the Century*.[40] Around the same time, they also competed on *The Weakest Link* (22 August) on Channel 7. It seemed that both channels were trialling *Big Brother* contestants in case they won the bidding war that was going on behind the scenes. After losing the bidding war, Channel 7 (in *Today Tonight*) and Channel 9 (in *A Current Affair*) aired negative segments about *Big Brother* on the same night (17 January 2002); though there were some positive statements, *A Current Affair* devoted more time to an interview with disgruntled Sharna West.

The night the first *Big Brother* aired on Channel 10, the ABC's *Foreign Correspondent* devoted 20 minutes to an examination of reality television. Using clips from the United Kingdom's *Panorama*, the segment focused on the detrimental psychological impact of the show. 'Nasty' Nick Bateman and 'flirty' Melanie Hill (from the United Kingdom's first *Big Brother* series) discussed how the show's producers had edited their characters. The segment debated the ethics of reality-tv shows and invoked the usual fears by mentioning the Jenny Jones and Jerry Springer 'murders'. After *Big Brother* ended, *Four Corners* followed up with 'Reality Check'.[41] It included clips from the most sensational reality-tv shows — such as *The Ex-Files* (in which ex-lovers come face to face) and the Japanese television show 'Sweepstakes Boy' — and managed to interview a number of the *Big Brother* contestants

(Peter, Christina and Todd). However, the ABC was probably still smarting after losing its bid for reality show *The Weakest Link.*

Various ABC radio shows discussed the *Big Brother* phenomenon; it was on 'Arts Today' (27 April 2001; 7 May 2001), 'Lateline' (25 & 27 April 2001) 'PM' (25 June 2001), Radio National Breakfast (17 July) and the Science Show (18 August 2001). Local ABC radio stations had numerous segments devoted to *Big Brother.*[42] The official *Big Brother* station, Triple M, kept listeners updated with events in the house (a minimum of nine updates per day). Then the station had its notorious 'Save Andy' and 'Johnnie Rotten' campaigns. But the show wasn't only discussed by the young; *Big Brother* dominated radio talkback, traditionally a forum for older people.

Big Brother on the Web

The internet was integral to *Big Brother*'s success. In addition to the official *Big Brother* website, a number of websites catered to the internet interest in the show. Two newspapers had mini-websites devoted to *Big Brother*, but both were short-lived. One week after the show started, the online *Sydney Morning Herald* launched a *Big Brother* mini-website. The website had only four web pages of reprinted material (from the *Sun-Herald*) and nothing was added after 29 April 2001. The *Sydney Morning Herald*'s high-tech website, 'Icon', also contained a number of webpages about *Big Brother*; the articles concentrated on the computer aspects rather than the televised show. *The Age*'s mini-*Big Brother*-website lasted longer but still didn't manage to last until the end of the series; it stopped in Week Eight. Generally, *The Age* ran about three times the amount of material online as it did in print; however, this decreased considerably after mid-June when the weekly updates and general commentary by Hamish Fitzsimmons stopped. Despite the demise of the mini-website, *The Age*'s online site kept reprinting stories about the show.

Websites devoted to reality tv have blossomed since 1997. Reality Blurred gathers press and online articles about the latest shows (*Big Brother*, *Amazing Race* and *Survivor* etc.). Mighty Big TV and Reality TV World provide episode recaps for many television shows. Mighty Big TV has information on nearly 20 reality-tv shows; it is such a popular site that the writers have attracted the attention of producers and are often given access to the contestants after the shows have finished. In Australia, technical writer Angus Kidman provided episode recaps of *Big Brother* and later contributed an article on the internet and *Big Brother* to the *Bulletin*.[44]

As can be imagined, the type of material available on the internet varied considerably in quality and quantity. Some were single pages that exhorted visitors to vote for a certain contestant; others were multimedia pages complete with photos (sometimes unauthorised photos), videos and audio files. There's even a *Big Brother* conspiracy website that lists all the rumours and gossip about *Big Brother*.[45] One of the most notable features of the internet material is its ephemerality. Many of the websites simply stopped at a certain date; the internet became a virtual cemetery of dead *Big Brother* sites. Others, such as the newspaper sites, remained up but were not updated. Whether people lost interest in the show or found it too much of a task to keep updating is not clear. Certainly many of the sites with counters have registered thousands of visitors to their pages.

Of course, the most popular website of all was the official *Big Brother* website. The official website had something for all fans. It was a virtual repository that contained the latest information about the contestants and the show in multimedia formats (video and audio). The site still received up to 32,000 visits a day after the show finished; the second series of application forms were available online only.

Before the second show has started, already a host of websites are devoted to the discussion of the new series: in January 2002, there are nearly 50 *Big Brother* fanclubs at Yahoo actively sharing information about the next series.

The second series

Somewhere along the line *Celebrity Big Brother* was filed away, which disappointed viewers who hoped to see Bert Newton and Rose Porteous sharing the same house. Australian fans never did find out why the show didn't go ahead.

The contents of the house had barely been auctioned before the speculation about *Big Brother*, the second series, began. The first media ripples examined the bidding war among the three commercial stations. Then came articles about how the show was going to change; there was no detail too minor for the *Big Brother*-hungry media. There was brief speculation about whether Gretel was going to return as host; yes, was the final answer. The house at Dreamworld was closed for refurbishing; this set fans speculating about what changes would be made: was it time for a spa? would a love shack be added? Possibly the house would be divided into different sections, like those overseas. What about the old contestants? Was Peter really going to co-host the Saturday night shows? Although much of the speculation is done on the internet, the media printed *Big Brother* material.

Some of the media are already predicting that the second series will be a failure: 'the law of television sequels tells us that the quality of originals is never rivalled … I don't think Australians have the stomach for a second helping of *Big Brother*.'[46] That remains to be seen, but if the proliferation of gossip about the second show is any indication, then many fans are keen for the second series to start.

Despite the bad press and warnings that *Big Brother* wouldn't result in long-lasting fame, Southern Star was inundated with more than 27,000 online applications for the second series. These were whittled down to a mere 2,000 who sent in videotapes; Australia Post had to make two special deliveries to the production offices. The videos yielded a shortlist of 150 candidates who will be interviewed. This time it seems that a lot of hopefuls considered nudity a necessity — even though streaker Anthony Debijl failed to make the final cut the first time around. But the producers aren't impressed by nudity (neither were the audience) and are keener to include women over 25 and people of ethnic background.[47] One suspects that viewers will get an all-new-but-slightly-familiar feeling about the contestants.

What does the second series have in store? A more aggressive contest, like the 'The Battle', or a sexier one? Will the second series expose more about the television show, the audience or the media? Have audiences learned to play the game? Or is it in our psyche to vote off the loud, the aggressive, the boring? Recently, viewers have seen that nice guys can win — even in America (Ethan in *Survivor* 3; the lawyers in *The Amazing Race*). Will the next winner be a grinner or a sinner? Even gay guys can win, as long as they are witty (British second series winner Brian Dowling). Australia might be the first non-European country to have a female winner.

Because *Big Brother* launched one of the most determined media blitzes in Australia, it was worthy of investigation as a media case study. The huff and the puff from many critics failed to collapse the *Big Brother* house. Why, is the question which lingered on lips. It was a show of less-than-average production values; it lacked the drama of *Survivor* and the panorama of *The Amazing Race*.

Its clever marketing paid off for a television show which was, well, boring. *Big Brother* captured the public's imagination. It was, for many, compulsive viewing — a fact that confounds media critics, cultural luminaries and fans alike. Perhaps the second series will help us to understand if it is a case of *schadenfreude* or Scheherazade.

Notes

Chapter 1: The *Big Brother* Family

1. www.bigbrother.com.au.
2. www.thestar.com.
3. David Holley, 'Many Poles Watch, but Others Look Askance at *Big Brother*', *LA Times*, 6 May 2001.
4. 'Reality TV Sex Stuns Land of Big Brother', *Australian*, 26 November 2001.
5. David Bullard, 'It's Very "U" to say Bah to *Big Brother* — But Are You Watching in Secret?' http://www.suntimes.co.za/2001/09/09/business/columns/columns.htm.
6. Jean Ritchie, *Big Brother: The Unseen Story*, London: Channel 4 Books, 2000.
7. Tara Conlan, 'Plans for Big Brother 3', *Daily Mail*, 30 July 2001.
8. 'Big Brother Creator Talks TV', Associated Press, 14 February 2001.
9. 'Big Brother Is Still Watching', www.etoline.com
10. Holley, op. cit.

Chapter 2: Behind the Scenes

1. Sally Stockbridge, 'The Strategies of Audience Capture', in *The Australian TV Book*, eds Graeme Turner and Stuart Cunningham, Sydney: Allen & Unwin, 2000.
2. Associated Press, 14 February 2001.
3. John de Mol, 'The Man Behind the Camera', in Joe Schlesser, *Broadcasting and Cable*, 3 July 2000.
4. *Courier-Mail*, 19 July 2001.
5. ibid.

6. Jean Ritchie, *Big Brother: The Unseen Story*, London: Channel 4 Books, 2000.
7. The production team included:
   Tim Clucas: Network TEN Head of Factual Television
   Denis Spencer: Chief Executive Southern Star Endemol
   Errol Sullivan: Director Southern Star Entertainment
   Peter Abbott: Executive Producer
   Howard Parker: Production Executive
   Chris Blackburn: Supervising Daily Show Producer
   Erik Steen: Executive Director/Compile Producer
   Karen Dewey: Supervisor Live Show
   Simon Francis: Director Live Show
   Michael Bridges: Production Designer.
8. Interview with Ms Vanda Leigh, 11 October 2001.
9. Interview with Dr Sally Stockbridge, 10 October 2001.
10. Figures come from Southern Star Endemol — Interactive Division.
11. David Katz 'Webcasting of ''Big Broz'' Shows Net Can Be Profitable, *Variety*, 27 September 2001.

Chapter 3: Genre

The shows mentioned below aired on Brisbane television channels.

1. From *Dragnet*, *Perry Mason* and *The Untouchables* (1960s) to *The Saint*, *Division 4* and *Homicide* (1970s) *Charlie's Angels* and *Hart to Hart* (1980s) and *LA Law*, *In the Heat of the Night* (1990s).
2. From *I Love Lucy*, to *Brady Bunch* and *Malcolm in the Middle.*
3. From *Pick-a-Box* to *I've Got a Secret*, *$6,000 Question*, *Sale of the Century* and *The Weakest Link.*
4. *Consider Your Verdict* and *Meet the Press* (1961), *People are Funny*, *Divorce Court* and *Roller Game* (1971), *That's Incredible* and *Candid Camera* (1981), *Blind Date*, *Totally Hidden Video* and *Australia's Funniest Home Videos* (1991).
5. In 1971 *Peyton Place*, *Love Is a Many Splendored Thing*, *Where the Heart Is*, *General Hospital* and *Days of Our Lives* ran consecutively on Channel 9.
6. *Jeopardy* and *Temptation* (1971), *Family Feud* and *Personality Squares* (1981), *Wheel of Fortune* and *Let's Make a Deal* (1991).
7. In one week in May 1961 over a dozen westerns aired after 6 pm: *Rin Tin Tin*, *Lone Ranger*, *MacKenzie's Raiders*, *Broken Arrow*,

Wild Bill Hickok, Lawman, Kit Carson, Rifleman, Tombstone Territory, Outlaws, Rawhide, Wagon Train, Bonanza, Whiplash, Stagecoach West.

8. *Petticoat Junction, Patty Duke Show, Courtship of Eddy's Father, Father Dear Father, Brady Bunch, Partridge Family, Flintstones.*
9. *Rockford Files, Quince MD, The Professionals, The Sweeney, Chips, Hart to Hart, Barnaby Jones, Charlie's Angels, Police Story.*
10. *Home and Away, Neighbours, E Street, Flying Doctors* and *Country Practice.*
11. Genres reflect their historicity. *Seinfeld* is very much a 1990s comedy; how would it have been perceived in the 1950s?
12. *West Wing* viewers may not 'read' the soap elements because of the low cultural value of soap operas.
13. In November 2001 half of the Top Twenty programs came under the reality rubric:

    2 *This Is Your Life*
    4 *Burke's Backyard*
    5 *Great Outdoors*
    6 *Better Homes and Gardens*
    8 *Backyard Blitz*
    10 *Getaway*
    12 *Who Wants to be a Millionaire?*
    14 *The Weakest Link*
    17 *Surprise Surprise*
    19 *Survivor (OzTam 2001)*
14. The rise and role of realism has been the subject of many long and learned debates. Generally realism is considered to represent middle-class values and social mores and strives ultimately to closure.
15. The definition offends many documentary purists. Stuart Kaminsky has defined documentary as 'Film which through certain conventions creates the illusion that the events depicted were not controlled by the filmmakers.' A consensus about a definition for documentary? Unlikely. I am going to treat documentary as a noun. There are shows made in the 'documentary mode' (i.e. those that reconstruct elements and are referred to as docudramas, such as *Unsolved Mysteries*) and shows that have doco elements (i.e. the reconstructions of crimes in *America's Most Wanted*). I realise 'documentary' is a mode of representation but for many it remains a generic label.

16. Accents are important; they should be educated for shows that wish to 'educate' (Richard Attenborough in *The Blue Planet*) and working class for those that wish to relate to the 'common man' (Michael Moore in *Roger and Me*). Somewhat less obvious is prosody (a person's intonation pattern), and the ironic tone that undermines statements.
17. The host does not have to be an expert, but he (generally males are preferred) should speak well and be appropriately dressed: khaki for the wildlife host (*Bush Tucker Man*, *Crocodile Hunter*) and lab coats for the medical documentary (*The Human Body*).
18. A shot of a drop of water falling off a leaf cuts to a shot of a drop falling onto a plant; there is nothing to suggest that the falling drop is the one that landed on the leaf (*The Secret Life of Plants*). Another technique is to pile clip after clip of an event (from different angles) or to have a number of people repeat the same assertion — these increase dramatic impact. Sometimes unrelated events are included for dramatic effect (e.g. the inclusion of the woman who skins rabbits in *Roger and Me*).
19. In *The Human Face*, John Cleese was reduced in size so that he could explore Liz Hurley's face; in *The Making of the "Human Body"*, Robert Winston demonstrated some of the computer software used to resconstruct a baby's skeleton.
20. http://www.tvchronicles.com/docusoap.htm
21. Dione said this happened in *Sylvania Waters*; see Sue Turnbull 'Return to *Sylvania Waters*', *Melbourne Report*, October 1992: 22.
22. 'Highlights' of the show were the Loud's divorce and the coming out of their son, Lance.
23. Noeline Donaher in particular felt that the editing reduced her to a drinking, smoking harridan.
24. See David Nichols, 'The Joy of Bex', in *ALR*, November 1992: 39–40; Graeme Turner, 'Suburbia Verite', *ALR*, October 1992: 37–39.
25. There are nearly 20 Dallas fansites, one of which campaigns to 'get *Dallas* back' — over 20 years after the show started (1978).
26. They even parody themselves. In a recent episode of *The Bold and the Beautiful* one of the male characters referred to a previous love who lived in Genoa City (the fictional setting for *The Young and the Restless*) and said that their romance didn't work because she

was 'young and she was restless' (episode aired on Channel 10 in August 2001).

27. For further reading on soaps see: Suzanne Frentz, ed., *Staying Tuned: Contemporary Soap Opera Criticism*, Bowling Green, Ohio: Bowling Green State University Popular Press, 1992; Richard Kilborn, *Television Soaps*, London: Batsford, 1992; Tania Modleski, *Loving with a Vengeance: Mass-produced Fantasies for Women*, London: Routledge, 1990; Carol Traynor Williams, *It's Time for My Story: Soap Opera Sources, Structure, and Response*, Westport, Conn.: Praeger, 1992.
28. Examples are *Rosalinda*, *Provocame*, *Betty La Fea* and *La Vida en el Espejo (Life in the Mirror)*. Telenovelas tend to run for only a few months rather than years.
29. See Sue Turnbull, 'Soap Opera', in *The Australian TV Book*; Kate Bowles and Sue Turnbull, eds, *Tomorrow Never Knows: Soap on Australian Television*, Melbourne: Australian Film Institute, 1994.
30. Sue Turnbull, ibid.
31. For further reading, see *Can We Talk? The Power & Influence of Talk Shows* by Gini G. Scott; *Freaks Talk Back: Tabloid Talk Shows & Sexual Nonconformity* by Joshua Gamson; *The Talking Cure* by Jane M. Shattuc.
32. Talk shows could roughly be divided into two main types: variety talk shows and issue talk shows. Variety talk shows (such as *The Midday Show*, *Good Morning Australia* and *Rove Live*) have a number of discrete segments and a variety of guests. Generally the tone is humorous and thus the shows are often hosted by comedians; usually the show opens with a comic routine which examines contemporary issues. Guests are generally promoting their latest book, film, concert etc.
33. Sally Jessy likes scientific tests administered by experts. Typical shows are 'Take the Test' and 'One Child, Two Men. Who's the Father?' Jenny Jones has adopted rhyming titles: 'It's the Bomb, When You Party with Your Mom!', 'My Child's Mouthy and Violent, Help Set Him Straight and Silent'.
34. For example, 'Pregnant by a Transsexual!' His website elicits guests for the following shows: 'Do you live in a trailer park and are you in a bizarre love triangle?' 'Do you have a sexy freaky fetish?' 'Do you have a strange or unusual sex job?'

35. Not only can the guests be violent but they have a penchant for removing their clothes. One guest in November 2001 on the show titled 'Extreme Ex-Lovers!' 'will win him back by proving she can be a ''dirty'' girl ... in a tub full of actual dirt with buckets of worms added for good measure'. Jerry has released *Too Hot for TV* and *Bad Boys and Naughty Girls* videos.
36. There have been some revelations from actors who have appeared on talk shows; but generally, the guests are perceived as 'real'.
37. I am not going to separate quiz shows from game shows, though there is a subtle difference. The quiz show asks questions and the game show requires some demonstration of skill.
38. The UK GameShow Web page lists nearly 20 subgenres.
39. These can test everything from general knowledge (*Sale of the Century* and *Weakest Link*) to in-depth understanding of a field (*Mastermind*) or a topic (sports, television, songs).
40. It is worth noting that a female host was introduced for the 'bitchiest' show, serving to reinforce stereotypes of women.
41. In the United Kingdom, *Sale of the Century* came under the scrutiny of the government watchdog, Independent Television Authority. The show was reprimanded in 1971 because it 'gloated over the high value of its prizes too much'.
42. There's anecdotal information that Brothers was not meant to win; so when she reached a certain level the questions became outlandishly difficult, but she knew the answers to them all.
43. Dan Enright, producer of *Twenty One*, was exposed by a disgruntled contestant, Herbert Stempel. Stempel revealed that Enright selected contestants not on the basis of skill but on who he thought would attract viewers. He coached contestants in how to act (when to stutter, mop their brow, bite their lip) and how to dress and provided contestants with the answers to the questions.
44. *Castaway*, *Shipwrecked* or *Treasure Island*. Ukraine became the twelfth country to air *Last Hero*, a version of *Survivor*.
45. There are a cluster of travel-oriented survival shows. In 2000, *The $20 Challenge* put a group of people in London with a variety of tasks to perform and only $20 a day to live on. The United Kingdom has *The Race* (which sounds exactly the same as *The Amazing Race*) and NBC has *Lost*, in which a group of people are stranded somewhere and have to get to the Statue of Liberty. In Europe a number

of people are trapped together on a double-decker bus. They are evicted at 'stops' along their route. In *Fear Factor* contestants undergo some gruesome challenges (eating insects, lying in a vat full of snakes or rats, etc.), and they are eliminated if they fail to complete their challenges or refuse to attempt them. In *Scream Test* (Channel 10) contestants had to complete tasks while in haunted places. In the United Kingdom's *Boy Meets Girl* four men and four women cross-dress and have to convince a member of the opposite sex; failure to do so means elimination.

46. *Boot Camp*'s mimicry of *Survivor* landed the producers in court. In an effort to protect its product, *Survivor* producers took legal action against *Boot Camp*. *Boot Camp* was not a success in Australia, perhaps because there was less cultural currency in its militaristic style. *Boot Camp* is almost a parody; at the very least it is high camp.

Chapter 4: The Show

1. The television hour is only 40 minutes long.
2. Which also explains why *The Secret Life of Us* was aired directly after the *Big Brother* finale.
3. Christina told Johnnie that her dad freaked out when he found out that *Big Brother* would be replacing Seinfeld (Week 4).
4. Responses to *Big Brother* questionnaire (see Chapter 6 for more information).
5. Personal email, 26 August 2000.
6. In his study *Rabelais and His World*, the Russian philosopher and literary scholar Mikhail Bakhtin explores the carnival and its manifestations.
7. Ben Elton, *Dead Famous*, London: Bantam, 2001.
8. There were twelve Big Brothers who worked in shifts. They did not make decisions — the chief Big Brother, Peter Abbott, did that. Instead they conducted much of the day-to-day communication with the contestants.

Chapter 6: The Contestants

1. *Big Brother Is Coming?*, 20 November 2000.
2. Australian New Zealand Reference Centre.
3. 'Today's TV', *The Age*, 17 May 2001.

4. 'Not Just Big Brother will be Watching', *Australian*, 25 April 2001: 3.
5. Ross Warneke, 'Truth Is, Ten's Reality Is Really Boring', *The Age*, 3 May 2001.
6. Geoff Roach, 'The State as You Have Never Seen It', *The Advertiser*, 28 July 2001: 28.
7. 'It's a Web Feat', *Sydney Morning Herald*, 1 May 2001.
8. 'Wall Flies' Feeding Frenzy', *Australian*, 3 May 2001: 28.
9. Amanda Meade, 'Screen Watch', *Australian*, 24 May 2001.
10. Ian Oshlack, 'All in the Mind games', *The Age*, 5 July 2001.
11. Amanda Meade, op. cit.
12. www.mistressandy.com
13. http://www.suntimes.co.za/lifestyle/bigbrother/
14. *Sunday Mail*, 2 September 2001: 10.
15. 21 May 2001; 28 July 2001.
16. *Sunday Telegraph*, 20 May 2001: 24.
17. 30 July 2001.
18. *Juice*, September 2001.
19. *Cosmopolitan*, October 2001.
20. *Daily Telegraph*, 27 August 2001.
21. 'We Love a Bit of Humility in Our Heroes', *Australian*, 20 July 2001: 13. *Sunday Telegraph*, 8 July 2001.
22. 'Would you Vote Yourself Off?', *Australian*, 14 July 2001: 16.
23. Jennifer Dudley, 'Intensity Not Enough to Stave Off Boredom', *Courier-Mail*, 11 June 2001.
24. Bantam House, 2001: 31.
25. www.blaircentral.com
26. Amanda Meade and Ashleigh Wilson, 'Oh Brother, What's Next', *Australian*, 18 July 2001: 13.
27. Kate DeBrito, op. cit.
28. 'Inside the Brotherhood', *The Age*, 26 April 2001.
29. Jon Hart, 'Viewer Exposed', Hobart *Mercury*, 18 July 2001.
30. *Juice*, op. cit.
31. Jean Ritchie, *Big Brother: The Unseen Story*, London: Channel 4 Books, 2000.
32. Nat, personal email, September 2001.
33. It's a pity that more of the contestants' conversations were not aired.

They discussed topics such as abortions, the US crisis in China and Timothy McVeigh's execution.

34. Jon Hart, op. cit.
35. http://www.mightybigtv.com
36. Drew Lambert on Peter's website: www.geocities.com/peterloversanon/
37. 'Big Brother says Nice Things About Us', *The Age*, 17 July 2001.
38. *Who*, 28 May 2001: 31.
39. Which equates the loss of a lock of hair with rape and is based on a true story. Lord Petre cut off a lock of Anabella Fermor's hair causing an estrangement between two powerful families.
40. Jon Hart, op. cit.
41. Tiffany Dunk, 'Celebrity Big Brother', *NW*, 4 June 2001: 16–17.
42. http://www.csmonitor.com/durable/2000/06/02/p13s1.htm
43. *Who Weekly*, 21 May 2001.
44. *Who Weekly*, 2 July 2001.
45. www.ancientrealm.com/andy.htm
46. P. Groffman and G. Likens (eds), *Integrated Regional Models: Interactions between Humans and Their Environment*, Melbourne, Chapman & Hall, 1994.
47. Meade and Wilson, op. cit.
48. Published 20 May 2001.
49. http://legendben.cjb.net/
50. Poems by 'Kidgalore' were often posted on the official *Big Brother* website, www.bigbrother.com.au.
51. *Who Weekly*, 28 May 2001; *NW*, 23 July 2001; *NW*, 30 July 2001; *NW*, 3 September 2001.
52. 10 September, 2001.
53. http://www.geocities.com/christina_bb_web/index.html
54. Ross Brundrett and Greta McMahon, 'Lookin' Grim for Gordy', *Herald Sun*, 24 May 2001: 16.
55. http://www.flashgordon1.com/; http://www.geocities.com/chick_muska_15_au/gordon.html
56. http://www.geocities.com/bb_princessjemma/; http://www.justjemma.com/
57. 'Zoo Inmates Raise a Stink About Todd', *Daily Telegraph*, 10 May 2001: 5; 'Backstabbing Johnnie Rotten to the Core!', *Daily Telegraph*, 24 May 2001: 5; *Daily Telegraph*, 21 June 2001: 5; 'Irwin

Spotlight on Real Culprit — Big Brother!', *Daily Telegraph*, 28 June 2001: 3.

58. 'Evicted Johnnie is Not that Rotten', *Advertiser*, 26 June 2001: 20.
59. http://www.johnniecass.com
60. *NW*'s 'Inside *Big Brother*', 23 July 2001; 'Secrets of *Big Brother*', 28 May 2001: 27; 'Life After *Big Brother*', 7 July 2001: 8–9.
61. http://www.geocities.com/lisastandingfan/
62. http://www.accaq.org.au/features/peter.htm
63. http://www.geocities.com/peterloversanon/
64. Fleur Michell, 'Big Brother: Where Are They Now?', *NW*, 3 September 2001: 18-22.
65. www.i7entertainment.com.au
66. 'Brits Do the Bubbles Better', *Australian*, 19 July 2001: 3.
67. *Cosmopolitan*, October 2001.
68. Sara-Marie said she took those sayings from Jerry Lewis's *The Nutty Professor*.
69. Hamish Fitzsimmons, 'Week Three', www.theage.com.au, 14 May 2001.

Chapter 7: The Audience

1. Peter Wilmoth, 'Spicy Bits', *Sunday Times*, 29 April 2001.
2. OzTAM, *Discovery Guide.*
3. There are 750 in Sydney, 700 in Melbourne, 600 in Brisbane, 475 in Adelaide and 474 in Perth.
4. *Discovery Guide* 5.
5. Taken from OzTAM website, www.oztam.com.au.
6. Eds C. Lee Harrington and Denise D. Bielby, *Soap Fans*, Philadelphia, Temple UP, 1995: 68.
7. Leo Howard Vacation School, Ipswich campus visit.
8. 'I'm Ashamed to Admit It —', *Media Culture and Society* (14), 1992: 561–82.
9. www.angelfire.mypic
10. Soap fans 168.
11. email BB Addict, 28 August 2001.
12. Peter Lovers Anon website.
13. Whit4You, The ClubHouse.
14. Gusworld website: www.gusworld.com
15. www.bigbrother.com.au

16. Email, Dr L. Ferrier, 16 October 2001.

Chapter 8: The Media

1. The News Limited 'Armchair Guides' caused some controversy because they were not marked 'advertorials'; the eight-page guide had been paid for by Channel 10. This breeches Press Council guidelines, but the guidelines are vague and the Council recognises there are instances when 'products or services are the proper subject of news reports'. Anne Davies debated the issue in 'Big Brother Is Watching', *The Age*, 2 May 2001.
2. Ed O'Loughlin in 'Oh, Brother, Who Stole the Gnome?', *The Age* 6 October 2001.
3. The *Observer*, 24 June 2001; The *Guardian*, 9 June 2001; The *Guardian*, 15 September 2000.
4. For example: Gary Levin, ' "Brother" Contestant Cut after Wielding Knife', *USA Today*, 21 July 2001; Brian Lowry, 'CBS Defends "Brother"; Ratings Up After Incident', Los Angeles *Times*, 12 July 2001.
5. Taken in part from the Australia/New Zealand Reference computer database.
6. Mike Colman, 'Foul-mouthed Warne Stars in His Own TV Program', *The Courier-Mail*, 17 May 2001: 38; Shaun Phillips, 'Superstar of the Pool Lives Life in a Fishbowl', *Herald Sun*, 31 July 2001: 8; Stuart Martin, 'State of the Art', *Daily Telegraph*, 28 July 2001:47.
7. Liam Bartlett, 'Reality Will Bite Voyeur TV's Callous Ratings Ploy', *Sunday Times*, 29 April 2001.
8. Lynden Barber, 'Death Race May Provide Reality Check', *Australian*, 26 May 2001.
9. Liam Bartlett, op. cit.; Michael Duffy, 'How Boring People Get All the Thrills', *Daily Telegraph*, 25 April 2001: 27; Ross Warneke, 'Truth is Ten's Reality is Really Boring', *The Age*, 17 May 2001.
10. Phil Bartsch, 'The Human Zoo', *Courier-Mail*, 10 April 2001.
11. *The Observer*, 24 June 2001.
12. 'What the TV Cameras Really See', *Sunday Times*, 20 May 2001.
13. David Brearley, 'The Illusion of Reality' *Australian*, 14 July 2001:17, and Karen Brooks, 'Winners in Reality', *Courier-Mail*, 18 July 2001: 15.

14. Amanda Meade, 'Screen Watch — Boozy Sleaze, Yes Please', *Australian*, 24 May 2001.
15. Dale Paget, 'Big Brother Immoral and Dull', *The Age*, 1 May 2001, emphasis added.
16. Shane Danielsen, 'Watch Big Brother's Siblings', *Australian*, 19 July 2001: 3.
17. Garry Mansfield, 'Prime Time's Sex Drive', *Herald Sun*, 9 May 2001.
18. 'Social Experiment?', *The Age*, 12 May 2001.
19. Andrew Bolt, 'My Vote: Dump Them All', *Herald Sun*, 30 April 2001.
20. Simon Johanson, 'Ten Denies ''Reality'' Sex Storm', *The Age*, 5 May 2001; 'Reality TV Around the Globe' at BBC News online at http://news6.thdo.bbc.co.uk/hi/; Mark Day, 'Big Brother Should Spark Debate', *Australian*, 14 June 2001: 4.
21. Geoffrey Newman, 'Reflecting on *Big Brother*'s Dark Side', *Australian*, 1 May 2001; Sacha Molitorisz, 'Here's Looking at You', *Sydney Morning Herald* and *The Age*, 14 May 2001.
22. Nick O'Malley and Julia Baird, 'Reality Shows Infiltrate Schools', *Sydney Morning Herald*, 7 July 2001; Mandi Zonneveldt, 'Obsessed by *Big Brother*', *Herald Sun*, 2 June 2001.
23. Corrie Perkin, 'It May be Real Life, but It's Death for Drama', *Sydney Morning Herald*, 15 July 2001; 'Shier Attacks Cheap Local Content', *Australian*, 4 May 2001; *Sydney Morning Herald* 4 May 2001; Mark Latham, 'Why Local Content Is Now a Farce', *Daily Telegraph*, 9 July 2001: 21; Amanda Meade and Ashleigh Wilson, 'Oh Brother, What's Next?' *Australian*, 18 July 2001.
24. 'Life Somehow Left Behind', *Sunday Telegraph*, 29 April 2001: 96; *Who Weekly*, 28 May 2001: 32; 'Switch Off', *Australian*, 17 May 2001: 20; 'Would You Vote Yourself Off?', *Australian*, 14 July 2001: 16; Danny Katz, 'Social Experiment?', *The Age*, 12 May 2001; Michael Boland, 'Big Bro Is Blah Down Under', *Variety*, 7 May 2001: 85.
25. Tim Pegler, 'How Big Brother Fuels Our Fantasies', *The Age*, 1 May 2001.
26. Desmond Morris op. cit.; Tim Pegler, '*Big Brother* Says Nice Things About Us', *The Age*, 17 July 2001.
27. 'Social Experiment?', *The Age*, 12 May 2001; 'How Realty TV Taps

a Basic Human Instinct', *Sunday Telegraph*, 22 July 2001; 'All in the Mind Games', 5 July 2001.

28. Red Symons, 'Me on Celebrity *Big Brother*?', *Sydney Morning Herald*, 4 August 2001; 'Life Begins at 40', *Sydney Morning Herald*, 19 November 2001; 'Fame Firm Favourite', *The Age*, 10 November 2001.
29. 'Ben wins Cash, Ten Wardrobe Unit Loses Plot', 19 July 2001.
30. 'Big Brother Is Watching', 3 May 2001; and 'While Big Brother Wasn't Looking', *Sydney Morning Herald*, 19 July 2001.
31. 'Voyeuristic Licence', *Courier-Mail*, 16 May 2001: 15.
32. Quoted in Molitorisz op. cit.
33. 'Inside the Home of *Big Brother*', *Sunday Times*, 22 April 2001: 9; 'Inside the House', *Sunday Mail*, 22 April 2001.
34. 'Crime Runs Riot as Police Cover Their Backsides', *Sydney Morning Herald*, 22 July 2001.
35. 'Fifteen Minutes of Fame or Life-Long?', *Herald Sun*, 11 July 2001: 10; 'Suddenly Famous Suddenly Forgotten', *Sydney Morning Herald*, 19 May 2001; 'Fame Fleeting for Evictees', *Herald Sun*, 5 July 2001: 24; Ross Brundrett and Peta Hellard, 'Big Sister Sparks Up', *Herald Sun*, 19 September 2001:22; Peta Hellard and Luke Dennehy, 'The Opening of an Envelope Award', *Herald Sun*, 28 December 2001: 25.
36. Jennifer Dudley, 'Dream of Fame Turns to Reality', *Courier-Mail*, 9 June 2001: 11. Singer Leah Haywood also attributed her success to a *Big Brother* appearance (Michael Duffy, 'Recognising Talent', *The Advertiser*, 2 August 2001).
37. Renee Mickelburgh, 'Even the Minder Is a Star by Association', *Sunday Mail* (Brisbane), 15 July 2001.
38. 23 March 2001; 'The Naked Truth', 29 May 2001; Angus Kidman, 'Big Brother Is Watching — The Web', 17 July 2001.
39. 25 April 2001.
40. 29 July 2001.
41. 30 July 2001.
42. The author was interviewed on ABC channels in Bundaberg, Adelaide, Wollongong and Brisbane.
43. www.smh.com.au/icon.
44. http://www.gusworld.com.au/tv/bigbro.
45. http://www.bbconspiracy.cjb.net.

46. Kate Jones, 'Big Brother, Big Yawn', *Daily Telegraph*, 11 December 2001.
47. 'Deadline Looms for Housemate Hopefuls', *Herald Sun*, 16 January 2001.